DEALING WITH AN ANGRY PUBLIC

The Mutual Gains Approach to Resolving Disputes

LAWRENCE SUSSKIND
PATRICK FIELD

The MIT-Harvard Public Disputes Program

THE FREE PRESS

New York   London   Toronto   Sydney   Singapore

THE FREE PRESS
A Division of Simon & Schuster Inc.
1230 Avenue of the Americas
New York, NY 10020

Designed by Carla Bolte

Manufactured in the United States of America

10   9   8   7   6   5   4   3   2

Library of Congress Cataloging-in-Publication Data

Susskind, Lawrencce.
    Dealing with an angry public: the mutual gains approach to
resolving disputes / Lawrence Susskind, Patrick Field.

        p.   cm.
    Includes bibliographical references and index.
    ISBN 0–684–82302–0 (hardcover)
    1. Public relations—Corporations—United States.   2. Issues
management—United States.   3. Corporate image—United States.
I. Field, Patrick, 1963–   .   II. Title.
HD59.6.U6S87   1996
659.2'85'0973—dc20   95–52831
                                                      CIP

ISBN 0-684-82302-0

Contents

Concluding Remarks   238

Acknowledgments

We thank our colleagues, especially Michael Wheeler and William Breslin for reviewing the manuscript. Howard Raiffa was instrumental in shaping our thinking about fairness, power, and compensation. Donna McDaniel completed extensive early research on the breast implant, animal rights, Jacksonville, and Three Mile Island cases. Her initial efforts were important in getting this project off the ground.

Several other associates provided much needed help under pressure. Sid Straley not only lived through the TMI crisis, but lived through the final production of this book. She straightened out verb tenses, restructured sentences, replaced our original internal citations with endnotes, and offered many helpful suggestions. David Greene checked facts, helped draft Chapter VII, edited numerous chapters, and pointed us to Greider's version of the Alar case. Antony Lucas helped proofread the final full manuscript.

A number of people reviewed the cases in which they were intimately involved, including Charlie Lord of Alternatives for Community and Environment, Robert O'Conner of the Metropolitan District Commission, and Gary Gilson of the Minnesota News Council. Michael Wheeler and The Program on Negotiation at Harvard Law School provided support for the preparation of the Rhone-Poulenc case.

Other friends and colleagues provided aid of still other kinds. Michael Garland and David Santomenna sent us newspaper clippings. Sarah McKearnan encouraged us to include more examples of real success stories. Numerous librarians at Harvard and MIT provided much needed research assistance.

Larry Susskind: For several years, Jack Connolly and Ira Alterman at the Center for Management Research in Wellesley, Massachusetts have helped to organize two seminars a year entitled "Dealing With an Angry Public." More than 1,500 public and private sector managers have attended. Their feedback has been crucial to my emerging sense of what to do and what not to do in the middle of a public controversy.

The forbearance and encouragement of my wife, Leslie, and my children, Lily and Noah, are always important to getting anything done. I thank them.

Patrick Field: Thea Sahr provided good humor, tolerance, and support during much of the writing of this book. My early teachers as well as my professors at Carleton College and MIT were instrumental in teaching me how to both write and think with clarity, depth, and breadth. I hope that my father's sense of humor and practical intelligence inform this book, as well as my mother's great curiosity about the world. Lastly, I want to thank Marc McGarry, whose insights about anger and love, as well as his honesty and convictions, have powerfully influenced my thinking about human nature.

We thank everyone listed here, as well as other colleagues and friends who offered encouragement and advice. However, the flaws, errors, and weaknesses in our argument are, in the end, all our fault!

Lawrence Susskind
Patrick Field

Chapter I

Introduction

There are many reasons for the public to be angry. Business and government leaders have covered up mistakes, concealed evidence of potential risks, made misleading statements, and often lied. Indeed, our leaders have fueled a rising tide of public distrust of both business and government by behaving in these ways. Consider the following:

- After oil poured from the torn hull of the *Exxon Valdez*, the public found that Exxon had actually reneged on the promises it had made when it was given the right to build the Alaskan pipeline. There was no adequate emergency response plan in place in case of a spill. Clean-up equipment, what little there was, was buried under several feet of snow. To make matters worse, the state had apparently known about these deficiencies since the early 1980s, but had not rectified the situation.
- Only after thousands of lawsuits had been filed against Dow Corning did it come to light that the company had not only obtained, but had sponsored biological research indicating, as early as the 1960s, that the silicone used in breast implants might impair the immune system. All that time, the company claimed that silicone was biologically inert and wouldn't hurt anyone.
- Citizens speaking out at public meetings to discuss large-scale residential and industrial development projects, who oppose these projects on environmental and other grounds, have been slapped with libel suits by wealthy corporations trying to scare them into silence.

Wouldn't you be angry if you had been hurt, misled, or threatened?

1

A New Way of Interacting with the Public

We want to challenge the way that many corporations and government agencies interact with the public. Through numerous examples, detailed case studies, logical arguments, and plain common sense, we want to make a case for a better way of handling these interactions—particularly with groups that are already angry because of the way they have, or think they have, been treated. More specifically, we offer suggestions for avoiding crises when the risks associated with new products or policies come to light, and for responding when mistakes—even disasters—have occurred. Furthermore, we suggest ways in which companies and government agencies ought to respond to those who are unalterably opposed to what they stand for.

Our intended audience includes senior executives of large and small companies who must deal with organized public-interest groups, midlevel managers who often face crises first hand, elected and appointed officials who must respond to unhappy constituents, and entrepreneurs who must take substantial risks to bring new products or ideas to market. Moving past the conventional wisdom, we want to suggest to those who advise these decision-makers—attorneys, issue managers, public-relations consultants, and others—that there is a different way to successfully interact with—indeed, to negotiate with—their critics.

Why We All Should Be Concerned About Angry Publics

Some readers might ask, "Why should I care if people are angry? Dealing with them is the responsibility of my company's public relations people. I never have to deal with the public directly." Others might say, "Why do I care? At my company we have been putting out our product for thirty years and we haven't had a problem yet."

There are two important reasons why all of us need to be concerned about a society in which the public's concerns, fears, and anger are not adequately addressed. First, a continually angry public undermines American competitiveness in the international marketplace. That is, it can sap the productivity of corporations and government agencies who must spend inordinate amounts of time and human capital rehashing every action to defend each decision they make. Second, an angry public contributes to the erosion of confidence in our basic institutions. When important decisions must be made, especially in times of emergency, no one will give the relevant decision-maker the benefit of the doubt if the public's trust has eroded.

They Undermine American Competitiveness

Because the battle lines are often drawn quickly and sharply in a crisis, companies and government agencies do not talk with those who are or might be angry at them. In turn, the public does not communicate its concerns directly to those responsible. Instead, the drama is enacted through the press, and soon thereafter in the courts. The public's anger is all too often translated into lawsuits. Between 1985 and 1991, 107,000 personal-injury suits, 48,000 asbestos liability suits, and almost 38,000 other product-liability suits were filed in the U.S.[1] In 1991 alone, 1,500 product-liability suits were brought in federal district courts against Fortune 1000 companies. These Fortune 1000 companies were defendants in 95 percent of personal-injury cases.[2] These do not include cases working their way through state courts, where a majority of such lawsuits are filed.

While attorneys and their firms gather data, haggle over procedural rules, and prepare for battle, dollars that could fund research and development, additional investment in infrastructure, or wage increases are eaten up in costly legal battles. Fighting fire with fire, so to speak, undercuts the profitability of business and adds to the cost of operations. It's been estimated that U.S. companies spend some $300 billion annually on litigation involving environmental claims, product-liability suits, class-action securities suits, medical malpractice suits, and Americans with Disabilities cases.[3] Du Pont Chemical alone spends some $75 million annually to defend itself against plaintiffs who have brought suit against it.[4]

Resources expended to fight an angry public cannot be used to solve other pressing problems. Money poured into defending past actions cannot be used to improve future performance. Embattled executives, managers, and their staffs are less likely to take risks, think creatively, and perform effectively if they are distracted from their primary responsibilities. Workers who doubt their employer's honesty are likely to work less hard, report more sick days, and generally be less invested in the success of their organization. Furthermore, because each unsuccessful attempt to address the public's concerns leads to increased skepticism and anger, executives, managers, and workers find themselves confronting the same problems in progressively more potent forms.

The expenditure of dollars and efforts to deal with an angry public are eventually folded into the costs of products. In the international marketplace, American products and services cost more. The Organization of Economic Cooperation and Development estimates that direct and indirect legal costs in 1987 amounted to 2.7 percent of the U.S. GDP, compared with only 0.5 to 0.7 percent of GDP for other OECD countries.[5] In a 1994 survey, 800 U.S. CEOs and CFOs estimated that liability-prevention measures increased the price of products and services by at least 5 percent.[6] One former commissioner of the Securities and Exchange Commission has stated that, despite attempts to attract foreign companies to list in the United States, such companies often refuse, citing fears of litigation.

In addition, lost time and effort, as well as ideas left untried, impose incalculable opportunity costs. Companies, cowed by the public's anger at others' mistakes, may be reluctant to introduce new products or ways of working. American companies lose their technological edge, and American workers lose the jobs that innovation provides. In an increasingly competitive and relentless international market, dealing poorly with an angry public means that American business and American workers lose out.

They Erode Public Confidence

It is not just business that loses out when the public is disenchanted or angry. Government loses, too. A public, frustrated or angry, loses faith in the institutions that govern everyday life and permit collective action. Americans expect the government to defend their country's interests abroad, pave highways, build bridges, prevent crime, provide for the needy, protect public health, and assure prosperity for workers and their families. In 1966, University of Michigan researchers asked Americans, "Do you trust the government in Washington to do what's right? How far do you trust it?" Seventy-six percent of those polled responded, "Yes; most or all of the time." In 1992, the same question was asked. Only 28 percent gave that response.[7] People do not feel they can count on government—regardless of which party is in power.

In anger, citizens have turned against their governing institutions and the individuals who represent those institutions. Thus, voters are easily rallied around such slogans as "Throw the bums out." In a 1994 New York Times/CBS poll, only 13 percent of the public said they believed that members of Congress deserved reelection.[8] Referendums to limit the terms of those gridlocked in Washington were on the ballot in ten statewide elections and in the District of Columbia in 1994. Sixteen other states previously passed such referendums.[9]

Thwarted by a paralyzed, partisan congress, a diminished presidency, and large and complex bureaucracies, citizens feel alienated and are tempted to "throw out" the whole system. Such anger, absent a response, may lead to smaller government and lower tax levels, but it will undoubtedly also lead to cutbacks in essential public services, rising costs associated with privatization, holes in the safety net meant to guarantee public protection to those least able to fend for themselves, enormous increases in the cost of insurance, and huge losses in the value of private property currently protected by regulation and government action.[10]

There are other hidden costs, too. Fewer capable candidates want to run for office when there are insufficient resources set aside to do the job correctly. Consequently, fewer talented and competent individuals are likely to rise to positions of power and influence. As California is discovering, disenchantment expressed through term limits creates unintended consequences when cutbacks tip the balance of power in government to long-time civil servants and lobbyists who face no limits to their length of time on the job.

When anger is directed, in a blunderbuss fashion, at the way in which government operates, civil society quickly erodes. More citizens join the ranks of the health-care uninsured. More youths are randomly killed in the mean streets of our cities. Wages for the middle class remain stagnant. The gap between rich and poor increases. Government's past failures to listen to and address the concerns of its citizens has led to an unprecedented lack of involvement in the electoral process and paralysis in vision and action when we most need it.

We believe that dealing with an angry public honestly, seriously, decently, and effectively is good for both business and government. Government officials and business executives must find a better way to listen to the public's concerns, respond to criticism, and engage citizens and consumers. Conversation and negotiation, rather than a sales pitch and a fight, are what are required.

The Public Is Not Easily Appeased

Imagine, for a minute, that you are the hard-working, able plant manager of a chemical plant that produces, recycles, and disposes of chemicals used in the petroleum industry. One day your attorney tells you that it's time to renew the environmental permit for the incinerator at your factory. Since you have not changed your operations since the last time, your attorney assures you that the filing will be routine and that there is nothing to worry about. However, when you attend the usual perfunctory public meeting at the local school, fifty vocal and angry neighborhood residents appear. They ask you, in no uncertain terms, why there is an incinerator in their neighborhood, what they don't know about what you've been doing, and how many other secrets you've been keeping from them. Surprised? Shocked? Since you haven't done anything, you can't imagine why they are so angry. And not just angry, but angry at *you!*

Now suppose that none of those fifty citizens have ever been inside your plant. But they know that several workers have died in the last several years in the petrochemical industry, and that big petrochemical companies seem to continue on with their business without remorse. And almost every day, the residents read about or hear of new cancer-causing chemicals and how their manufacturers have either not known about their toxic effects, or worse, have covered up suspected risks.

Fueling the Fire

What faces the plant manager, or anyone in a similar position, is not merely dealing with those fifty angry people at that moment, but rather putting a process in motion that takes account of past mistakes by others. The public has been lied to, talked down to, ignored, and manipulated for so long that those fifty people are not likely to take seriously anything that plant manager says at the meeting. This is not necessarily the plant manager's fault. The public has seen business and government respond to their concerns in the past with slick advertising campaigns, denials of risk, misleading information, and false fronts. Now, anything that plant manager says, even if he or she is totally new to the situation, will be suspect.

Take Brown & Williamson Tobacco Company executives. They privately wrestled with how to deal with the health risks of smoking for over forty years while publicly denying that any such risks existed at all. During the 1950s and 1960s, the company sponsored research on how to minimize the risks of smoking through filters, additives, and delivery devices. However, in public the company denounced epidemiological studies linking nicotine to lung cancer, terming the studies merely "statistical" and "emotional." If you think times have changed, consider a group known as Restaurants for a Sensible Voluntary Policy. The group, with connections to the Tobacco Institute and a public relations firm that serves Philip Morris, claimed restaurants had lost 30 percent of their business from a smoking ban. However, a study of sales receipts commissioned by one municipality involved found restaurant revenues actually increased by 2.4 percent during the period the smoking ban was in effect, while a survey sponsored by Beverly Hills restaurants found a more modest drop of 6.7 percent.[11]

Many past public-relations efforts have done less to address the concerns of the public and more to minimize and ignore those concerns. These efforts have succeeded in fueling citizen anger. For instance, when the Three Mile Island nuclear power plant malfunctioned in the spring of 1979, Metropolitan Edison (Met Ed) announced to the public, "The entire system was systematically shut down and will be out of service for about a week." According to the company, there were no recordings of significant levels of radiation nor were any expected. But within days, the Nuclear Regulatory Commission (NRC) announced detection of radiation off the plant site and in nearby Harrisburg. After that news, rush hour in Harrisburg ceased to exist as fear kept people at home. Even the NRC was engaged in spin control of its own. While the NRC had sufficient information to indicate that there was a potential for severe damage to the core of the reactor within hours of the accident, the Commission failed to notify either the citizens living in the vicinity of the plant or Jimmy Carter, the President of the United States.

It is no wonder, given the history of many public-relations efforts, that the public is not easily appeased. Too many mistakes have been made, and too many situations have been mishandled for the public to trust the opinions and reports of high-level executives and government officials. With good reason. From the beginning of a crisis, the public assumes they are not getting the basic facts, let alone the full story.

Who Is the Public?

In a large and technologically complex society, it is difficult to identify just who your audience is and with whom you should be talking. Every public relations practitioner, senior executive, and high-ranking government official faced with an angry public must answer the short but difficult question: Who are these people?

Consider the plant manager's story once again. While the fifty angry citizens before him are certainly the public, how accurately do these citizens represent the larger community? Are these just a few malcontents or troublemakers? Is public anger nothing more than "minor" dissatisfaction amplified by advocacy groups with their own agendas and the media looking for a story? Are there other members of the public, not at the meeting, who have totally different concerns and interests? If the plant manager—active in the community—doesn't recognize anyone in the audience, does that mean that he or she is not really in trouble?

After the tanker *Exxon Valdez* ruptured, the executives of Alyeska and Exxon U.S.A. encountered strong public reaction and continuous news headlines. Which public should they have been most concerned about? The millions of Americans sitting in their living rooms watching the disaster unfold? The residents, fishermen, local officials, and Native Americans who would bear the brunt of the spreading oil? Visitors who had come to sightsee and fish? The environmental advocacy groups who immediately attacked the company? Or the federal and state officials who were supposed to have helped prevent such a disaster in the first place, but now were sure to blame Exxon?

Who should you talk to in a crisis? Whose concerns should you address first? Which people and organizations must be convinced of the legitimacy of your actions? Until these questions are answered, it is not possible to appease an angry public.

The Typical Approach to Public Relations Does Not Work

If you were to sit down in a classroom with some of the 18,000 college students majoring in public relations today, you might very well like what you hear.[12] The theory of public relations sounds well reasoned, responsible, and pragmatic. One textbook, in use since 1975, offers such proven maxims as: "A source of information regarded as trustworthy, expert, or authoritative is most likely to be believed"; "Personal contact is the most effective means of communication"; and, "Participation in, or awareness of, the decision process increases the likelihood of acceptance."[13] Another classic text, first printed in 1952, defines public relations as "the management function that identifies, establishes, and maintains *mutually beneficial relationships* [emphasis ours] between an organization and the various publics on whom its success or failure depends."[14] Public relations, according to the textbooks, sounds as simple as companies relating honestly with the people they serve and the people affected by their actions.

But something often happens between the classroom and the boardroom. The ideas disseminated in the classroom are not what the public experiences when the pressure of real-life events requires a quick response. In practice, business leaders (and their governmental counterparts, who are equally concerned about public relations) all too often fail to acknowledge the public's anger. Indeed, they attempt to blunt or undercut the public's concerns by dredging up countervailing "facts" or rebuttals from pseudo-independent experts and unscientific polls. They commit to nothing and admit to nothing. The public is often treated like an angry mob rather than as concerned customers or citizen with legitimate fears, concerns, and needs. Relying on obfuscation and concealment, both public and private leaders tend to make matters worse, compounding the initial difficulty.

While public-relations textbooks may highlight the need for quality information, effective communication, and mutually beneficial relationships, public relations as practiced often employs techniques such as stonewalling, whitewashing, as well as blocking and blaming. We have highlighted these well-practiced public relations ploys below. This is not a comprehensive list. Nor do we mean to suggest that most public-relations practitioners would advocate these techniques. However, someone is advocating for these techniques, or, at least acceding to their use, because we see them all the time.

The Stonewall. All too often, in the face of crisis, attorneys advise their corporate clients to keep quiet. The threats of lawsuits and substantial financial liability can often muzzle a well-intentioned company's sincere attempts to communicate with the public. After methyl isocyanate (a poisonous gas) leaked from Union Carbide's plant in Bhopal, India in late 1984, the chairman of Union Carbide, Warren Anderson, rushed to Bhopal in what we consider an exemplary fashion. Anderson was quoted at corporate headquarters as saying: "We can't show our concern about this tragedy by me staying in Danbury."[15] However, his public-relations handlers soon squelched such attempts at accountability and forthrightness. By December 7, three days after the leak, the press reported that Union Carbide had repeatedly refused to provide a detailed description of the system used to store and process the lethal gas. Here's a slice of a press conference held by the company's director of Health, Safety, and Environmental Affairs.

> *Reporter*: I think you've said the company was not liable to the Bhopal victims?
> *Director*: I didn't say that.
> *Reporter*: Does that mean you are liable?
> *Director*: I didn't say that either.
> *Reporter*: Then what did you say?
> *Director*: Ask me another question.[16]

The Whitewash. Too often companies and agencies attempt to minimize the effects of their actions, or downplay the public's worries. Months after the *Exxon Valdez* ran aground, the State of Alaska helped launch a $4-million ad campaign paid for by Exxon. One ad used a retouched photo of Marilyn Monroe, her mole airbrushed away. The ad read: "We changed this picture to make a point about a legendary beauty. Unless you look long and hard, you probably won't notice her beauty mark is missing. Without it, the picture may have changed, but her beauty hasn't."[17]

The Smokescreen. If stonewalling and whitewashing don't work, then some companies and agencies will attempt to erect a smokescreen to conceal the truth. As one tobacco company public-relations manager stated as far back as 1971, "Doubt is our product, since it is the best means of competing with the 'body of fact' that exists in the mind of the general public."[18] Of course, in a free and open society such as the United States, rarely do such schemes work out. Somebody, often the press, finds out the truth behind the "truth."

One classic smokescreen was created by several tobacco companies back in 1953. That December, top tobacco company executives, with the help of public-relations experts Hill and Knowlton, hatched the Tobacco Industry Research Committee, now known as the Council for Tobacco Research. The new committee promised that it would look into the reported link between cancer and smoking and offer "aid and assistance to the research effort."[19] It would also, apparently, look after public relations. Twenty-eight of Hill and Knowlton's staff were transferred to the new group within a year. Half of the first several years' budget was allocated for public relations. While the Council claimed to sponsor legitimate scientific research, actual participants, testifying before Congress in 1994, finally admitted that at least some of its research had been directed by the participating companies' attorneys. The Council sought out obscure researchers who agreed with the industry's stance. The Council promoted the research results through magazines and newspapers, not through scientific and academic journals.

The False Front. Sometimes, organizations enter into a debate under false pretenses. A company or trade association sets up a front, which then goes about lobbying for one cause or another in a seeming spirit of citizen activism. Organizations like the "Coalition for Health Insurance Choices" or "Citizens for Sensible Acid Rain Control" sound reasonable enough. But these organizations were funded, respectively, by the Health Insurance Association of America and public utility companies. Often, this false-front strategy backfires. A group called Nevadans for Fair Fuel Economy Standards attempted to fight a federal fuel-economy bill sponsored by a Nevada senator. What the group didn't publicize was its connection to U.S. automakers in Detroit. When the press ultimately publicized the industry connection, the public was angry and surprised. One individual, who had originally agreed to have his name printed on the group's letterhead, denounced the organization. Many who had written letters to the Senator opposing the bill wrote again to apologize.

The legislative version of the False Front is very familiar. Elected officials propose legislation, knowing full well (and being quite relieved) that the opposition party will kill the bill in committee. This allows the officials who introduced the legislation to claim that they did their best to respond to a particular constituency. They know, though, that nothing will happen. They sometimes even admit in informal meetings with opponents of the proposed legislation that this was their strategy.

The Block-and-Blame. When all else fails, public relations practice seems to suggest that businesses and government leaders ought to distance themselves from the problem and blame somebody else. "If we didn't cause it," the conventional wisdom goes, "we can't be blamed for it." Union Carbide first told the press that its Bhopal plant had been designed and built by Americans under American standards. Days later, with the crisis out of control, Union Carbide tried to distance itself from its Indian counterpart, UC India, Ltd. The U.S. company claimed it did not have a detailed understanding of the foreign facility's design. Union Carbide stated that the plant had not been supervised by Americans in over a year. The company also argued that the poorest residents in Bhopal had moved too close to the plant over the years.

Shortly after the *Exxon Valdez* spill, one Exxon USA official said of the tanker's captain: "You can't be any more legally qualified to do this work than Captain Hazelwood."[20] The Coast Guard soon found out that Hazelwood had been drinking. Quickly, Exxon management distanced themselves from the captain. They fired him and reconsidered footing his legal bills. The president of Exxon USA told the press: "This incident should never have happened. In my view, it was a human failure that it did happen."[21] In the public sector, the block-and-blame strategy is as easy to use—one official or party needs only to accuse the other(s) for unpopular action or the failure to act. "They made me do it," and, "They wouldn't let me do it," both offer an easy excuse.

The Slash and Burn. When worst comes to worst, some public-relations practitioners suggest all-out warfare against their critics. In 1991, a crisis management document prepared for the Clorox Company came to light. It suggested strategies the company could use in case they were attacked by environmentalists challenging the safety of household bleach products. For example, if a newspaper columnist noted the environmental hazards of household bleach, and Greenpeace suggested a boycott, the plan enumerated several countermeasures. First, "independent" scientists should immediately conduct media tours. Second, the industry should initiate an advertising campaign called "Stop Environmental Terrorism." Third, the legal staff should be told to conduct research into the possibility of a slander suit. Above all, the company was advised to avoid a debate on the scientific merits of the case because the issue would become "too emotional." In another imagined scenario, if the National Toxicology Program (NTP) concluded that chlorine was indeed an animal carcinogen, the plan called for Clorox to bring several "objective" scientists from the Chlorine Institute to testify in front of Congress that the NTP report would require reevaluation and further study (this before any study was ever published)![22]

A Different Approach Is Needed

Clearly, a different approach is needed. Business and government must find a better way to negotiate with their critics. With American competitiveness and faith in our governing institutions at stake, business and government leaders must go back to the basic tenets of public relations. We do not suggest that this will be easy. Given legal liability, the difficulty of identifying representative publics, increasingly complex technological risks, diverse values and beliefs, and the age-old unpredictability of human nature, all filtered through a complex lens of press, radio, and television, the work ahead is formidable. However, we believe there is a better way. We have developed an alternative approach that we believe can provide a means of navigating the turbulent waters churned up by an angry public.

Consider once again the predicament of the plant manager standing before fifty angry citizens. What should he or she do? At every turn, the manager is likely to be heckled and doubted. Should the plant manager hold a community day with free food, drink, and balloons for the children? The public will surely see this as a paltry attempt to make friends at a time when opponents are not feeling friendly or conciliatory. Should the manager sponsor a scholarship at the local high school, or maybe volunteer to rehabilitate a local playground? The public will see the offer of such funds, particularly for items that are not the primary concern of those who raised the issue, as nothing less than a bribe. Most residents will not be bought off, certainly not at the expense of their own self-respect or the respect of their peers. Should the manager then simply assure them that their fears are unfounded, and offer independent reports and manuals outlining operating procedures to appease them? However accurate such information might be, a skeptical citizenry is not likely to believe these reports or trust what they are sure to view as biased material. Furthermore, the citizens are likely to feel that their concerns have been brushed aside if they are not given an opportunity to meet face to face with the top leadership of the industry and regulatory agencies involved.

We have different advice for this plant manager. In fact, we have what we believe to be the most practical advice for most business people and government officials who face an angry public We believe that they should adhere to a simple set of principles that we call the *mutual-gains approach* to dealing with an angry public. The gist of the mutual-gains approach is to think of the interaction with the public as a multiparty, multi-issue negotiation. In that context, the plant manager should:

- acknowledge the concerns of the other side.
- encourage joint fact finding.
- offer contingent commitments to minimize impacts if they do occur, and promise to compensate knowable but unintended impacts.
- accept responsibility, admit mistakes, and share power.
- act in a trustworthy fashion at all times.
- focus on building long-term relationships.

These concepts have been developed over many years at the MIT-Harvard Public Disputes Program and at the Program on Negotiation at Harvard Law School. They have been honed and refined through numerous face-to-face interactions among government agencies, private businesses, technical experts, consumer advocacy groups, environmental organizations, and the public at large, as well through dozens of intensive workshops with more than fifteen hundred top-level business leaders and government officials.

These concepts are especially likely to resonate with those familiar with total quality management (TQM) or continuous quality-improvement techniques, through which companies strive to organize themselves around their customers' and suppliers' wants and needs. We'd like to borrow from the President of SAS Airlines, who wisely said that his company exists only in the eye of the beholder, in those moments when a company employee and a customer interact. Like the key concepts of total quality management, these six guiding principles focus on quality, responsiveness, and problem-solving. Like proponents of total quality management, we advocate listening hard to the concerns of consumers, customers, and clients so that problems can be spotted ahead of time. We also advise that there be a premium put on building long-term relationships. What is notably different about our prescriptions is that we propose applying them in the most difficult kinds of conflict situations.

The following chapters illustrate and explain these six ideas in more detail. Chapter II probes further the various reasons why different publics are angry. Unless the different causes of anger are carefully distinguished from each other, mistakes will be made in applying the mutual-gains approach. Chapter III discusses why the mutual-gains approach is more effective than the typical practice of public relations. In Chapters IV, V, and VI, the real heart of the book, we illustrate and expand on the six principles through well-known examples of accidents or mistakes, potential risks, and philosophical disagreements. We let the events of real crises unfold and discuss how the mutual-gains approach might have helped to produce positive outcomes in each of these circumstances. Because of the importance of the media in shaping the way the public understands what is happening, in Chapter VII we suggest ways of interacting with the media that are consistent with the six mutual-gains principles. Finally, in Chapter VIII, we discuss the most important element for pulling all these ideas together into a coherent and useful whole: the leadership that corporate and government managers can and should provide. Our advice is simple. But implementing our advice requires innovative, courageous, principled, and sophisticated leadership.

Chapter II

Why Is the Public Angry?

The public can get angry about all kinds of things. After the *Exxon Valdez* spill, thousands of Exxon customers mailed their plastic credit cards back to company chairman Lawrence G. Rawl. The Indian government, incited by enraged advocates of the thousands left alive but still suffering in Bhopal, unsuccessfully attempted to extradite Union Carbide's chairman Warren Anderson to be tried for murder. After a Pittsburgh surgeon transplanted a baboon liver into a dying man, protesters gathered around his house to chant, "Animals are not spare parts!"[1] When a state agency in Massachusetts decided to hold a controlled deer hunt to help protect the forest that surrounds Boston's drinking water reservoir, protesters camped out at the edge of the forest with signs exclaiming, "Stop the slaughter!" After the hunt, one protester wrote to the local paper, "Left on those rocks was the innocent heart of a once-living, breathing, feeling creature whose only sin was survival."

What Is Anger?

Anger takes many forms and arises from many different circumstances. Anger is fists thrust into the air, yelling, screaming, and in its extreme, physical violence. Anger can take the form of political expression—picket signs, petitions, and get-out-the-vote campaigns. Modern-day "tar and feathering" such as editorials, paid advertising, and *60 Minutes* exposés are all means of expressing anger, as are "tea partying," when consumers say "Hell, no!" through boycotts of gasoline, tuna, and even travel to states which pass laws that some people find offensive. Anger can take many forms, but what is it? What causes it?

The *American Heritage Dictionary* defines anger as "a strong feeling of displeasure or hostility." The *Webster's New International Dictionary* adds that anger suggests "no definite degree of intensity." Thus, anger might be slight displeasure or out-of-control rage. Anger may be wrath seeking punishment, or indignation provoked by something mean or offensive.

A working definition of anger that we find helpful builds on these standard definitions, but adopts a more psychologically-nuanced perspective. We believe that anger is a defensive response to pain or the threat of pain, real or perceived. Much as a mother bear will attack a hiker crossing between her and her cub, individuals, perceiving themselves or those they love to be in danger, rear up and fight. To the hiker, walking innocently through the woods, a ton of charging fur and muscle is terrifying. For the bear, though, the hiker is no less threatening. While the hiker views the bear's charge as purely offensive (and deadly), the bear is motivated by fear.

Of course, human motives are even more complex. The form, cause, and use of anger is as complicated and unpredictable as any human behavior. We do not want to rule out the possibility that anger can be used strategically and consciously to build or maintain power. However, in the many public disputes that we have studied, anger seems most of all to be a natural human response to pain or the threat of pain.

Why Are People Angry?

We have identified at least six types of anger that are typically displayed in public disputes. People who are already hurt often express anger out of frustration with wrongs that cannot be righted. People who suspect they will be hurt in the future are driven in part by fear, which easily takes the form of anticipatory anger. At least one type of anger, on the other hand, does not grow out of physical or other types of pain already incurred or clearly perceived. Indignant, self-righteous anger arises when fundamental values and beliefs, and not simply life and limb, are challenged or threatened. People will fight, sometimes to the death, for the beliefs that give meaning to their lives.

Thus, we see three basic circumstances when anger is likely to arise—when people have been hurt, when they feel threatened by risks not of their own making, or when they believe that their fundamental beliefs are being challenged. In each of these circumstances anger can be compounded by related factors. For example, when people feel weak in the face of others who are more powerful, their anger is increased. When people feel they have not been treated fairly, or with respect, their anger multiplies. If they have been manipulated, trivialized, ignored or, worse still, lied to, the initial source of their anger may be less important than their sense of unfairness. People are angry in these situations not only because someone lied to them, but also because they feel duped or fooled. Lastly, anger may be part of a carefully thought-out strategic plan aimed at manipulating the reactions of others. Public displays of anger can be an effective means of "rallying the troops," altering the perceptions that others have of us, or bullying others into accepting our demands.

While these categories are useful for analysis, we want to stress that many, if not most, real-life events involve a combination of circumstances. A confrontation that may seem to be about risk, is—at another level—a conflict over values. Anger that takes the form of moral outrage might actually be a defensive response triggered by fear. While the case studies we present focus on only one type of anger at a time, in almost all circumstances it should be obvious that events and explanations are interconnected. Our intention is not to develop rigid categorizations for describing public anger, but rather to show how the six principles of the mutual-gains approach can and should be applied differently in different sets of circumstances.

Rational and Irrational Anger

Many commentators cannot avoid the temptation to add still another distinction among types of anger. They want to differentiate between rational and irrational anger. During the many seminars for top-level executives and government officials, almost always at least one participant will come to the podium and ask, "But what do I when I'm dealing with really crazy people? How do I deal with people who rant and rave, throw themselves in front of bulldozers, and chain themselves to trees?" While some anger is accepted as rational and normal, some is seen as irrational and abnormal.

Some kinds of anger seem to make sense. If your child were hurt in an industrial accident, you would have a right to be angry. In fact, when people don't display a kind of rage at extreme circumstance, others think they are "not normal." In the 1988 presidential debate, Michael Dukakis was asked, if his wife were raped and murdered, would he favor the death penalty? A distasteful question, indeed, but the candidate's response drew even wider criticism. "No, I don't," Dukakis calmly replied, moving quickly to a discussion of the war on drugs.[2] The press and the public were horrified that a presidential candidate would approach such a terrible situation with so little emotion and so little outrage. Dukakis's answer left one pundit to exclaim: "Well, he became—at least the presence there seemed to be a man half-formed—a big, cold brain and no heart."[3]

Yet other kinds of anger are often met with disbelief. A Cambridge, Massachusetts man recently went on a hunger strike to protest the local cable television station's lack of a Portuguese-language channel. In November of 1993, a Minneapolis meat wholesaler's trucks were firebombed by animal-rights extremists, causing $100,000 in damage. To most people, such behavior seems radical and extreme.

During the Cold War, protesters of the U.S. military build-up judged the seemingly rational discussions about the "missile gap" between the former Soviet Union and the U.S. to be irrational and self-destructive. In fact, many academics pointed out the faulty logic of such thinking. If each side believed it had to close the gap, the end result could only be mutual proliferation of deadly nuclear weapons. To these opponents, the "missile gap" was insanity masquerading as cold, calculating reason. But for at least some strategists promoting the build-up of weapons, "mutually assured destruction" was a powerful means of avoiding nuclear war. Proponents of "closing the gap" believed that the chances that either side would use nuclear weapons were extremely small. In the eyes of these strategists, the protesters were caught up in an uninformed and emotional reaction to a strategic action with a clear rationale and a high likelihood of success. Who was right?

We argue this: It simply doesn't matter whether you think that someone else's anger is rational or irrational. Someone else's behavior may appear bizarre to you, but from where they are standing, "zealots" see their outrage as quite logical and rational. The young woman tying herself to a tree may be acting in the way that she thinks is most likely to attract the attention of the press. She may sincerely believe that unless she takes this action, the things she loves—trees, forest, and animals—will surely die. Others, compelled by circumstances and motivations not easily understood by the rest of us, may appear irrational. Yet, it is almost always a mistake to treat someone else's anger as irrational.

The problem lies in how we perceive the actions of others in relation to our own. Lee Ross, a social psychologist at Stanford University, points out that most people operate from a position of "naive realism." This perspective is rooted in the belief that we are able to interpret reality objectively, and that our social attitudes, beliefs, preferences, and priorities are rational, un-emotional, and unbiased. Consequently, because of, and in order to maintain this belief, when others disagree with us, we must assume one of three things. We assume our opponents were exposed to or had access to limited information. That is, we know something they don't. Second, we may decide that our opponents are simply biased due to mistaken beliefs, ideology, or self-interest. For example, "They are misinterpreting the facts because they are liberals. Of course they cannot understand!" If these two explanations don't fit, we must assume that our opponents are too irrational to arrive at the proper conclusions given the evidence at hand. We conclude that they are not only biased, but perhaps unstable as well. They must be divorced from reality or else they would see things as we do.

Dale Griffin and Lee Ross illustrate the problems of naive realism through a study undertaken by Elizabeth Newton, a doctoral candidate at Stanford University. In her study, the subjects were given two roles, as either tappers or listeners. The tappers were given 25 well-known songs and asked to tap out the song to a listener sitting across from them at the table. In addition, the tapper was asked to estimate the percentage of her peers likely to succeed at the task. The listener was asked to identify the tune. The study then compared the tappers' estimates with the actual success rate of the listeners. While tappers estimated, on average, that the song would be identified 50 percent of the time, the listeners only succeeded in three out of 120 times, or less than 3 percent! The tapper, the melody clear and plain in her head, could not identify with the kind of information the listener actually received. The tapper, secure in her knowledge of both the tune and her ability to convey it, had failed to account for the very different stimuli the listener would receive. "It's obvious!" the tapper would exclaim with great frustration. "No. You are making a series of random taps without any melody," the listener might reply. Griffin and Ross conclude, "Issues look different to opposing partisans, who think their own perceptions—and emotional reactions—are the only 'natural' ones."[4]

The dangers of labeling your opponents as "irrational" are substantial. First, by discounting their behavior as irrational you may shore up your own self-confidence, you may also limit your ability to absorb new information. For example, the "other side" may have additional insights that could aid both of you in bringing the dispute to a close. But you must remain open to hearing and considering what they have to say for the information to be of any use. Second, you may discount plausible arguments or evidence that require you to change your mind. The "trap" of the self-fulfilling prophecy (i.e., what you hear and see are what you expect to hear and see because you ignore or discount everything else) is very dangerous. Keep telling yourself that you are not necessarily more likely than they are to fully grasp the full complexity of the situation or to draw the proper inferences from the facts at hand. Third, by starting down the path of defining anger as irrational, you are more likely to exacerbate "irrational" anger by asserting and arguing that you are the only one who is rational. The more rational you attempt to be, the more likely you are to provoke the other side. By attributing other people's anger to insanity or maladjustment, you will undermine your own attempts to deal with an angry public.

Thus, we argue, it is not helpful to distinguish between rational and irrational, justified or unjustified, appropriate or inappropriate anger. Our definition is: Anger is a response to pain or threat of pain, real or perceived. Whether or not it seems rational to us does not matter. Even though we may not understand (or agree with) the reasons for someone else's anger, and even though we may be certain that we have not injured anyone or threatened to injure anyone, angry people believe that they are, will be, or have been threatened. This is what is important: If people believe they are threatened or think you have hurt them, whether you have or not, they will instinctively react in anger.

We believe that there are many advantages to employing our definition of anger. First, rather that writing off someone else's behavior to "emotion," "hysteria," or "nerves," we will immediately focus on finding the causes or perceived threats that underlie their anger. This underscores the need for problem-solving. Second, by assuming that anger is legitimate, we force ourselves to emphasize the concerns of the other side, rather than devaluing or downplaying them. We believe that acknowledging the concerns of others offers many advantages that we will detail later. Third, by viewing anger as defensive, rather than as offensive, we are more inclined to look for ways of easing people's pain. This will forestall counterproductive actions on our part that escalate rather than deescalate conflict.

Typical Responses to an Angry Public

What are the conventional responses to the six different kinds of anger we have enumerated? We will illustrate them, with brief vignettes that highlight the advantages and disadvantages of the conventional response to public

anger. Many responses represent what intelligent, capable, and competent people have found works for them. In some instances, the conventional response is adequate. However, we believe public officials and private managers can do better. More importantly, what has worked in one situation for a particular manager may not work in another, or may not work again. Most responses to anger, in our view, do not grow out of a well-honed theory of action. We will highlight cases in which the "typical" approach has not worked well or has led to long-term (unintended) consequences that have been quite problematic. Finally, we will use the vignettes that follow to sketch a very different way of thinking, which will be elaborated in more detail in Chapter III.

Anger and Hurt

People are usually angry if they have been hurt severely. This hurt may take the form of bodily injury or financial loss. Human error may set off a chain of uncontrollable events that leads to disaster. Systematic failure to plan ahead, on the part of institutions or their leaders, can often exacerbate disasters. In other cases, accidents have happened or injury has been inflicted because both producers and consumers could not anticipate what would occur. In still other instances, criminal or malicious behavior may lead to or compound disasters. Whatever the cause, when people have been hurt, they look to the cause of their hurt, and want compensation for the pain they have had to bear. People quickly become victims who want to know who is responsible for their plight, what can be done to ease their suffering, and what kind of compensation they will receive for wrongs committed.

Consider, for instance, the methyl isocyanate that leaked from Union Carbide's plant in Bhopal, India, in the early morning of December 4, 1984. An estimated 7,000 people died from the accidental poison leak and 200,000 were reported injured.[5] To this day, many residents still report symptoms such as breathlessness, blurred vision, inflamed eyes, and fatigue, not to mention continued panic attacks and nightmares. What was the response to this "crisis" as the *New York Times* called it? In one of its first press releases, The Union Carbide Corporation stated that it was "deeply concerned about this incident." Less than a week later, the company announced it would contribute $830,000 to a special relief fund for disabled survivors. The company also contributed $1 million to the emergency efforts. In addition, Union Carbide pledged to open an orphanage for children left without parents.

What are the strengths of this approach? Direct compensation, such as the company's $830,000 pledge, may help alleviate the suffering of the victims. It may also forestall or ease the flogging that will certainly follow in the press. If the company offers money, or something else of value—like technical assistance—they will at least be seen as doing something. Payments to charities and "good causes," such as Union Carbide's offer to establish an orphanage, appeal to people's concern about the plight of the helpless and innocent and put a human face on a faceless corporation. In more pragmatic terms, direct offers of compensation may very well establish a "first offer" of what a company or an agency is willing to pay, before the victims flock to waiting injury attorneys. The fact is that early and speedy offers of compensation can improve a company's chances of limiting liability if a case does go to court.

There are, however, serious weaknesses to this approach. In such a tragic situation, offers of money will be seen as not just inadequate, but unfeeling and insulting, particularly in the face of death and human suffering. Furthermore, any direct, specific, and unilateral offers of compensation will immediately be devalued because they come from the presumed cause of the suffering. Those who accept offers of financial assistance, especially when their neighbors refuse money on grounds of principle, may feel they have been bribed or paid to shut up. Someone is also sure to ask, "Where in the world did that $830,000 figure come from, and who decided it was enough?" Thus, immediate offers of money will be suspect and undoubtedly seem arbitrary. The company will appear to be jumping the gun, or hosing down the fire. If the company does not base monetary compensation on a formula for determining what is fair given the injuries inflicted, it will lose all credibility. Since there are no standard formulas, it is not possible for the company to develop a quick or a unilateral response that will be accepted by all parties.

What is a "better" response to the same situation? First, the company should acknowledge responsibility for the disaster, express genuine compassion for those who have been hurt, and apologize for the pain and suffering the company may have caused. At least one Union Carbide official had the right idea when he said, on viewing the plant with Mr. Anderson, "We want to find out all that is possible on what happened and why it happened . . . . Believe me, it's shaken me to the core . . . . I knew many of these people who worked here, and this is something that really tears me up."[6] Second, the company should talk directly to those who were injured about some act of contrition that they, not the company, would deem appropriate. Third, as attempts to develop a compensation package get under way, the company should formulate and test various general principles for determining fair compensation. This should be done in conjunction with the victims and state explicitly what financial resources are available.

Anger and Risk

Sometimes people are angry because they are afraid they will be hurt. In our highly complex technological society, there is a great deal of uncertainty as to the risks associated with drinking the water, eating the food, and utilizing highly engineered products that take years to develop but become readily available over time. This uncertainty often leaves citizens feeling that they have very little control over the risks they encounter. The situation is further exacerbated when the risks are difficult to quantify, or when the only explanations available are presented in the arcane language of science. All anyone wants to know is what dangers they face and whether these dangers can be avoided. They want answers to their questions from people they can understand and trust. Unfortunately, it is not that simple.

Consider the choices facing the residents of Jacksonville, Arkansas. Some of the town's inhabitants, many of them poor, live next to an abandoned Vertac Chemical plant that once produced Agent Orange, a defoliant used during the Vietnam War. One day in 1985, the parents of a three-month-old boy awoke to find the child dead in his crib. The night before, he had been fed infant formula mixed with tap water. While the official death certificate listed Sudden Infant Death Syndrome (SIDS) as the cause, the parents and their doctor believed toxins from the Vertac site were to blame. Tissue samples from the baby indicated elevated levels of chlorophenols. The Centers for Disease Control proposed a study of 100 tissue samples from other SIDS babies in Arkansas. The test results were thrown out because the independent laboratory conducting the test failed quality-control inspections. Tests of the tap water were inconclusive. Although one study conducted in 1986 suggested no significant difference between the chemical exposure experienced by children in Jacksonville and by children in another town used as a control, some scientists who visited the site stated that merely breathing the air was likely to be harmful.

The response of the community leadership to the potential risk of living next to this major superfund site was typical. With the help of Hercules, the former owner of the site, and a hired public relations consultant, prominent citizens formed Jacksonville People with Pride (JPWP). The group produced a booklet stating that there was no proven link between dioxin (the incinerator emission of greatest concern at the site) and human disease. The mayor of the town, in an attempt to trivialize the concerns of the abutters, asserted that, "There's a health risk to everything."[7] The city's representative in the state legislature said that he was "far more concerned about toxic journalism than he was about toxic waste." The City Council passed a resolution condemning *Family Circle* magazine for printing an article about the risks of environmental contamination in Jacksonville, and told its reporters to "stay in the kitchen." Twenty Jacksonville doctors signed a letter denying any link between dioxin emissions and serious health danger. The U.S. Environmental Protection Agency (EPA) stated that no clear link had been established between the Vertac site and the deaths in the city.

The response of Hercules, their public relations firm, and the town—as well as state and federal officials—was, unfortunately, what we have come to expect. A 1987 study of risk communication by the National Research Council found "almost no success stories" of successful risk communication by industry or government.[8] The typical response to anxious residents worried about the safety of their children involves several time-worn techniques. First, those defending the facility seek to minimize or deny the claims of those who think they, or the public at large, are in danger. Second, they seek endorsements of respected community leaders or famous celebrities to add to the "credibility" of their counterclaims. Third, they blame the press for stirring up residents unnecessarily, disturbing the peace, and threatening the reputation and economy of the community. Fourth, they respond to scientific uncertainty by throwing up their hands and pointing out that even the experts cannot agree among themselves.

What are the strengths of this approach? The fears of some residents may be assuaged, at least for a short period. "Don't worry, it's not as bad as you've heard," residents are told. As one Jacksonville citizen said, "We've got to trust somebody."[9] Respected spokespersons may lend credibility to corporate or governmental claims. For example, if twenty doctors in the town support your statements, most people will assume you cannot be entirely wrong. You might also succeed in isolating some of the community activists from the rest of the population by pointing out that they have overreacted, given the uncertainties. In the Jacksonville case, no one had proven anything, not even the respected Centers for Disease Control. According to JPWP, "the poor people across town" were reacting out of fear, not reason. By blaming the press, JPWP sought to focus the debate on what others were or were not doing, rather than on the steps they might take to reduce whatever risks did exist. If the media were, indeed, rabble-rousing, then the public might be less likely to believe what the press had to say.

However, there are many other weaknesses in this approach. By not recognizing and acknowledging the legitimate fears of the residents, town leaders multiplied them. The residents' fears were not allayed by arguing that they were unfounded; in fact, quite the contrary. As the probable agent(s) of the risk(s) involved, JPWP was not likely to be believed. Each denial heightened the anxiety of some members of the community. While inconclusive evidence might be enough to prove to an academic scientist that something is not yet known to be true, uncertainty only magnifies the nightmares of those actually facing grave risks. Finally, blaming the press for fanning the flames of mistrust usually increases the level of negative coverage. After city leaders condemned *Family Circle* for publishing the article listing Jacksonville as one of many communities at risk for contamination-caused disease, the magazine initiated a full-length investigation highlighting the Jacksonville situation.

What would have been a more intelligent and self-interested response? First, the local leadership should have acknowledged the concerns of the community. Though the community's fears might or might not have been well founded, their concerns were real enough. Second, local and state agencies should have promised to put all the information they had on the table, perhaps offering to host a panel of experts chosen together with residents to sort through the facts. Third, they should have offered to jointly develop contingency plans for addressing various problems, assuming independent investigations confirmed the worst. Fourth, they should have created a public forum in which short-term steps aimed at minimizing or managing risks, regardless of subsequent findings, could be discussed. Finally, they should have worked with the press, particularly the ownership and the editorial boards, to keep everyone informed of all actions being taken.

Anger and Belief

Anger emerges not only out of physical hurt already incurred or danger clearly perceived. Indignant, self-righteous anger often arises when people's values and beliefs, and not simply life and limb, are threatened. Continued war in the former Yugoslavia, unrest in the diverse ethnic republics of the former Soviet Union, the decades-long battles in Northern Ireland, and the lasting Palestinian-Israeli conflict all serve to showcase the violence that can erupt when people's fundamental beliefs, values, and identities are challenged. Closer to home, the shooting of physicians who perform abortions, violent confrontations over court-imposed school desegregation, and the destruction of long-term medical research projects because they involve experimentation on animals, show that value conflicts all too frequently escalate into violence and killing. Arguments over principle are perhaps the most difficult to address, even when no one has been injured. As the old adage goes, politics and religion ought never to be brought up in polite conversation. In the realm of public discourse, however, they arise regularly, and often, with a vengeance.

People take their beliefs very seriously, and they want others to take them seriously as well. Many groups seek opportunities to explain their beliefs and to convince others of their merits. Any attack on their fundamental beliefs will be seen by many groups as a direct and dangerous attack on the group itself. As we all know, some people are even willing to die for their beliefs rather than be forced to compromise. The Revolutionary orator Patrick Henry was not the last person who would yell, "Give me liberty, or give me death!"

In late 1992, a reporter and a photographer from *People* magazine went to extraordinary lengths to pursue an article. Picked up by a windowless van at the airport, their watches taken away, they were jostled back and forth through traffic by two subsequent drivers to a small, nondescript suburban home to meet a women in a strawberry-blonde wig and rose-tinted glasses. They had arrived at the hideout of the head of the Animal Liberation Front (ALF), a group claiming responsibility for millions of dollars of damage to U.S. scientific laboratories. ALF has raided almost 100 research facilities and fur farms on behalf of the rights of animals. "I don't think that destroying a building can really be classified as violence. I think that burning an animal is violent," the woman told *People*.[10] "Valerie" (her pseudonym) concluded: "I don't think we should ever take an animal's life, ever. For me, compassion is indivisible."[11]

What has been the response of the medical establishment, whose pursuit of cures for human suffering depends, at least in part, on the testing of animals? In 1991, the American Medical Association (AMA) officially censured a far less radical group, known as the Physicians' Committee for Responsible

Medicine (PCRM), for "misrepresenting the critical role animals play in medical research."[12] PCRM had a membership of about 3,000 physicians and 50,000 others as of 1992. In 1993, the AMA sponsored a series of workshops to enlist physicians in the "fight" against animal-rights activists. The workshops had three goals: to establish a nationwide network of like-minded physicians to speak up on the matter, to provide information these physicians might need to support the importance of animal research, and to establish further links with other "right-minded" organizations. "If this [animal rights] movement is successful, untold millions will suffer the ravages of disease," a senior vice president of the AMA said in one of the workshops.[13] The vice president told physicians to draw a line in the sand. An attending physician told the *American Medical News*, ". . . I can't join in the argument that animals have the same rights as humans."[14]

What are the "tricks of the trade" usually prescribed today when a clash over fundamental beliefs is involved? Most importantly, posit your own beliefs in direct opposition to "theirs." Second, couch the debate in terms of a fight, drawing a line between "us" and "them," and dramatize the worst possible outcome if "their side wins." Third, seek to convince others of the reasonableness and righteousness of your cause. Fourth, challenge your opponents' credibility by accusing "them" of misrepresenting or falsifying facts. Finally, never enter into a dialogue with extremists or you will legitimize the very claims you are trying to defeat.

Of course, there is some merit to these prescriptions. You are more likely to become a "player" in a public debate, if that is your goal, by framing issues in terms of right and wrong, or good and bad. And raising fears about the worst possible outcome may well scare some people into supporting your views. It is possible to raise doubts about the credibility of others by pointing out their "mistakes." And, indeed, it boosts morale within your own group if you can show that you have taken a position, not out of selfishness, but out of concern for the betterment of humankind.

Of course, there are also serious problems with this approach. Most importantly, by couching your points in "fighting terms" and asserting first principles, you pick up the gauntlet tossed down by your attackers. By pushing your principles in opposition to theirs, the debate is polarized, making it unlikely that any kind of reasoned conversation, leading to the discovery of common ground, will be possible. Instead, the persons on the attack must continually shore up "their side" of the debate. Opinions in the "middle," however reasonable, tend to become casualties of the battle between two stark, but captivating extremes. Worst of all, partial solutions that might actually alleviate public concern are ignored or attacked. Any sign of weakness must be avoided. Dissent within the ranks (i.e., reasonableness) must be quashed in order to win the war.

What might you do instead? First, acknowledge that there are legitimate differences between you and those who oppose your ideas. Second, seek to understand the key differences between the two by entering into a dialogue in a neutral setting where more information and, perhaps, understanding might be achieved. Third, when attempting to solve the problem at hand, seek outcomes that respect everyone's principles. There may be a "third" way to solve the problem that respects the principles on both sides. For instance, large ski areas in the East, such as Killington, Vermont, have fought with state agencies and environmentalists over the amount of water they are permitted to withdraw from rivers and streams for snowmaking. However, Okemo, another ski area in Vermont, built a pond in a natural low-lying basin to collect snowmelt in the spring for the following season. The ski area got its snow. The trout and other aquatic life got the stream flows they needed to survive. In the language of negotiation, this is known as avoiding a zero-sum game, or "expanding the pie" so that mutual gains can be maximized. Last, do not paint people into corners. Attempt to avoid the pitfalls involved in labeling one side right and the other wrong. Such polarization tends to obscure both the complexity of the issue and the path to a possible middle ground. Efforts to vilify the "other side" only encourage "them" to vilify you, escalating the conflict.

Anger and Weakness

Anger may also arise when people feel weak in the face of others who are more powerful than they are. When people feel impotent or are unable to control circumstances, they are likely to rise up in anger. At too many public hearings, the public officials describing a proposed law or a private developer sketching a new development are calm and composed. But the lonely citizens, without political clout or extensive resources, are upset. They are the ones who shout. They are the ones who stand up and shake their fists. They are angry because they are frustrated. They do not have the power to impose their views. (Sometimes they don't even know who is making decisions or how they are made.) Often, they do not have the resources or information to judge whether a proposed decisions is really good or bad for them.

Consider, for example, the conflict between the Cree Indians of northern Quebec and Hydro-Quebec, the province's electric utility. The Cree are a small band of indigenous people who inhabit the subarctic eastern shores of Hudson Bay. Until the 1970s, many of the tribespeople earned their livelihood in traditional ways, fishing in the numerous rivers and following traplines deep into the rugged interior of the peninsula. Hydro-Quebec, a publicly-owned utility, reported assets of 36 billion Canadian dollars in 1990, serving over 3 million customers with a work force of 20,000. In the 1970's, the corporation embarked on an enormous hydroelectric project in the Crees' homeland. The project was dubbed the "project of the century" by then Quebec Premier Robert Bourassa. If fully completed, it would generate over 20,000 megawatts of electricity at a cost of some sixty billion Canadian dollars. Despite a 1975 agreement ceding lands to the utility, the Cree have been fighting the project ever since.

This represents a fierce clash between the vision of a modern, highly technological society and a long-standing, less technologically complex culture. The conflict is about the potential risks the Cree will face if development encroaches further on their native lands. The conflict is also about the very strong and the very weak. The Cree are not just angry because they fear the death of their culture; they are not just angry because their natural resources will be diminished by development, leaving them no way to make their way in a cold and harsh land. The Cree are angry because they feel powerless. As one member of the council in the town of Chisasibi said, "What we have said is that yes, our life is in many ways much easier than it used to be. But we are also prey to all the social diseases of the South. We are no longer in control of our lives."[15] In part, the Cree are angry because they no longer have the final say over what happens to them.

How did Hydro-Quebec respond to this small band of indigenous people, most with little or no formal education and limited exposure to modern urban life? First, in a court-ordered 1975 agreement, the province of Quebec paid the Cree and the Inuit $170 million for ceding much of their land to the Province. When questioned later about the impacts of the proposed Great Whale Project in the Cree territory, corporation officials responded that the lands had already been paid for and that the Cree had been adequately compensated. When attacked in the press by environmentalists and allies of the Cree, Hydro-Quebec asserted that their project was "truly one of the seven wonders of the world," and denied that there would be any major impacts on the environment or the Cree. Bourassa, in his second term as premier, said, "Seven million Quebecers cannot be wrong." The Cree chief in the village of Great Whale responded, "The premier seems to have suggested that it doesn't matter if you kill one thousand people—there are seven million people who need this."[16]

As the debate over the Great Whale Project intensified, corporation officials and provincial ministers attempted to speed up construction before provincial and federal environmental reviews could be completed. Ironically, while opposing the Crees' attempts to interject themselves into the formal decision-making process, Hydro-Quebec fought all federal attempts to impose national environmental assessment regulations, arguing, as one provincial official put it, "Hydroelectricity is a strategic sector of Quebec's future. It is absolutely essential that all elements of this future are controlled by Quebecers."[17]

When one party wields far more power and resources than another, we can almost always predict what will happen. The more powerful party offers compensation, or is forced to offer compensation; it then assumes that the matter is settled, and that it has acquired unencumbered rights to the property or goods purchased. The stronger party elaborates on the immense value of its undertaking and the benefits it will bring to the many. At the same time, the stronger party minimizes or ignores the concerns of the weaker party. Resisting all claims by weaker parties to participate in joint decision making, the stronger player invests tremendous resources fighting off all other powerful parties that attempt to inject themselves into the situation.

There are tremendous advantages to this strategy. After all, "might makes right." By ignoring the claims of the weak, and fighting off claims by those equally or even more powerful, one side can maintain and even increase its power or control. Those who are weaker may eventually give up and go away. Their lack of resources will make it difficult for them to build alliances or plead their case in the court of public opinion. If no one can hear their story, no one will respond. Despite its unattractive implications, the argument that overall benefits outweigh costs (regardless of their distribution), or that the majority should rule (regardless of the concerns of various minorities), may be convincing to the public.

But, as the Cree–Hydro-Quebec case suggests, there are certainly disadvantages to this strategy too. First, ignoring the weak tends to fuel their anger, not extinguish it; consequently, they may be able to build alliances that extend beyond the reach of their powerful adversaries. While Hydro-Quebec was winning the war of public opinion in Quebec, the Cree took their case to the United States, and even to Europe. Several U.S. environmental advocacy groups took out a full page ad in the *New York Times* to attack the "most destructive energy project ever in North America." As soon as events were recast in terms of David vs. Goliath, numerous advocates stepped forward to defend the defenseless. Such rock stars as Jackson Browne, Dan Fogelberg, and David Byrne played at a New York City benefit for the Cree called "Ban the Dam." Claiming that Hydro-Quebec was running roughshod over the weaker Cree, the tribe was able to garner numerous sympathetic stories in the American press. As one political leader in Quebec angrily stated, "Vicious, dishonest and mischievous propaganda has turned the James Bay agreement into a symbol of an intolerant Quebec which oppresses its aboriginal minorities."[18] As David Kuechle, a professor of labor relations at Harvard, has pointed out, while corporations may prevail on technical grounds, in court cases for instance, they can easily be "victimized by a commonly-held presumption: that corporations, through superior legal acumen and financial power, always win over the downtrodden and underprivileged."[19]

Last, but certainly not least, a strong case may be made that ignoring the concerns of the weak is simply wrong. Belief systems as diverse as Judeo-Christian ethics, Buddhist philosophy, and English common law, as well as many other systems of ethics and law, all assert some protection for the weak in the face of the strong and condemn the uncontrolled exercise of power— if for no other reason than to avoid an ungoverned life that is, according to Hobbes, nasty, brutish, and short.

What should the powerful do instead? First, listen to the concerns of the other side. People's frustrations at having little say in their lives will only be increased if their attempts to explain the situation as they see it go unheeded. Second, cede power to gain power by involving the weaker party in decision making. This does not mean, as we will explain later, giving up control. This does not mean handing over power unilaterally. That would be foolish. It does mean helping to balance the accessibility of information. It means practicing the principles of democracy, as terrifying and uncertain as that may be, to garner support and achieve superior outcomes. It means recognizing that power, in a pluralistic society, is as much about perception as about resources. Power, as Fisher, Ury, and Patton remind us in their book *Getting to Yes*, is multifaceted.[20] While one side might have greater power in the eyes of the law, or in terms of financial resources or technical expertise, the other side may have greater power in terms of moral persuasiveness or public sympathy.

Anger and Lies

Most people are quite indignant when they believe they have been lied to. Indeed, any sense that we have been manipulated, trivialized, ignored, or made to look the fool, fuels our feeling of rage. Nothing is more damaging to a relationship than having expectations of honesty, clarity, decency and good faith dashed by either lack of concern or outright lies.

Consider, for instance, the case of Dow Corning and silicone breast implants. In 1976, a researcher for Dow Corning quit in protest over the implant's purported safety problems. When the researcher stepped up his campaign to reveal the company's seeming cover-ups years later, Dow Corning officials told the press that since he was a disgruntled employee, his motives should be questioned. In 1984, a San Francisco federal court jury ruled that the company had committed fraud in marketing the silicone implant as safe. This ruling was upheld upon appeal. While an injured woman was awarded $1.5 million in punitive damages, much of the legal file was put under protective order. In addition to ensuring that any damning information was not released, the company labeled the ruling "a highly charged emotional piece of litigation."[21] Shortly after this case, in 1985, Dow Corning did include in its product literature a warning of possible immune-system sensitivity and potential migration of the silicone if the implants were to rupture. But in 1987, the company distanced itself even from this warning by asserting that such risks were linked to a less pure silicone not used by the company.

With concern growing rapidly in 1990 and 1991, Dow Corning set up a hot line in the fall of 1991 to address the concerns of women. But the hot line told women the devices were one hundred percent safe, and the U.S. Food and Drug Administration (FDA) soon after warned the company that information from the hot line was often misleading and sometimes false. In January of 1992, the *Washington Post* reported that the results of a 1973 study on four implanted beagles was misreported by the company. Although company scientists stated that the beagles remained in normal health after the implants, the laboratory that conducted this study reported that one of the dogs died and another developed a tumor.

As public outcry spun out of control, Dow Corning began to change direction. A new chief executive was appointed, a veteran of Dow Chemical's handling of the Agent Orange crisis. The company released documents that revealed some company personnel had been informed about the possible hazards of the implants. The company announced it would stop criticizing the FDA's investigations into the matter. The company also floated the idea of paying for removal of the implants for those who desired such an operation. The company hired former attorney general Griffin Bell to review its handling of the safety of its product. But a year later, the company seemed back to its old ways, refusing to turn over Griffin Bell's report to the FDA. An FDA official told the *Wall Street Journal,* "'Dow Corning has tried to create the public impression that they're cooperating fully with us. While they have sent us hundreds of thousands of documents that were reviewed for the report, they are not organized in any useful order."[22]

What is the typical response when evidence arises that a company has either ignored potential risks or lied to its customers about the safety of a product? Too often, the company attempts to conceal evidence while putting on a happy or at least a benign face for the public. When whistleblowers question the company's position, the company attempts to discredit them. The company mounts a public-relations campaign asserting its innocence under the guise of providing accurate scientific information. Even when the evidence mounts that the company has lied, it continues to assert that it has done no wrong. New policies of openness may even be announced, but as the company's fear of exposure to liability grows, damaging information is suppressed.

What can possibly be the advantage of lying to the public? Regardless of the accumulating evidence, by admitting no wrong or denying any mistakes, a company may shore up its legal position; at least that is what its general counsel is likely to argue. By denying all allegations and withholding information, critics and plaintiffs' attorneys will have less evidence to use against the company. Since public perception is more important than the truth—or so some company spokespeople would have us believe—what does a lie matter if it casts doubt in the public's mind about evidence implicating the company? Since the lie is often a sin of omission, as opposed to the commission of an act, it can be blamed on scientific uncertainty and inconclusive experimental results. "It's not that we didn't tell the truth, it's that we didn't know the truth," companies can say. The public can sometimes be forgiving, forgetful, and fickle. At his death, Richard Nixon's lies to the American people were placed by the national media in the larger context of his great political acumen and foreign-policy success. In the District of Columbia, Marion Barry's supporters were willing to forgive him in a 1994 mayoral campaign couched in the language of second chances and religious redemption. Many voters in Virginia didn't care, didn't believe, or had forgotten

Oliver North's lies to Congress. If you can ride out the storm, some media advisors assert, what does a little lying hurt over the long run?

Clearly, though, this approach can backfire. Lying to the public or concealing evidence, when exposed, severely damages if not destroys relationships. The press soon smells a scandal. The public feels they have been manipulated once again. Customers directly affected believe they may have made a potentially fatal decision and ask for their money back. Customers and consumers run to their attorneys. When private and public officials lie, not only is trust lost and relationships maimed, but reputations are destroyed. A company can not only lose millions of dollars in sales, it can face billions of dollars in litigation and injury payments. If a company loses its reputation, it sacrifices the very thing on which its business depends. Investors won't invest. Consumers won't buy. Talented employees will go elsewhere. Government agencies that lie will be faced with skeptical constituents when they attempt new projects. The public will reject governmental efforts when they discover that authority has been abused.

What might they do instead? By all means, they should tell the truth and admit mistakes. The costs of not telling the truth are simply too high. In a society with a strong press, strong independent academic institutions and advocacy groups, and a skeptical public, most lies will eventually be found out. It is much harder to gain credibility than to lose it, and it is much easier to destroy a reputation than to build one. Ultimately, regaining what has been lost by unintended or poorly-thought-out actions is even more difficult when the truth has been hidden.

Anger and Show

Anger may also be for show. Public displays of anger may be a device for shoring up or improving a bargaining position, and for intimidating others. Advocacy groups often find that the best way to build political credibility, increase membership, and raise funds is to engage in a fight and to eschew civil discourse.

For years, the EPA has attempted to formulate regulations to protect farm workers in the field from the spraying of pesticides. The EPA is required to regulate how long workers should remain away from newly sprayed areas and what kinds of precautions employers must take to ensure worker safety. After years of failing to draft acceptable rules, the EPA brought the divergent interests—farm workers, pesticide manufacturers, farmers, state regulators, and others—together to jointly craft guidelines. The parties met for several months. As the final draft approached completion, suddenly and unexpectedly, the farm workers' representatives pulled out of the impending agreement. The other parties, surprised, asked the farm workers what had happened. "The facilitator was biased," they claimed. "We didn't trust the process."

In most cases, everyone but the farm workers would be left wondering exactly what had transpired. In this case, an answer came from an unexpected source. Since the interested parties had used an on-line computer bulletin board to share information, and the farm workers had kept the computers they were given, the EPA was privy to the farm workers' internal communications for a while before it became clear that these transmissions were accessible to everyone. Farm worker exchanges on the bulletin board made it clear that they had walked out because the negotiations were going to succeed. That is, there was going to be an acceptable agreement, one that responded reasonably to the concerns of the farm workers. They decided their interests would be better served by pulling out than by going along. The group had used this particular conflict to politicize its membership and to raise funds for its organizing and lobbying efforts. They were about to lose the very thing that kept them together. They engineered what the others took to be a hostile walkout because it better served their interests to pursue further litigation.

Dealing with an Angry Public: The Conventional Wisdom

We believe that many managers and officials in the public and private sectors have been getting bad advice from their public-relations advisors. These officials are caught between public-relations practitioners with sophisticated suggestions regarding spin control and litigators dispensing legal advice in the un-courtlike realm of public opinion. All too often, the advice goes something like this.

> Don't talk to the public. Conceal information. Reveal as little as possible. Those angry people are crazy extremists. Whatever you do, don't give them an official forum. Don't legitimize their views by meeting with them. If you are forced to converse, do it on your own turf. Have low-level staff or hired public-relations experts handle these discussions. Make sure they are private and quiet. You don't want conversations you can't control occurring in full view of the press. If word does get out that you've done something wrong, draw a line in

the sand and start fighting the battle for public sympathy. Let public figures (like rock stars, movie actors, former public officials, and upstanding members of the community) take your case to the public. Discredit and denounce your critics. Ignore, or at least minimize, their claims. Hide behind scientific uncertainty, and if that fails, hire your own experts to discredit theirs. If the truth about what you've done becomes obvious, offer compensation to make it go away. Maybe money will shut them up.

We believe there is a better way; one that can help American business compete more effectively in the global market and that can help restore faith in our governing institutions. What we are proposing is completely consistent with such innovative business strategies as total quality management and the main thrust of recent efforts to reinvent government. What we are proposing is at once pragmatic and ethical. The actions involved are simple and adaptable. They flow from the six basic principles that comprise the mutual-gains approach to dealing with an angry public. The next chapter elaborates on the ideas hinted at in the previous examples, and explores them in more detail.

CHAPTER III

The Mutual-Gains Approach

When the citizens of Jacksonville, Arkansas, expressed grave concerns about the risks of living near a toxic waste site, they were told, "Don't worry, there's a risk to everything." When Cree leaders challenged the proposed Great Whale hydroelectric project, the Premier of Quebec replied, "Seven million Quebecers cannot be wrong." A noted public-relations firm advised Clorox to avoid any debate on the scientific merits of chlorine safety because the public would be "too emotional." Clearly, many companies and many governmental agencies are going about public relations in the wrong way. They only make matters worse when they try to convince concerned citizens "not to worry" or explain to the minority that the majority is right. They certainly do not help their cause when they refuse to interact directly with the groups that are angry about what they have done, might do, or seem to stand for.

The Mutual-Gains Approach: Six Principles

In lieu of the conventional approach, we offer the *mutual-gains approach*—six simple guidelines that provide a framework for dealing more effectively with an angry public:

- Acknowledge the concerns of the other side.
- Encourage joint fact finding.
- Offer contingent commitments to minimize impacts if they do occur; promise to compensate knowable but unintended impacts.
- Accept responsibility, admit mistakes, and share power.

- Act in a trustworthy fashion at all times.
- Focus on building long-term relationships.

These six principles sound remarkably simple, and at first blush they are. When we review, however, the way they translate into concrete actions, it will be clear that they reflect a profound shift from traditional ways of doing business.

When companies and agencies are pitted against opponents in painful and protracted conflicts, or when an adversary has been demonized or ridiculed as a "money-grubbing capitalist pig" or a "ecofascist femi-Nazi," it becomes almost impossible to listen to, let alone acknowledge, that group's concerns. Yet the group being challenged must follow the first principle: *Try to look at the issue from the standpoint of others.* Indeed, it is only by taking a step back from one's own interests, and "walking a mile in the other side's shoes," that underlying interests (as opposed to positions) can be identified. In the words of negotiation theory, the players will be stuck in a zero-sum bargaining game—where the only common ground is the need to perpetuate the conflict—if they fail to appreciate the needs and concerns of the contending stakeholders. As Max Bazerman and Margaret Neal conclude in their book *Negotiating Rationally,* "In a negotiation, if each side understands and can explain the viewpoint of the other, it increases the likelihood of reaching a negotiated resolution."[1]

The second principle also seems quite straightforward: *Encourage joint fact-finding.* In other words, try to generate information that is believable to both sides. For parties used to operating in the traditional mode, this can be worrisome. Attorneys, in particular, spend a lot of time advising clients not to release information that might be damaging. Dow Corning spent at least fifteen years and countless dollars to keep the evidence in damning lawsuits from escaping the confines of the courtroom. Business innovators do not want to let proprietary information enter the public domain; their competitors might use it to undercut them.

On the other hand, decision-makers want to have the best possible information to be certain they are making wise decisions. But the "best possible" information might not be the most convincing. In fact, it might be counterproductive to share information, if the "other side" is going to reject the content because of the source. Thus, decision-makers must decide what information others will find compelling. What should they share? What should they not reveal? What should be left for others to discover on their own?

Information gathered, analyzed, modeled, and carefully packaged behind closed doors may have no credibility when it appears, even if it is quite accurate. The answer is to open the doors wide and pursue fact-finding together. This means gathering data, analyzing data, and drawing conclusions together. This is a frightening proposition for someone who wants desperately to control the outcome. But in a world of a skeptical public, ready with instant expertise and a ready conspiracy theory, joint fact-finding is far more likely to lead to believable findings.

The third principle states: *Offer contingent commitments to minimize impacts if they do occur; and promise to compensate unintended but knowable effects.* It does make sense to minimize impacts up front, when they occur, rather than to wait and to pay a premium later. For example, we, the authors, were involved with a dispute that arose when a regional hospital decided to relocate to a different neighborhood. The abutters at the new site complained, "With all the traffic and the noise of ambulances, our property values will be reduced." Under most circumstances, the hospital would have answered either, "It's not our problem, we have the permits we need to move," or, "Don't worry, property values won't be affected." The right answer would have been for the hospital to encourage residents within an agreed-upon perimeter to file credible home appraisals well before they planned to sell. Homeowners could then file these appraisals at a local bank. The hospital would establish an escrow account. If a landowner sold any time within five to ten years after the hospital was built, and if they didn't realize the appraised cost of their property plus cost-of-living increases reflecting the changes in economic conditions in the area, the escrow account could be tapped to cover the difference. Such an offer of property value insurance would have settled the debate about what would or would not occur in the future. Up-front contingent commitments ensure those at risk that they are "held harmless." Such commitments do require corporate and government actors to put their money where their collective mouths are. If a company or an agency promises that something will not happen, or cannot happen, they should stand behind that promise with a contingent offer of compensation.

The fourth point is also quite succinct: *Accept responsibility, admit mistakes, and share power.* Consider the story of the hospital once again. The hospital's initial proposal for a new structure called for a very large facility, with an estimated price tag of $120 million for 120 beds. After a state regulatory agency urged the hospital to initiate a public advisory process and reconsider its proposal, a revised $70-million, 90-bed facility emerged. More importantly, the new, smaller structure more closely reflected the rapidly changing and competitive health-care market, which assumed shorter stays, more emphasis on ambulatory care, and increased reliance on a network of home-based and community-based services. The initial proposal would probably have been a financial failure. The community felt that it had saved the hospital $50 million in capital costs, not to mention continuous operating losses, through its opposition to the original proposal. But when the hospital leadership had the chance to thank the community for helping to come up with something smaller and more attuned to both local circumstances and the broader health-care market, they couldn't bring themselves to do it. They were smarting from the state's rejection of their initial proposal. Moreover, they resented being forced to sit side by side with their critics and "being told what to do by nonexperts" (even though that's not what happened). The goodwill the hospital could have bought by graciously admitting that their initial proposal was not nearly as good as the one that emerged from the public advisory process, was enormous. The positive effect that a simple "Thanks" would have had on hospital-community relations evaded the grasp of the public-relations professionals hired by the hospital. The hospital administrators found sharing power, even though they retained the final authority to decide, totally distasteful.

The fifth point is closely related to the previous point: *Act in a trustworthy fashion.* The concept of trust is elusive. What is it? How can it be created? Does it differ from situation to situation, or culture to culture? While the debate surrounding the concept of trust continues, we think the mechanics of trust-building are relatively straightforward. Trust, or the lack of it, relates primarily to expectations. Thus, to inspire trust one must shape expectations; or, to put it as simply as possible, we must "say what we mean and mean what we say" if we want to hold on to the trust we have or build more. If we camouflage our intentions, sugarcoat the truth, or spin the story to make it "sound better," we are not saying what we mean. This is not to say that subtlety and sophistication in communication are not important. Rather, the authors put the highest priority on the age-old maxim: "Honesty is the best policy." It is also crucial to mean what we say; that is, we should never make promises we do not intend to keep. Nor should we ask for commitments we know that others will be unable to honor. Not only are reputations ruined by exaggerations and misstatements that must be retracted or contradicted later on, but trust, once lost, is almost impossible to regain.

Despite the difficulties that many American managers have in accepting these five ideas, the last is harder still: *Focus on building long-term relationships.* With the emphasis on quarterly reports, annual shareholder meetings, short-term stock market fluctuations, shifts in monthly cost-of-living and balance-of-trade reports, and the latest opinion polls, top managers in both the public and private sector seem utterly unable to look beyond their immediate situations. Indeed, there are tremendous incentives, especially in an increasingly decentralized, international, and competitive marketplace, to ignore long-term relationships. But, as companies like Saturn (the automaker) are finding out, tending to the long-term needs of customers actually pays off. While the costs of not paying attention to long-term relationships may not, in the short term, be obvious, over time disgruntled customers, frustrated constituents, and an angry public can and will buy elsewhere. Consumers sent such a message to Detroit automakers in the 1970s, as did the voters in the 1992 presidential election. If you care about your reputation, if you care about your credibility, if you want to affect the bottom line two years from now, focus on building long-term relationships.

There they are: the six principles of the mutual-gains approach. Now that we have pointed out just how hard they might be to implement, we have to make a convincing case that they can be put into practice. The remaining portion of this chapter examines a composite case study, combining the details of a number of real life cases under the title of "The Old Plastics Factory." This case is meant to animate the six principles and to contrast the differences, not just in theoretical terms but in practice, between the conventional wisdom and the mutual-gains approach. This case has been used to teach the mutual-gains approach to over fifteen hundred high-level public- and private-sector managers and executives over the past several years.

Practitioners sometimes choose to adopt bits and pieces of this approach, but the authors advocate using the total mutual-gains approach as a comprehensive strategy for dealing with an angry public. Each of its six points is related to and informs the others. Together, they comprise a principled approach. Abiding by some but not all of the principles may undermine their overall effectiveness. Discounting one principle or another will likely lead to actions that contradict one another and exacerbate, rather than adequately address, the public's anger. In short, this approach is best understood as more than the sum of its parts. Of course, blindly marching ahead with a short set of instructions, without taking account of the uniqueness of each situation, will surely cause even more problems. Thus, the six principles must be used to guide and inform experienced judgment, and not merely serve as a cookie cutter to be applied to the raw material of any and every dispute.

The Old Plastics Factory

Background

Halcyon Chemical Company, a multinational firm, purchased a plastics manufacturing plant in 1979 with every intention of operating it. However, with the recession of the early 1980s, demand decreased for the plastic valves the plant produced. Furthermore, advances in carbon fibers soon made the heavier and less sturdy plastic valves obsolete. After mothballing the plant and carrying the financial liability for two years, Halcyon sold the facility to a developer, Marvin Associates. As the real-estate market heated up, this developer razed the plant in the hope of selling the land. With a bustling new business center, including high-technology companies, forming at the intersection of two major freeways, Marvin decided to build a shopping mall to serve both the daytime workers in the business center and the many residents of the surrounding towns.

In 1990, Marvin's attorneys contacted Halcyon's legal department. In the final phases of construction, during work on a corner of the parcel, the construction crews uncovered various kinds of waste containers filled with toxic waste. While the wastes were known to be on the EPA's list of toxic contaminants, the extent of the leakage into the surrounding environment and the potential risks to businesses and residents remained unknown. The chief counsel of Halcyon informed her C.E.O. that the company might attempt to release itself from any liability as a potentially responsible party under the Comprehensive Environmental Response, Compensation, and Liability Act (CERCLA) given the short period that Halcyon had owned the property as well as the terms of the sale to Marvin. But, as likely, the strict-and-joint-liability clause of the federal act would lead to a lengthy legal battle. After calls to several other companies that had found themselves in similar situations, and after hearing about the protracted litigation and costs involved, Halcyon decided to take responsibility for the clean-up.

Halcyon contacted Marvin Associates. After almost a year of negotiation and failed efforts to bring the former and bankrupt owners of the original plastics plant into the cleanup process, the two companies agreed to a 60/40 split of the costs (with Halcyon accepting the larger share). The two companies hired a contamination expert to help them. He reported that the contamination, as they feared, was substantial. Numerous solvents deemed potential carcinogens had seeped into the soil and were still in the many barrels that had been buried. Fortunately, the consultant noted, the risks to public health in all likelihood were not very great, since nothing was found in the soil at the edges of the site. The site itself sat in a small depression in the landscape, and fortunately a bed of clay underlay at least part of the site. Thus, according to the consulting engineers, there was only a small likelihood that the contaminants had migrated off-site into adjacent soils or reached the underground aquifer that supplied the community's drinking water. The consultant recommended that Halcyon (which had assumed primary responsibility for the cleanup) apply for a state waiver. If the company could prove that contamination and its associated risks were "not serious," they could avoid elaborate state regulatory review procedures prior to remediation of the site. That is, the potentially responsible parties could themselves make most of the decisions and assume most of the responsibilities for cleaning up a site. The state would still confirm, at the end, that the cleanup has met all the relevant standards, but the choice of cleanup technology and the like would be less confining. The consultant assured Halcyon that the waiver would save a great deal of both time and money.

Applying for a Waiver

The Traditional Response

Marvin Associates was very relieved to hear about the waiver process. They suggested to Halcyon that a waiver application should be submitted as quickly as possible so that they could get on with construction of the mall. The consultant suggested to Marvin and Halcyon that a waiver might shave as much as one to two years off the full state review process. Both companies agreed to retain the initial consulting engineer to ensure that the waiver was technically correct. Marvin, not a novice in dealing with the state bureaucracy and local politics, suggested that they take two additional steps: hire a lobbyist with strong ties to the governor, to "grease the skids" for the waiver; and have Marvin's press agent prepare a stream of news stories announcing that the preliminary studies had found a very small risk of any danger at the site. "We've got to deal with public opinion," he pointed out.

While others in the region had, indeed, applied for waivers in the past, only a quarter of them had been granted by the state. Furthermore, requests for waivers in some communities had led to charges that the applicants were trying to shirk responsibility for cleaning up the sites properly. Several applicants had taken a beating in the local press.

The Mutual-Gains Approach. A sophisticated public-relations vice president at Halcyon's home office was assigned to assist. He recommended holding off on the waiver request. Indeed, he urged that Marvin and Halcyon establish and consult with a community advisory board comprised of local officials, elected state representatives, abutters, and concerned citizen groups. The two companies would also be represented. He urged them not to leave out anyone who might be interested in the process, pointing out that if they did, these groups might cause trouble later on. Since anyone serving on the group would probably see an invitation from Marvin or Halcyon as an attempt at cooptation, Halcyon's vice president suggested that they find a well-respected resident to serve as chair of the advisory board and hire a professional facilitator to help assemble the group and assist them in formulating ground rules and an agenda. This would ensure the neutrality of the process.

The vice president went on to suggest that the advisory board should meet with state officials in order to learn about both the waiver process and the regulatory process that would apply if no waiver were granted. He urged Halcyon and Marvin to provide funds to underwrite the work of the advisory board. Indeed, he suggested that they turn over about $50,000 for the board to hire its own expert to prepare an assessment of the potential risks and to cover the costs of facilitation. To ensure the absolute neutrality of the process, he suggested that the advisory committee and the companies have an equal say in deciding which technical experts to use. Furthermore, he urged that the funds be held in a separate account administered by a five-person executive committee of the advisory board once the money had been contributed by the companies.

The vice president urged Halcyon and Marvin to suggest to the advisory board that the waiver would save time and money, and that this would mean that additional money would be available to pay for cleanup, and that the cleanup could start sooner. He stressed that both the companies and the community had a mutual interest in getting the site cleaned up as quickly as possible. Finally, he recommended that the decision about whether or not to apply for the waiver should be put to the advisory board, not for a vote, but for a decision by consensus. As members, Halcyon's and Marvin's representatives should try to make their case directly to all the stakeholders.

At first, the Halcyon manager on site and Mr. Marvin were incredulous. "How can we let other people make decisions for us? It's our project and our necks, we should make the decisions. Besides, this will just delay things even more," they argued.

The vice president pointed out that while they were indeed in charge, the contaminated site and the new project affected not only company profits, but also the long-term well-being of residents in the surrounding community as well. Thus, local representatives should have a say in any decision to apply for the waiver. He also pointed out that the local papers had not taken an editorial position, but if local interests were excluded from decision making, that might be the issue that could turn the local media against them. Most of the members of the local city council had not yet jumped into the debate, the vice president pointed out. Nor had they tried to use their connections to the governor. He argued, "Why line all these groups up against Halcyon and Marvin by preempting local involvement in an important decision like applying for a waiver?"

Marvin did not agree. "You'll just be stirring up trouble. You'll be unleashing a monster!" The vice president agreed that the process made him a bit uneasy, too, but he had seen it work elsewhere. Besides, the so-called monster might be unleashed anyway, once the community got wind of the waiver proposal. Even though it was adopted by the legislature to lighten the "heavy hand" of government, it was sure to be reinterpreted in this case as a device for allowing companies to shirk their duty. Furthermore, because they were not consulted, residents and local officials might well accuse the companies of operating behind their backs.

Marvin, warming to the idea, said: "O.K., you've made some good points. But what about the money? How can we just hand over the cash?"

Because the vice president had thought a lot about these questions, he calmly replied, "If we control the purse strings, the process will be viewed as tainted. 'If they control the money, they control the committee,' will be the way most people in the community see it. You have to give up a little control now to ensure that your interests are met later." Grudgingly, Marvin and the local Halcyon representative agreed.

Further Study

A 25-member advisory board was created. A retired businessman who had run for local office many years before agreed to serve as chair of the board. The group interviewed several firms that provided facilitation services before finding one it liked. Despite the many concerns raised by the advisory board, after two months of productive discussion, the group encouraged Halcyon and Marvin Associates to move forward with the waiver request. The turning point came when the companies agreed to consult the advisory board at each step in the waiver process. In the meantime, the state environmental and public health agencies required the companies to investigate potential remediation technologies and strategies. The results of these investigations were required as part of the waiver request. After the advisory board helped select a new consulting firm (the group felt that while the initial consultant was competent, they did not want to leave the larger community with the impression that they were merely a rubber stamp for a process already underway), the consultants got to work.

The Traditional Response

While Marvin Associates had gone along with the idea of creating a community advisory board and retaining the services of a neutral facilitator, Marvin grew increasingly fearful of the costs of remediation. A knowledgeable engineer from Marvin Associates told them that the consultant would probably recommend two potential remediation strategies: mobile incineration or transferring the waste material to an off-site facility. Mobile incineration involved either constructing on site, or hauling in, a small incinerator to burn the contaminated soil. Off-site remediation entailed digging up, loading, and transporting the contaminated soil to an existing large-scale incinerator or landfill. After hearing more of the details, Marvin was sure he preferred mobile incineration. It would be far cheaper than transporting the material off site. Furthermore, the companies had no guarantee that they would find an off-site incinerator able to handle their contaminated material. The backlog for incinerating such materials tended to be years, not months. Furthermore, by disposing of the material in a licensed landfill, the companies' exposure to future liability would, most likely, be increased. There would be no absolute guarantees that contaminants might not leach out of or migrate from the landfill site in the future.

Although the consultants selected in conjunction with the advisory group had not yet produced a report, Marvin suggested that the companies prepare a technical memorandum addressed to the state government justifying the use of mobile incineration. Marvin argued that once the options were laid before the community, both companies should advocate for the most cost-effective means of remediation. "Democracy is all well and good," Marvin said, "but Marvin Associates and Halcyon both have real costs to minimize, employees to pay, and profits to earn for their respective shareholders. The community is free to indulge in unrealistic and inefficient practices because they won't end up having to pay the bills." To ensure the success of his strategy, he also suggested that Halcyon and Marvin locate several experts to testify in favor of mobile incineration at the hearings the state would ultimately hold before approving the waiver request and the cleanup plan. Marvin had a friend whose wife's uncle was a professor of environmental engineering at a nearby university. Marvin was sure he would be willing to testify in favor of mobile incineration.

Marvin said that his friend also told him that the professor had mentioned a sophisticated technique called *comparative risk assessment.* This technique would indicate that even if there were an elevated health risk associated with mobile incineration as compared to off-site incineration, the increased risk would be negligible compared to that of driving a car at night or sitting in a smoke-filled restaurant. Finally, Marvin again offered the use of his press agent to get a story out highlighting the multiple benefits of mobile incineration. The local Halcyon manager was beginning to feel like a ping-pong ball being batted back and forth between Marvin and the vice president at headquarters.

The Mutual-Gains Approach

Though he agreed with Marvin's estimate of the benefits of mobile incineration, the vice president had raised doubts in the local manager's mind about Marvin's strategy for convincing the public. He suspected that Marvin's focus on the bottom line was short-sighted, and that he had not considered the community's likely reaction to this conventional "decide-announce-defend" approach. Once one side began hauling out advocates, the others would do the same. Halcyon and Marvin Associates would only inflame their critics and inspire them to locate "extremists" to push their positions. Ultimately, this would lead to a battle of computer printouts and to massive confusion and skepticism in the public's mind.

The vice president outlined the mutual-gains alternative. Rather than commissioning a technical report with a predetermined outcome, he suggested that the advisory committee jointly request that their consultant prepare a report estimating the costs and benefits associated with each cleanup option. As part of this strategy, the advisory board would explore fully the methods and techniques that would be used to determine these costs and benefits, and even have input into the final methodological assumptions. If the advisory board were to serve as a witness that the companies were proceeding in good faith, they would need to understand the sensitivity of the study findings as they applied to each assumption and to the choice of techniques.

"What?" Marvin cried. "You're going to let the cat out of the bag before we've got a good look at the information and can shape it to our needs? We can't do that. That information is proprietary."

The vice president tried once again to explain to Marvin that, yes, this was a different way of accomplishing his goals. The less the community understood about the way the study was to be conducted, the less likely they would be to believe in its objectivity, fairness, and accuracy. If the intent was to convince the skeptics that the health and environmental risks are small, then handing them a final, completed report—no matter who had prepared it—would not work. "If we hand over a finished report, no matter how objective it is, they'll assume it's biased in our favor. It won't change anyone's mind," the vice president pointed out. Marvin wavered.

The vice president also suggested that the advisory board should aim to reach a consensus on the choice of a remediation strategy given the information available as well as the various interests at stake in the community. Finally, because, as Marvin had suggested, the mobile incineration option was in their best interest but might pose greater risks for nearby residents than off-site incineration, the vice president recommended that the companies offer to compensate any unintended, but knowable, side effects of mobile incineration.

"Mitigate and compensate all unintended effects!" Marvin exclaimed when the Halcyon site manager presented these ideas. "Are you out of your mind? How can we take the blame for something that hasn't even happened, and probably couldn't be proven in court anyway?" Marvin, of course, was partly right. The companies could not be expected to take the blame for every illness or problem that might plague the surrounding communities. With air pollution, second-hand smoke, asbestos, leaking underground storage tanks, oozing PCB transformers, lead in tap water, and other contaminated industrial sites in the area, it would be crazy for Halcyon and

Marvin to take the fall for all the hazards anyone might face. However, it would be in everybody's best interest, including the companies', to do everything possible to mitigate potential risks and to enumerate the adverse impacts that might (but probably wouldn't) occur, and to spell out the contingent compensation they would promise to provide for each specific harm—should it occur and should it be clearly attributable to their site or their project.

While mobile incineration might be far less costly, the vice president suggested that the companies ought to be willing to take all reasonable precautions when using mobile incineration to decrease the chances of any damage. For example, a higher stack on the incinerator, while more expensive, would allow for better (and safer) dispersion of emissions. Furthermore, if at some time in the future sufficient evidence accumulated to suggest that mobile incineration caused harmful effects, the companies should promise, up front and jointly, to compensate the victims. In principle, the vice president argued, people ought to offer compensation for any harm they (wittingly) caused. The community would not agree to something unless they felt it would leave them better off. Thus, only an offer to compensate potential harm in the future would extend the prospect of support for the use of mobile incineration. Besides, the Halcyon representative suggested to Marvin, if the risks were less than sitting in a smoke-filled restaurant, as the consultant has contended, they should have little to worry about.

After a week to consider his proposition, Marvin once again agreed. "Either the mutual-gains approach is the best thing since sliced bread," Marvin told the folks from Halcyon, "or you're leading me down the path to hell with good intentions."

The vice president replied, "I'm only doing the logical thing."

The Public Presentation

To Marvin's relief and the vice president's quiet delight, the state agreed to grant the companies a waiver, releasing them from the cumbersome process of filing endless forms over a period of two or three additional years. At the same time the state would no longer tell them how to proceed; Halcyon and Marvin Associates would have to figure out on their own how to interact with the community. Granted, the state would not be there to slow things down. On the other hand, neither would the state be there to take the heat if mistakes were made. However, the state would still maintain an oversight role and would be able to force the companies to do the job over if regulatory standards were not met in the end.

Everyone involved knew that the time had come to meet with the community at large. The advisory board had met for months. While meeting summaries had been made available to the public, and some of the meetings had even been broadcast on the local cable access channel, that was not tantamount to presenting the draft risk assessment, proposed remediation strategy, and site management plans for public review and comment. Even the adjacent communities wanted a chance to be heard. The advisory board, while leaning toward mobile incineration, decided not to make a final recommendation until they heard everyone's reactions. The town manager of the largest community adjacent to the site had already booked the largest available auditorium at a local community college.

The Traditional Response

Marvin, who was on vacation, turned the responsibility for the meeting over to his public-relations firm. They prepared a highly polished presentation. Indeed, they were ready with color overheads, a graphic package—including four-color pamphlets to hand out to everyone, and an action plan in gold-embossed binders. They were all set to hire Meeting Management, Inc. to handle the audiovisual pitch. "Don't worry," the public relations people told the companies, "We'll keep the engineers from boring the residents with needless details and incomprehensible jargon. We have lots of photographs and jazzy graphs showing the comparative risks that people in the community already accept." The front page of the brochure (which the advisory board had not seen) read, "After exhaustively carrying out state-of-the-art studies and compiling all the available scientific evidence, Marvin Associates and Halcyon—in conjunction with their community advisory board—are firmly convinced that mobile incineration is the safest, most effective, and most practical technology for removing the contaminants from the Springdale Mall site."

The Mutual-Gains Approach

When the chair of the advisory committee saw a copy of the brochure a week before the scheduled community forum, he was furious. "The community will never buy your glossy presentation," he fumed. "Furthermore, we haven't reached a consensus yet on the choice of a cleanup technology." He called for an emergency meeting of the advisory board to discuss and jointly design the best possible public presentation. He also insisted that the professional facilitator hired to assist the advisory committee be the one to facilitate the community forum. From the standpoint of both the chair and the facilitator, the last thing they needed was a stage-managed and tightly controlled presentation. Those with strong opinions contrary to the companies' needed not only a chance to speak, but also to feel that their comments could have an impact on the decisions that had to be made.

The vice president argued that the companies should promise residents that Halcyon and Marvin Associations would work with the advisory board (adding still other members if necessary) to reach a consensus on how best to meet all state and federal requirements.

Not surprisingly, Marvin was very worried about this approach. "I'm honor bound to advocate for Marvin Associates' interests, not to work toward some lowest common denominator agreement that pleases everyone," he explained.

The public-relations firm chimed in, "We cannot serve two, or three, or fifty masters at once." If the choice were between advocacy and consensus building, they knew where they stood.

However, the Halcyon vice president didn't see the choice as starkly as the public-relations firm. It was fine, the vice president pointed out, for the public-relations firm to advocate for Marvin Associates, but that didn't answer the question of how best to win support for a cleanup strategy. Since the medium is the message, as Marshall McLuhan said decades ago, a "slick" campaign might convey the message that the company was trying to put one over on the public. This, in turn, would suggest to some that the company had something to hide. Why not let representatives of the various stakeholding publics help shape the medium as well as the message? Furthermore, many of the residents were likely to see themselves as customers of the mall and would be interested in doing what they could to help the project succeed. If the mall were shoved down people's throats it would be harder to establish a positive image that attracts customers. The public-relations firm preferred a more controlled presentation, but they were willing to give the mutual-gains alternative a try.

A Disaster Threatens

Two months later, after a successful public meeting, a woman in the audience asked to speak at a routine advisory committee meeting. She had not been present before. "I have here," she said, standing up and shaking her fist, "a list of families in this area whose children have suffered various childhood cancers." She turns first to the audience to say, "I don't know about you, but I think there's a link between these poor, sick children and those rusting barrels they found several months ago." She then turned to the representatives of Halcyon and Marvin and said, "And you're to blame. These deaths are on your shoulders!"

Sure enough, in the next day's paper, a front-page picture of the woman appeared. She was waving the list. The headline, "Another Love Canal?" ran in large type over the picture. No one was very happy that the press had shown little or no interest up until then in the work of the advisory committee. The members of the advisory committee were irritated that the paper barely mentioned that several advisory-board members had called upon the woman who spoke to produce concrete evidence to back up her charges. The Halcyon site manager was reading the article when the phone rang. "We just got creamed in the paper. Did you see that picture?" Marvin said. "This means war."

The Traditional Response

"I've hired a specialist to deal with this disaster," Marvin said. He outlined the strategy the crisis management specialist had suggested. "First, we've got to get an expert in to dampen this hysteria, someone who can testify that the causal link between childhood cancers, such as leukemia, and the particular solvents at the site is hardly understood at all. He has a list of scientists from across the country we can release to the press who will challenge the scientific merits of her claims. Furthermore, we have someone in-house who can have charts and diagrams ready by tomorrow that will show that there is absolutely no way that anyone living more than a hundred yards from the site could have been affected in any way."

Marvin went on, "My attorney told me this morning that we should immediately deny any and all liability beyond the cost of cleaning up the contaminants. After all, that is something both companies have already agreed to do. For God's sake, we've only owned the site for a couple of years. We don't have responsibility for what the earlier owner might or might not have done." Marvin's attorney had advised him to do everything possible to protect the company against future lawsuits. "No more talk of compensation," Marvin exclaimed. "That implies we might have done something wrong. We're looking at a legal nightmare here."

Finally, Marvin said in a somewhat conspiratorial tone, "We've got to raise doubts about that woman's credibility."

"What do you mean?" the Halcyon manager asked.

"Well, she's the one doing the rabble-rousing," Marvin says. "I found out from someone I know that she's just angling for political office. She was a political science major at the state university. She's been involved with all kinds of radical environmental groups like Greenpeace." The Halcyon site manager and Marvin had no trouble convincing themselves that they ought to denounce such radical and irresponsible accusations. They tried to think of ways of convincing "reasonable" people in the community that she did not know what she was talking about.

Marvin said, "We've got find some *reasonable* people to put our arms around. If the upstanding citizens in the area say they believe in us and intend to shop at our mall, and that they think this woman is crazy, maybe other will trust us, too."

The Mutual-Gains Approach

The company representatives, as well as the members of the advisory committee, were worried about the fallout from the accusations and the political headlines. If there really were an elevated cancer rate and it had something to do with the old plastics plant, Halcyon and Marvin could well have liability of some sort (although causal links for legal purposes are very hard to establish). And, if children in the community were at risk, someone ought to do something immediately. No one knew what the agenda of the woman leveling the charges really was, but her accusations certainly cast a cloud over the community advisory process. Moreover, the advisory-committee members were frustrated to find that all their hard work, serious thinking, and good intentions had done nothing to prepare them for this.

For a moment, even the Halcyon vice president thought Marvin might be right. After all, they wouldn't be doing anything different from what almost everybody expected them to do anyway. Maybe Marvin had been right all along.

The events of the advisory-board meeting and the preceding months told a different story, however. Both companies had generated a lot of goodwill among advisory-board members. The company representatives had earned the respect of the members of the advisory board and had spoken freely with them. The cleanup effort had received little, if any, negative press—even the decision to seek a waiver. No one had challenged the technical information presented at the community forum. The board matter-of-factly endorsed mobile incineration by consensus. Until the woman's charges were made, the community had accepted the advisory-board process as a legitimate way of ensuring that public concerns were met. Even at the advisory-board meeting, rather than discounting the woman's charges outright or pointing out that Halcyon had not operated the plastics plant in the first place, everyone acknowledged the seriousness of her concerns. They agreed to devote the next meeting of the advisory committee to the issue, although both companies insisted that a public-health expert from Halcyon's staff be given a chance to speak. It was the member of the advisory committee who had pressed the companies the hardest over the preceding months who asked the woman to explain her charges and provide documentation. That was real progress.

The Halcyon vice president pointed out that Marvin's proposal to discredit the woman might very well backfire, destroying Marvin Associates and Halcyon's credibility instead. If the woman had a valid point, all the spin control in the world would not erase the facts. If she had none, it would be better to let the advisory committee take the lead in questioning her claims.

If the companies reverted to a traditional approach and adopted a "bunker mentality," the members of the advisory committee would surely doubt that they had ever been completely honest. Given that the companies had already suggested that they would take compensation seriously in the event adequate evidence arose concerning anticipatable harm, the community would accuse the companies of going back on their word.

After a lot of back and forth, the companies proposed several next steps to the advisory board.

- Sponsor a day-long panel open to the public, organized by the companies and the community advisory board, to explore the recent charges. The advisory board's facilitator would manage the meeting. A respected nearby university would be asked to help identify a panel of technical experts to provide comments on the charges once they were presented in writing.
- Commit to short-term measures to make the site totally secure, given the increased level of community concern. Measures might include erecting a cyclone fence around the site to keep children out or interim linings or concrete fill to prevent any possible leakage from the barrels. Once again,

the companies volunteered to work with the advisory board, as well as state regulators, on each of these decisions.

- Agree to joint monitoring of the site in response to community concerns. The technical consultants had indicated all along that when the site was excavated, monitors would have to be placed around the barrels and contaminated soil to measure any further discharge of solvents. There was no reason why this could not take place immediately.

- Work with the state public-health agency to verify the incidence of childhood cancers in the surrounding communities in a professional, thorough, and objective manner *after* committing to interim protective measures. Once again, the advisory committee would help select the study team. A respected neutral party, agreed upon by those affected or potentially affected, would be needed to manage the inquiry.

The Halcyon vice president urged Marvin to stay with the mutual-gains approach. If they found at a later time that the strategy was not working, he argued, they could always revert to the approach recommended by the PR firm.

"Nothing in the law calls for us to do any of this," Marvin said to him. "You keep encouraging me to give away the store, and, I suspect you are increasing our exposure. You know what my PR man told me?" Marvin continued. "He said he's an advocate. He's paid to represent my views. To do less would be to emasculate his role as a PR professional. I feel you and your PR staff are advocates for the other side!"

The vice president tried to get Marvin to see things from the other side's perspective. "As long as the residents feel unsafe," he pointed out, "they will continue to be angry. Even worse, if they think their children are at risk of death, they will be especially enraged. The first step in reducing their anger is to reduce the threat behind it. To do nothing at this point would be perceived as ignoring their concerns. That will only strengthen their belief that the company is acting irresponsibly."

The vice president pointed out that he was only asking to put in place relatively inexpensive interim measures to secure the site. He was not suggesting huge outlays, but rather, modest spending that might help bring the project back on track. He pointed out that they were not (yet) bound by the formalities of legal proceedings and should do whatever they could to ensure the safety of citizens, to protect their customer base, and to preserve one of their most valued assets, their reputations.

The Fallout

The advisory board decided to stick with the mutual-gains strategy in dealing with the charges leveled by the one vocal citizen. As the health study got
underway, a study the state estimated would take two to three years to complete, the advisory board suggested that Halcyon and Marvin Associates hold
still another full community meeting. One of the most involved members of
the advisory board, a local banker, pointed out, "People are scared. Who
knows whether there is an increased risk of cancer? I suspect that as the study
drags on, people will get frustrated and consider filing lawsuits. That's what
I've heard, anyway. Don't disappear now."

Halcyon and Marvin Associates held the extra forum. This time, angry
citizens engaged outside advocates to speak for them. Several young, fresh-
scrubbed attorneys appeared at the back of the room. A local environmentalist mentioned that his group had engaged the help of a state-wide
advocacy group known as Citizens United Against Toxics. Staff from a
state senator's office as well as the congressional district office were present.
At this meeting, several residents pressed for compensation to the municipality as well as nearby residents. Some citizens contended that housing
prices were already starting to plunge. Others were worried about the dangers to themselves and their children and wanted to know who was going
to do something to protect them. Some said the companies should compensate them for the emotional stress the whole situation had already
created. "We want compensation for the risks we face," they demanded.
"We don't want to wait for a study that will probably be flawed anyway.
We want action now!"

After the tough meeting, Marvin and the Halcyon vice president sat
down with their company attorneys. Both attorneys point out that the abutters would have an almost impossible time proving in court that Halcyon
and Marvin Associates were responsible for anything but the cost of the
cleanup. While the study that was just getting under way might indicate
excess cancers in the community, the attorneys argued, because of the long
history of industrial activity in the region it would be unlikely that anyone
could scientifically point the finger at the leaking drums and contaminated
soil at the specific mall site. The attorneys did point out, too, that the compensation mentioned by the disgruntled abutters might not total much more
than the estimated legal costs of defending the companies were the case to
drag on for several years in state and federal court.

The Traditional Response

"Well," Marvin's top aide told him, "the answer is clear. We are only liable for the clean-up. The probability of losing in court for proven damages caused by the leaking barrels is less than five percent, and more likely, less than one percent. I say we state exactly what our attorneys told us. Our liability is negligible. If you don't believe it, take us to court. We'll go ahead with the cleanup, but that's it." To his surprise, Marvin remained quiet. "We can also," his aide said lowering his voice, "discreetly offer a few key individual homeowners abutting the site a reasonable fee for them to cool down. We can have them quietly sign a statement agreeing that payment of such funds in no way constitutes an admission of guilt on our part. In addition, they will have to agree not to seek further damages individually or as part of a larger suit. And, maybe, if everyone does what they're told, we can build the community a baseball field."

"Anything else?" Marvin asked.

"I guess," the aide said, "we should hire outside counsel to prepare a legal defense in the event that we are taken to court. We should probably expect those outside environmental agitators and hungry injury attorneys to stir up more trouble. It might be worth checking to see if we have the basis for a slander suit against the rabble-rousers. That would teach them a lesson."

The Mutual-Gains Approach

"Well," Marvin said, turning to the vice president, "What does Halcyon think?"

"I have a slightly different strategy in mind," he said. "Halcyon and Marvin Associates should

- "continue with the cleanup as planned. In addition, the companies should agree to subsidize the cost of long-term monitoring of health and environmental impacts after the cleanup is completed. The monitoring might best be administered locally through the nearby state college.
- "make a public offer to compensate all those individuals who can reasonably demonstrate that the contamination actually caused them harm. The companies would only cover real economic losses—the actual costs of harm.
- "work jointly with the advisory board to seek agreement on the standards and methods of proving actual harm.

- "encourage the advisory board to establish a joint arbitration panel to review disputed claims. This joint arbitration panel might be comprised of three arbitrators: one picked by the companies, one picked by the advisory board, and a third selected by the first two.
- "agree to set up a community trust fund administered through the advisory board or its executive committee. If these funds are not awarded by the joint arbitration panel within ten years, the moneys would be returned to the company. While the companies should strive to limit this fund to the estimated cost of avoided litigation, they would first consult with the advisory committee to see if a reasonable initial allocation could be determined."

The attorneys didn't like it at all. "With all due respect," Marvin's council said to the vice president, "I think this strategy is terribly dangerous. It's like we are blindly admitting fault. We will have every Tom, Dick, and Harry coming to us for money. The process will bankrupt us."

Marvin's aide supported this contention: "But we didn't do anything wrong. Why go to all that trouble? We didn't own the company that created this mess in the first place."

The vice president pointed out that the financial exposure was on a par with the estimated legal fees for taking the conflict to court. "If you are reasonably certain we can do better in court, saving money and time, then let's go ahead and encourage them to sue us," he said. He pointed out that litigation is sometimes the best alternative, especially when someone is not inclined to negotiate, but the companies in this case had not yet negotiated with the community to see what might be possible.

The vice president proposed that they negotiate directly with the advisory board regarding the procedures for proving harm. If the group failed to reach a satisfactory outcome, the companies could always go to court. If they could agree, though, the arbitration board could administer the agreement. There are successful private firms that make their living selling arbitration services to private clients. With enormously high legal fees billed by the hour and congested and clogged courts, businesses and government agencies have turned to such private dispute resolution providers to resolve their disputes. If they failed to reach agreement on the amount to put into the fund, he explained, we might be able to arrive at an initial amount to put aside, which could then be renegotiated after six months or a year.

"You're right," the vice president said to Marvin's attorneys and right-hand man. "We could do nothing. However, if we do not act, this does not mean our critics will fold up shop and go home. If people truly feel threatened or hurt, whether they are or not, they will continue to seek safety and redress. If some people believe they can benefit from the situation, fairly or not, they will continue to exploit any appearance of impropriety or denial on our part. If we attempted to quietly compensate individuals, the word would get out eventually. Rather than openly and fairly addressing the community's complaints, it would look as though we were secretly buying people off. Furthermore, we would create a rift in the community between those who accepted money and those who refused on grounds of principle. This would lead to even more community divisiveness and anger."

After further discussion, everyone turned to Marvin. "Well," they asked, "What do you think we should do?"

Marvin leaned forward, resting his elbows on his desk. "I've been hashing this out for almost a year now with Halcyon," he said. "We've disagreed. But, over time, I have come to believe that they have a point. Things have hardly gone perfectly. We still face some potential losses. Yet the first part of the mall is open and doing well. The advisory group, rather than being a loose cannon, has served us well. They might not always agree with us, but they respect us. I say we can always go to court. Let's stay with Halcyon's approach."

As they walked out of the meeting, the Halcyon vice president turned to Marvin privately and asked: "What really convinced you?"

"Well, to be honest, it's more personal than I'd like to admit," Marvin said. "I walked into a local restaurant and a long-time adversary, with whom I have butted heads often, said to me, 'You know, Marvin, I wasn't sure I ever liked you. But since this whole mess at the mall, the one thing I can say is that, no matter what, even if it's not in your favor, you call it like it is. No matter what, you're honest. That keeps me coming back.'"

CHAPTER IV

Accidents Will Happen

Accidents are a public-relations trial by fire for any organization. After an accident decision makers must address numerous questions from victims, journalists, public-interest groups, as well as the public at large. There are questions about the event from outsiders: What happened? Who is affected? Is there danger? How much? What should be done? What can be done? There are questions asked from inside the organization: What should we have done? What should we do now? Should we do anything? Who should we tell? What should we tell them? Who will do the telling? Before the leaders in charge, from CEOs to governors, know what is going on, events tumble out of control. If a crisis is mishandled, an organization's credibility and reputation, in the eyes of the public, can be lost.

Two newsworthy accidents over the last twenty years were the crisis at Pennsylvania's Three Mile Island nuclear-power plant in 1979 and the *Exxon Valdez* oil spill of 1989. While the actual consequences of TMI were, in retrospect, minimal, the prevailing fear of meltdowns and nuclear disasters made that event a seminal incident from which the nuclear-power industry has never recovered. The effects of the *Exxon Valdez* spill were so immediately visible, horrifying, and wide-ranging that six years later the litigation was still wending its way through the tortuous legal appeals process.

On the one hand it might seem inappropriate to use these two cases as lessons from which to draw generally applicable points. After all, nuclear disasters and mammoth oil spills are hardly the kinds of events which government or business face on a daily basis; how can anyone expect to handle the public anger arising out of such crises? The angry-public and crisis-management elements of these cases are not fundamentally different from those faced regularly by public bodies and corporations. They are perhaps only more intense. Furthermore, because the Three Mile Island and *Exxon Valdez* "accidents" were of such enormous proportions, they can help reveal the layers of assumption and supposition that undergird the conventional wisdom we criticize in this book. In these two cases, every decision was held up for intense scrutiny and often found wanting. If business and government want to more effectively deal with very angry publics, they must learn to handle better these roller-coaster rides of post-accident public relations.

Three Mile Island: To Tell or Not to Tell

After an accident occurs, while a crisis unfolds, companies and agencies must decide quickly how much to tell, as well as when and with whom to speak. If an accident is of national interest, media outlets pick up and spread the story almost immediately. In the case of the nuclear reactor malfunction at Three Mile Island, it took less than four hours for the management at the plant to find themselves in a crisis of national proportions. Management must be clear beforehand about what it will and won't disclose in a crisis. As the Three Mile Island case illustrates, concealing, hedging, and blandly re-assuring an angry public do not produce positive results.

In hindsight, the real and absolute dangers of Three Mile Island were not nearly as great as the imagined possibilities. The Kemeny Commission, appointed by President Jimmy Carter to study the accident, concluded that the physical effects of the accident on the off-site public were minimal at best.[1] The Commission found that there would be "no detectable additional cases of cancer, developmental abnormalities, or genetic ill-health as a consequence of the accident at TMI."[2] Despite the erosion of the nuclear industry's credibility after TMI, the fact that the safety systems held, was, in an ironic way, proof that the redundancies engineered into plants were highly effective. But Three Mile Island also confirmed the public's worst fears and proved wrong the proponents of nuclear power who said such an accident was practically impossible—after all, a malfunctioning valve had led to a national crisis. The events of the first few days of the crisis provide a glimpse of how quickly a company can lose its credibility with the public. Furthermore, the case highlights how one company's failure to establish and maintain public confidence can contribute significantly to the troubles of an entire industry.

The accident at Three Mile Island did not occur in a vacuum. The 1970s saw a rise in grave concerns about the safety of nuclear power; the

1950s promise of virtually free energy became the 1970s threat of leaks, meltdowns, and perpetually dangerous radioactive wastes. Citizens' advocacy groups protested both at operating nuclear power plants and at those under construction. Just days prior to the accident, the press reported on a trial pitting a power company against the family of Karen Silkwood. The family believed that in an attempt to cover up gross negligence and danger at the plant where she worked she had been forced off the road to her death. At the very same time the accident occurred at Three Mile Island, Jane Fonda was starring in *The China Syndrome,* a movie about a threatened fictional plant meltdown. In short, the public's attention was already focused on the hazards of nuclear power. Opponents of nuclear power were waiting, fearfully perhaps, for the event that would prove their point: human beings were not capable of safely harnessing nuclear energy.

The First Day: March 28, 1979

4:45 A.M.: It Begins

Three Mile Island was the plant name for two recently opened nuclear-power reactors operated by Metropolitan Edison, a Pennsylvania utility company. At 4:45 A.M. on Wednesday, March 28, 1979, George Kunder, Metropolitan Edison's Superintendent of Technical Support for Three Mile Island, Unit 2, arrived at the plant. From 4:00 A.M. on, the newly operable plant, situated on an island in the Susquehanna River (Three Mile Island) eleven miles south of the state capitol, had been shut down. Though Kunder expected the opposite, the primary coolant system appeared to contain too much water while the system pressure remained low. At 5:15 A.M., Kunder and Gary Miller, Station Manager, discussed the unusual plant conditions. Miller asked for a conference call with Jack Herbein, Metropolitan Edison's Vice President for Generation, and a technical representative from the plant's manufacturer, Babcock and Wilcox. At 6:15 A.M., the utility declared a site emergency. At 7:02, Metropolitan Edison (Met Ed) notified the Pennsylvania Emergency Management Agency (PEMA) that a site emergency had been declared. Soon after, the Nuclear Regulatory Commission (NRC), the governor of Pennsylvania, and various state agencies were notified.

Sometime around 8:00 A.M., a local reporter in Waynesboro, Pennsylvania learned from his morning check with the state police that there was a problem at Three Mile Island. At 8:25 A.M., the story was announced on WKBO radio in Harrisburg, the state capital. By 9:02 A.M., the Associated Press put out a national bulletin. Shortly thereafter, a flood of calls inundated offices of the Nuclear Regulatory Commission at its regional office in King of Prussia, Pennsylvania, and its headquarters in Washington, D.C. What was happening at Three Mile Island? The story had broken. What began as a private discussion among company personnel about confounding instrument readings was quickly becoming one of the most intensely covered news stories of the late 1970s.

7:00 A.M.: The General Emergency and the First Mistaken Public Statement

Two events prior to 9:00 A.M. had already began to erode Met Ed's credibility: a mistaken public statement and the lack of notification about the declared general emergency. At 7:15 A.M. Vice President Jack Herbein contacted Blain Fabian, Met Ed's Manager of Communications Services. Herbein wanted Fabian to be ready for press inquiries. Fabian quickly drafted a public statement that the reactor had tripped because of a feed-water malfunction and would be out of service for one week. This statement told the public little, but at that time, control-room personnel and managers were still attempting to sort out the exact nature of the problem. While the out-of-service notice may have reassured some that the company was tending to business, in retrospect, the highly mistaken statement suggested that the company had no idea of, or was not telling the truth about, the magnitude of the problem. As it turned out, it took more than ten years to clean up Unit 2, and it will never be operable again.

At 7:24 A.M. Station Manager Gary Miller declared a general emergency, as required by NRC regulations. Readings suggested that radiation in the containment vessel had reached dangerously high levels; the possibility existed for "serious radiological consequences to the health and safety of the general public."[3] This declaration was not passed on to the NRC until 7:40 A.M. The press was not notified of the declaration at all the first day. Whether by oversight or intent, this was an error Met Ed would repeat in the following days—Met Ed failed to provide regulatory officials and the public with timely and accurate information regarding public safety.

9:00 A.M.: The Information Gap Between the Company and Government

By 9:00 A.M., the gap between the knowledge gained by company personnel about the condition of Unit 2 and the information obtained by state and federal officials had widened. Around nine o'clock, William Dornsife of the state's Bureau of Radiological Protection (BRP) spoke with Gary Miller at TMI about the plant's condition. Despite the fact that there were temperature readings suggesting that the core might have been uncovered and that cooling was being achieved through an unapproved and unpracticed route, Dornsife was led to believe that all emergency systems had functioned as expected. Dornsife thought everything was under control, later telling investigators, "I didn't really question. I didn't have time to question that much the information he was giving. We were relying on their information at that point."[4]

In a 9:30 A.M. conversation with George Troffer, Met Ed's Manager of Quality Assurance, Miller told Troffer that he had not described certain aspects of the situation to Dornsife. The exact "aspects" were not made clear on the recorded transcript, but investigators were left with the impression that Miller had not been forthcoming with Dornsife. According to one investigation, Miller had known that some core damage had been sustained as early as 8:00 A.M.[5]

This information gap continued through the morning and afternoon of the first day of the crisis. At 10:15 A.M., TMI's George Kunder told the NRC's Donald Haverkamp that the right hot-leg temperature—a critical indicator of the condition of the core—was reading 571°F. (The hot leg is the portion of the primary coolant system piping that carries pressurized water away from the reactor core.) Later investigation showed that the hot-leg temperatures during this hour were actually between 730 and 780 degrees. The 200-degree gap meant the difference, given the system pressure, between water and steam. If there was, in fact, steam in the leg, the reactor coolant pumps would be vapor bound, cooling would be impossible, and the core could then be uncovered. According to a Senate investigation, the hot-leg temperature in one loop had actually increased from 680°F to at least 730°F, but NRC headquarters was never made aware of this.

Later in the day, about 4:00 P.M., Met Ed reported to NRC Region I that in-core thermocouple data, a more direct means of measuring the core's temperature than the hot-leg temperatures, were not available because the instruments were only printing out question marks. These question marks indicated one of two things: either the temperatures were higher than 700°F or the instruments were malfunctioning. Without the in-core data, Met Ed personnel would not have been able to corroborate what the high hot-leg temperatures suggested: that the core had been uncovered. However, an analysis of the computer printouts from the time indicated that two of the thermocouples were actually measuring excessive temperatures at approximately the same time Met Ed informed NRC to the contrary.

Part of the problem during the first hours of the crisis can be traced to insufficient data, confusion and differing opinions among control room staff, and lack of clear communication between the company and government officials. Yet the record strongly suggests that company personnel, determined to control the situation, withheld important information about the condition of the plant from both government officials and the public.

10:00 A.M.: Confusion Grows

At 10:00 A.M., while the control-room staff struggled to understand the problem and bring the temperatures back down, the company presented the best possible face to the public. Around ten o'clock, Met Ed released its second official public statement. "Radiation monitoring teams have been dispatched on and off site to monitor for possible external radioactive releases. None has been found, and we do not expect any. We are presently bringing the plant down to an orderly cold shutdown condition with no consequences to the public expected."[6] Although Gary Miller had personally drafted the release for the TMI public-information officer, he failed to pass on the fact that he had declared a general plant emergency two hours previously.

Before 11:00 A.M., Lieutenant Governor William Scranton had been briefed by the BRP's William Dornsife, who believed from his conversation with Miller that all was under control. At 10:55 A.M., a press conference was held at which the lieutenant governor said, "Everything is under control. There is and was no danger to public health and safety."[7] The lieutenant governor flatly stated that no increase in normal radiation levels had been detected. However, when Dornsife was called upon to answer technical questions he announced that small amounts of radioiodine had been detected. Just prior to the conference, too late to inform the lieutenant governor, he had learned from the head of the BRP that detectable levels of radioactive iodine had been found in nearby Goldsboro, Pennsylvania. This piece of contradictory news was a surprise not only to the press but also to the lieutenant governor.

Around noon, after finding out that above-background radiation levels had indeed been detected at the perimeter of the plant—not in Goldsboro as BRP communicated to Dornsife—Met Ed released its third public statement. "... [T]here had been no recordings of any significant levels of radiation and none were expected outside the plant."[8] With readings at levels above background radiation, and no apparent certainty as to why, Met Ed had decided to determine "significance" to its advantage. Once again, Met Ed mistakenly reassured the public that no further calamities would occur. Rather than bluntly stating the level of the recordings, the company chose to take a reassuring tack. The company attempted to soothe the public, issuing statements without regard to their accuracy or potential for causing later embarrassment.

At 1:15 P.M., Jack Herbein, after conversations with his boss, Met Ed President Walter Creitz, held an impromptu press conference. During this forty-minute conference, Met Ed failed to mention several indications suggesting that the core had been uncovered and the fuel damaged. In addition, Herbein failed to mention that Met Ed had vented steam into the atmosphere in an effort to cool the plant from approximately 11:00 A.M. until after 1:00 P.M. Herbein had ordered the venting stopped just prior to the conference, because he could not be certain that the steam was not radioactive. Yet, Met Ed did not notify the state of this steam release until, in a meeting with company and state officials in the lieutenant governor's office, the state asked about it. Thus Met Ed had already squandered much of its credibility.

2:30 P.M.: Losing the State's Confidence

The 2:30 P.M. meeting between TMI staff and the lieutenant governor was significant. At least three pieces of information available to state authorities led them to believe that Met Ed was concealing important information about conditions at the plant.

The meeting quickly became strained because it appeared that Met Ed was not planning to tell the governor, or the public, that radioactive steam had been released earlier in the day. The lieutenant governor had to ask Herbein directly, "Have you been venting radiation?"[9] Herbein hedged, but eventually answered in the affirmative. Because the company was anxious to predict an optimistic future of "no expected radiation," it had waited to see if the steam venting had actually released radioactivity into the Pennsylvania landscape. Met Ed had managed to exercise caution in exactly the wrong way. As Paul Critchlow, the Governor's press secretary, recalled, "[Herbein] was asked, 'Why didn't you tell the press?' He said he had never been asked, or the question did not come up, or something like that. That immediately led to a very quickly developing caution on our part in dealing with Metropolitan Edison."[10]

At the meeting, Met Ed maintained that there were no problems off-site. However, staff of Thomas Gerusky, Director of the BRP, informed Gerusky that they were measuring heightened levels of radioactivity off-site. To Gerusky, the company's denial signaled that Met Ed either was sorely lacking in pertinent knowledge or was simply concealing the facts. Third, while the company made no mention of an uncovering of the core or damage to the fuel rods, the state strongly suspected that the plant had at least some damaged fuel rods. This state officials had gleaned from earlier conversations. "I thought I had more information than they were giving me," Gerusky later told investigators.[11]

In addition to these factual discrepancies, state officials were particularly put off by the style of the Met Ed managers. Gerusky later told investigators, "I think it was more of an attitude than anything else. It was the way they phrased the words and the way they talked down to the people in the [BRP] office, rather than trying to lay it out—lay their cards on the table."[12] At the end of the meeting, Gerusky recalled, "When they left, everybody shook their head and we said, 'We don't trust them,' just from the way they presented the information . . ."[13] This opinion was later backed up by a House committee's investigation into the reporting of information at TMI. The report concluded, "The record indicates that the overall assessment of the situation presented on March 28 to state and federal officials by TMI managers was inconsistent with the managers' own perception of the severity of the accident and the prognosis for bringing the reactor to a stable condition."[14]

By 3:30 P.M., less than twelve hours after the reactor had shut down, the state had lost faith in Met Ed. Top state officials felt that the company had misled them, and in no time they passed this impression on to the general public. Word had spread: Met Ed could not be trusted.

4:30 P.M.: The State Undermines Met Ed's Credibility

State officials quickly decided to leave the company out of a 4:30 P.M. press conference. Lieutenant Governor Scranton told the press, "This situation is more complex than the company first led us to believe. We are taking more tests. And at this point, we believe there is still no danger to public health. Metropolitan Edison has given you and us conflicting information."[15] When asked by a reporter if Met Ed was misleading state officials, Scranton replied: "'I think there is a great deal of disappointment from our side that the company did not tell us that they were venting radioactivity, particularly when statements were represented that they made, that they said there was no radioactivity being put out in the atmosphere."[16] Scranton also notified the public that the state had not been aware of the steam release, but that the company had promised to notify the state in the event of further steam discharges. This promise would be broken in the next two days.

With the state discrediting Met Ed, the company decided to hold a press conference of its own the following morning. By 4:30, Met Ed Communications Manager Blain Fabian had worked out the logistics of the press conference and called the NRC to ask them to participate. Joe Fouchard, NRC Public Relations Director, said no. The NRC, he stated, wanted to remain in the investigative mode. This refusal was only one of Met Ed's growing public-relations problems. So many telephone calls were coming in that the company found it impossible to write additional public statements. Senior management staff began answering phone calls when public-affairs and technical staff became overwhelmed.

That evening most Americans first learned of the accident at Three Mile Island on the broadcast news. Walter Cronkite, then dean of TV newsmen, led with this story, saying, "It was the first step in a nuclear nightmare; as far as we know at this hour, no worse than that. But a government official said that a breakdown in an atomic power plant in Pennsylvania today is probably the worst nuclear accident to date."[17]

The Second Day: March 29, 1979

The Front Page News

On Thursday morning, March 29, the press reported that "details of the accident were in dispute."[18] An NRC official believed that the accident had been caused by problems with filters at the plant. Met Ed's Jack Herbein believed a valve had failed on a pump in the cooling system, but the pump's manufacturer, Bingham-Willamette, stated that there was no valve in their pump. In Washington, Colorado Senator Gary Hart stated that some human error was involved in responding to the emergency. Herbein focused only on mechanical error, stating that "the plant's backup system worked perfectly," but that overheating had caused a rupture in the drain tank, releasing radioactive steam.[19] The public and the press wanted to know what had caused the problem: fallible humans or failing machines? No one seemed to know.

The press raised concern that the utility had released radioactive steam into the atmosphere without notifying the state. When Herbein was asked about the steam releases, he stated that no escaping radioactivity was detected at first. In this first day, the *New York Times* seemed to be willing to give the company the benefit of the doubt. One reporter wrote, "Part of the confusion over the exact chain of events was due to the inability of the monitoring team to inspect the reactor because of the high levels of radiation within the reactor dome."[20]

However, the press was already beginning to question the credibility of Met Ed's designated spokesman. Jack Herbein emphasized and focused on the fact that the main safety systems in the plant had worked well enough to prevent a serious accident. "Look what didn't happen" was the impression Herbein left with the press corps. The *New York Times* described his comments as bland, not exactly a praiseworthy adjective. "Using bland terms, he described the series of events in the plant as 'not the normal evolution' in stating that there was 'some minor fuel failure.'"[21]

10:00 A.M.: The Press Grows Tired of Met Ed's Optimism

The public's confidence in Met Ed suffered another blow during the company's press conference on Thursday morning. One hundred reporters showed up for the briefing. Eventually, some four hundred area reporters would cover the story. The company was surprised by the attention. Met Ed President Walter Creitz told the *New York Times*: "We're simply aghast at the number of people we've had to deal with."[22]

At the press conference, Met Ed continued to maintain that emphasis should be placed on the fact that the plant's safety systems had averted a catastrophe. Jack Herbein provided a detailed overview of the previous day's events. Most of the paths leaking radiation from the auxiliary building would be closed off by the end of the day. The utility was not certain how long the core had been uncovered, but "there was nothing there that was catastrophic or unplanned for," and that the releases were "insignificant'" and "minuscule."[23] Herbein even stated that the mishap was not all that unusual in his eyes since similar accidents had happened at TMI-1 since it had opened in 1974.

The company's reassurances were not reassuring. Every effort to maintain calm only fueled the fires of doubt in the minds of reporters and left the impression that Met Ed was downplaying a major crisis. When asked by reporters if residents of the area ought to seek medical attention, Herbein replied: "No, I don't think they should see a doctor. There is nothing like that kind of concern. I can tell you that we didn't injure anyone, we didn't overexpose anyone, we didn't kill a single solitary soul."[24] According to observers, reporters seemed to be frustrated by Herbein's use of technical jargon and his inability to provide complete answers to their questions. His assurances, while factual, weren't helpful.

11:50 P.M.: The Second Day Comes to a Close

Just before midnight of the second day, the Pennsylvania Department of Environmental Resources issued a press release announcing the discharge of industrial wastewater containing trace amounts of xenon, a radioactive waste product, into the Susquehanna River. This public announcement would mar the state's and the NRC's reputation, and it also provided the final excuse for the press and the public to write off Met Ed as not being credible, legitimate, or trustworthy.

Shortly after the reactor's shutdown, Met Ed had stopped its normal practice of discharging wastewater from toilets and showers and overflow from the turbine rooms into the river. However, by the afternoon of the second day, 400,000 gallons of water, slightly contaminated but well within the limits set by the NRC, had accumulated in storage tanks. Two NRC officials had told Met Ed at midday that the release of the water was fine as long as it met NRC's regulations. However, no one downstream was informed of this release. Met Ed began dumping the contaminated water into the river. When informed of the release around 6:00 P.M., NRC Chairman Joseph Hendrie ordered it stopped immediately. Hendrie, already under attack from antinuclear activists, was very worried that the public would see the company acting unilaterally, without the agency's careful oversight and approval. The NRC, like Met Ed, had a growing public-relations problem on its hands.

After Hendrie's order, the NRC, gubernatorial staff, and the state's Department of Environmental Resources (DER) argued for six hours over the wording of a press release. Having stopped the discharge, the NRC did not want to take responsibility for restarting it. The state did not want to take public responsibility for the release, and thus become the NRC's fall guy, since the state had neither approved the release in the first place nor ordered it stopped. During this six-hour negotiation, the state soon found out that the NRC had the ultimate authority to approve or disapprove such discharges. After rewriting the NRC's draft release, the state issued a statement that said, in part, that the DER "reluctantly agree[d] that the action must be taken."[25] The remaining water was then discharged.

The Third Day: March 30, 1979

Front-Page News

On March 30, the *New York Times* entitled an editorial "The Credibility Meltdown." This editorial charged the nuclear industry with downplaying nuclear power's risk and accused all the players in the Three Mile Island incident—industry, agencies, and politicians—of damaging their credibility by the "profusion of explanations and of contradictory statements."[26]

Protests were erupting across the United States from the Rancho Seco nuclear plant in Sacramento, California to the Millstone reactors in Waterford, Connecticut. The President of Columbia University in New York City asked the faculty to agree to drop plans to operate a nuclear research reactor on the Manhattan campus. In West Germany, 35,000 demonstrators chanted "We all live in Pennsylvania." Other protests erupted across Europe. By Friday, the third day of the crisis, the value of coal stocks shot up between 10 and 15 percent as the New York Stock Exchange halted trading in the stock of General Public Utility, Met Ed's owner, after it fell some 10 percent.

In print, the NRC contradicted its initial estimation of human error, as reported by Senator Hart, and flatly declared: "There was no operator error."[27] Met Ed's position now appeared shored up by the NRC official's statement. Other officials at the NRC, however, said that a human error may have occurred after the equipment failure, but that their lack of complete knowledge about the events prevented them from making a final determination. The press now began to accept the company's original story that a failure of pumps and valves had caused the accident. Reporters, however, were still angry about the release of the water into the Susquehanna River. Even as federal and state officials worked to approve release of the wastewater, a spokesperson for the NRC had denied reports that water containing radioactivity would be released.

7:10 A.M.: *Another Unannounced Release, Another Broken Promise*

Friday morning, a supervisor of operations at Unit 2 ordered the transfer of radioactive gases from a make-up tank, part of the primary coolant system, to a waste-gas-decay tank in order to release pressure in the former. Without notifying other Met Ed officials or the NRC, the transfer began. Primarily because of leaks in the system, radioactive material was released into the atmosphere. At 8:01 A.M., the company's helicopter recorded readings of some 1,200 millirems per hour at 130 feet. This reading was released to the press and to the NRC, still without notice of the actual venting.

Coincidentally, NRC officials had grown concerned about a suspected overload of the waste-gas-decay tank. In a meeting held that morning, NRC officials had estimated that a planned release of gases from the waste-decay tank would result in an off-site dose of 1,200 millirems. Within seconds of the estimate, someone at the meeting announced that the company was reporting radiation levels of some 1,200 millirems. The meeting's atmosphere turned apprehensive. Without knowing that the release was from the tank-to-tank transfer, not from a direct release from the waste-decay tank, Harold Denton, Director of Nuclear Reactor Regulation, and others from the NRC ordered an evacuation.

The NRC contacted the state's Emergency Management Agency. An NRC official, apparently selecting a reasonable distance on his own, recommended evacuating people as far as ten miles downwind from the plant. Confusion broke out as local emergency preparedness officials received conflicting recommendations. Fire departments were notified. A broadcast warning went out over a local radio station. At the plant a NRC official checked various readings, and advised Region I and Washington officials to call the evacuation off. At 10:00 A.M., Governor Thornburgh contacted NRC Chairman Hendrie to discuss the matter. They reached a decision and the governor recommended that everyone within a five-mile radius stay inside for one-half hour. Later that morning, the governor warned all residents within a ten-mile radius to stay inside. In addition, he recommended the closing of schools and the evacuation of pregnant women and preschool children from within a five-mile radius. In their discussions, the governor asked Chairman Hendrie to send an expert who would be a reliable source of technical information and advice. Later that day, Chairman Hendrie apologized to the governor for recommending the evacuation. In addition, he sent Harold Denton, head of the NRC's reactor regulatory division, to the site to represent the NRC and help clear up the confusion.

11:00 A.M.: Another Press Conference, Another Mistake

Met Ed's Jack Herbein once again appeared before reporters, this time at the American Legion Hall in Middletown. Trouble quickly erupted. At 9:00 A.M., the Emergency Management Agency had reported an "uncontrolled" release of radiation. At the press conference, Herbein attempted to explain that the radiation from the "planned" venting had measured between 300 and 350 millirems per hour. Met Ed maintained that the hazards were "minuscule," "negligible," and not worthy of an evacuation.[28] Herbein told the press: "I am here today to try to ease the level of panic. No evacuation is necessary."[29] But the company's use of "not significant," "minuscule," and "negligible," once again, were not easing the level of panic.

The press was faced with two contradictory pieces of information. The state agency had called the steam release "uncontrolled," not "planned." In addition, the report released by the company earlier that morning, unknown to Herbein, had detected 1,200 millirems, not 350 millirems. When the reporters grilled Herbein, the situation was exacerbated because newly arrived reporters were asking him basic questions, which irritated the three-day veterans of the affair. Stumbling, Herbein said he had not known of the higher readings, and that he could not dispute them. The press, unaware of the feud between the state and the NRC over accepting responsibility for allowing the release, then began to question Herbein on the unannounced release of wastewater into the river. Herbein, tired and exasperated, retorted: "I don't know why we need to tell you each and every thing we do."[30]

That was it. Reporters' suspicions that Met Ed was withholding information were confirmed. The company's credibility was in tatters. At 12:30 P.M., the governor held a press conference, telling reporters: "'We share your frustration. We're getting conflicting reports, too. Our responsibility is to protect the citizens of central Pennsylvania. To protect their safety we need better information."[31] The governor announced that, in conversations with the president of the United States and the chairman of the NRC, it had been agreed that the NRC's Harold Denton would be dispatched to the site as the

President's personal representative. The governor also said, "I repeat that this [the closing of schools] and other contingency measures are based on my belief that an excess of caution is best."[32] Even though the company had exercised cautious optimism and repeatedly reassured the public that the situation was under control, state officials publicly expressed concern about the public's safety.

The NRC's Own Credibility Problems

Met Ed was not the only organization having difficulty communicating with the public. By Friday evening, the NRC reported that there was evidence of serious damage to the fuel rods, samples of primary coolant had been found to contain high levels of radioiodine, and a large bubble of gas had formed at the top of the reactor vessel. However, NRC interjected panic into the situation by suggesting that a complete meltdown was possible at Three Mile Island. The confusion began when Dudley Thompson, a senior NRC official in Washington, stated on Friday afternoon that there was the possibility of a meltdown. Though Thompson described this possibility as "very, very small," the UPI wired his quote across America: "We are faced with a decision within a few days, rather than hours, on means of cooling down the core. . . . We face the ultimate risk of a meltdown."[33]

Staff working for Senator Gary Hart and Representatives Morris Udall and John Dingell confirmed that the NRC had stated that the chance of a meltdown existed. Later, Thompson pulled away from his earlier use of the word "meltdown," suggesting only that some of the fuel rods could melt. The NRC commissioners, highly concerned about the inflammatory nature of the statement, issued their own press release assuring the public that there was no impending danger of a core meltdown. Jody Powell, President Carter's press secretary, stated that there had been "unwarranted and disproportionate amounts of speculation about this matter."[34] Later that evening, the NRC's Harold Denton reassured Americans that "There is no immediate danger to the public," and called a meltdown a "very remote" possibility.[35] Nonetheless, the word "meltdown" appeared in the *Times*' headline the following day.

Later investigations revealed that Denton's statement, given the divergence of opinion within the NRC about the hydrogen bubble in the reactor, was as optimistic and misleading as many of Met Ed's statements. Experts disagreed about the danger of the bubble, first with regard to the possibility of its growth exposing the core, and later about the possibility that a potential oxygen build-up might cause an explosion. As a commissioner of the NRC later said, "The reporting—where it was off base—was off base because we were off base."[36]

In order to maintain Harold Denton's credibility and reduce miscommunication between the accident site and the capitol, the White House and the NRC decided to become far more reticent and to close the NRC headquarters information center in Bethesda, Maryland. Thus, while the NRC was not necessarily more forthcoming than the utility, with the White House's help, it was certainly better at damage control.

The Final Days: March 31 and April 1, 1979

Denton Takes Charge. Met Ed is Shut Out.

Denton, through his technical knowhow and straightforward manner, was able to bring legitimacy and credibility to the position of spokesperson. On the first day of his arrival, Denton was described as the "president's representative."[37] By the second day he was deemed "the president's chief troubleshooter." Denton, and Governor Thornburgh, quickly became press heroes in the crisis. On his third day, the *New York Times* ran a glowing article stating that Denton filled in the details "in language that was measured, clear and straightforward."[38] The article mentioned that the president had personally ordered Denton's services, and that the president and Denton conversed several times daily.

As Denton's fortunes rose, Met Ed's continued to fall. On Saturday, March 31, Met Ed's President Creitz asked NRC PR Director Fouchard once again to participate in a joint press conference. Fouchard refused a third time. Creitz decided that Met Ed would therefore discontinue its daily news briefings. At Met Ed's Saturday news conference, Creitz announced that further public information would be provided only by the NRC. At this final briefing, Jack Herbein increased Met Ed's public-relations woes by telling the press that personally, he thought the crisis was over. One hour later, Denton told the reporters quite the opposite. "The crisis won't be over until we have the core in full shutdown mode."[39] Herbein stated that one-third of the hydrogen gas bubble had been dissipated, further reducing the danger of damage to the fuel, but Denton would not confirm that number. He would only state that he did not think the hydrogen bubble posed an explosion problem at that time.

Despite the fact that Met Ed had frequently been accurate in its reporting to the press, even in the face of wrong information from the NRC, the company had lost all credibility with the press and the public. The press quickly accepted Harold Denton's appointment as chief spokesman during the crisis. Met Ed officials were relegated to mute operatives in a drama of their own making. Despite the fact that Met Ed had its news center at the Hershey Convention Center operational by Friday at noon, by Saturday the company was essentially sealed off from the press.

Danger Is Averted, but Not for Met Ed

On the fifth day of the crisis, President Jimmy Carter donned cloth boots and toured the control room at Three Mile Island. In front of Middletown, Pennsylvania's Borough Hall, the president said, "The primary and overriding concerns for all of us are the health and the safety of the people of this entire area . . . . As I have said before, if we make an error, all of us want to err on the side of extra precautions and extra safety."[40] While still careful and cautious, Denton, among others, stated that they had reason to believe the situation had substantially improved. The crisis was coming to an end, but Met Ed's credibility had already met its demise.

Telling the Truth:
The Mutual-Gains Approach

As the Three Mile Island case so painfully reveals, it is extremely difficult to conceal pertinent information in a public crisis. It is equally hard to avoid the temptation to speculate when the key facts are still not known. Yet, speculation should be avoided at all cost. A corporation or agency in trouble must select an experienced spokesperson who understands the sources of company or agency credibility. If a corporation is at the center of an accident or disaster, corporate management should work especially hard to enlist the support of government leaders. If a government agency is at the heart of the controversy, elected and appointed officials should interact intensively with the parties they regulate. In addition, both public agencies and private corporations should work hard to ensure that honesty is, in fact, their policy, and that they have put in place sufficient incentives and controls to ensure full and accurate disclosure. This is a central tenet of the mutual-gains approach to dealing with an angry public.

The Advantages of Disclosure Outweigh the Disadvantages

Disadvantages

Consider for a moment the arguments against full disclosure: the legal argument, the technical argument, and the media-relations argument.

The legal argument advises: *protect* information. Protect the company and its stockholders from exposure to liability. Do not become a target for blame. Do not accept responsibility for things that the organization probably didn't do. Do not accept blame until all the facts are uncovered and the rules of engagement are arranged under the auspices of a court. Above all, protect the organization. Taking responsibility and admitting blame only increase exposure later on.

The technical argument advises: *control* information. Do not admit to a problem until it is clear what the problem is, and, better yet, wait until a solution is at hand. Systematically investigate the situation, logically identify the most likely causes, carefully rule out possibilities until the exact nature of the problem has been identified. Telling the uninformed and technically limited public about these efforts before they are completed only confuses matters. Moreover, identifying a problem without fixing it suggests either ignorance or incompetence; better not to say anything.

The media-relations argument advises: *Create* information. Whatever is said can and will be used by someone. So, by giving the public information in small doses—always cast in the best possible light—there'll be no dangerous weapon for someone else to use. Appropriate disclosure is about maintaining and creating image. In the age of MTV and 500 cable channels, the facts are only one of a number of possibilities. Truth is what we make it; events should be shaped to our advantage.

Advantages

While each of these arguments has some merit, we believe that the advantages of full disclosure outweigh the disadvantages. We advise: *Share* information. Why?

Disclosing information might save the public from further harm and protect an agency or a company from further liability. If the core of Unit 2 of Three Mile Island had heated up enough to melt not merely part of the reactor, but the containment vessel, hundreds of thousands of people within a wide radius would have been adversely affected. The sooner government officials and the public had information pertinent to making an evacuation decision, the more time everyone would have had to take appropriate precautions. The less information the public has, the less they will be able to protect themselves. In court, willful concealment of information that might have protected the public is likely to create more, not less, liability. Moreover, concealing information may make someone look far more guilty than they actually are.

Revealing information keeps channels of communication open. By being forthcoming about what it did and did not know, Met Ed might have established its bona fides. This could have encouraged further sharing of information—all of which would have been important to corroborate facts, better ascertain the reactor's actual state, and provide consistent information to the public. Had Met Ed worked to build relationships with the press, government officials, and the public, it would have had numerous parties' help in implementing solutions to the problems they faced. Furthermore, by revealing information early and accurately, and not overstating the bounds of its knowledge, Met Ed would have avoided having to eat its words later or having to retract optimistic assurances that proved to be false.

Disclosing information, both favorable and unfavorable, builds credibility. On numerous occasions, Metropolitan Edison did have the right answers. The company accurately stated the initial cause of the problem, i.e., a broken valve. They also correctly reported that the release of radiation was not dangerous to human health. Further, the company accurately predicted that there would not be a meltdown. Yet, despite the fact that Met Ed had the facts right most of the time, nobody believed them. By concealing information when they shouldn't have, admitting to actions only after others had discovered them, and acting as if they were the only ones who could understand the situation, the managers at Three Mile Island undermined their credibility. In the end, the company lost power by concealing information. They were forced to give control over their destiny to state and federal officials.

Revealing information may also generate helpful feedback that can lead to better solutions. By practicing openness rather than defensiveness, an agency or company in trouble can invite others to help them formulate an appropriate response. By laying their cards on the table, as Thomas Gerusky of the Bureau of Radiological Protection suggested, organizations can work together with others to piece together the best interpretation of all the facts available. In the Three Mile Island case, because the NRC did not have all the facts it made less than accurate assessments, such as the coincidental estimate of radiation from the gas-decay tank that never actually leaked. In turn, the NRC recommended an evacuation when one was not warranted. If its cards had been laid on the table for *all* the decision makers to see, better decisions could have been made.

In an open society such as the United States, with local newspapers, radio, national television, worldwide cable network news, computer networks, and the Internet, information is simply harder and harder to conceal. Ironically, just as Three Mile Island occurred, a federal court was considering whether or not to let *The Progressive* magazine print instructions for building a hydrogen bomb. That information was readily available. As Harold Denton said years later to a gathering of the Nuclear Energy Agency of the Organization for Economic Cooperation and Development, "With the growth in technological ability of all the media worldwide, no one can hide a major reactor accident."[41]

There are sound reasons why companies and government agencies should make full disclosure of their policy. We cannot improve upon Denton's formulation. As he told the Nuclear Energy Agency, "I believe we frequently underestimate the public's ability to understand the situation, and have therefore inadvertently or purposely withheld information because of our perception of the danger of a crisis mentality when none was warranted. This is exactly the wrong approach to take with the public. If we want the public's trust, we must trust the public."[42]

Prescription 1: Share information to build trust and credibility.

Act in a Trustworthy Fashion

What is trust? For an economist convinced of the rationality of individual actors, trust might best be understood in cost–benefit terms: an actor determines that sufficient benefits will flow from cooperation so he or she adopts a cooperative pattern of behavior toward another in exchange for reciprocity. From a sociological perspective, trust is a mode of behavior that allows individuals to interact in a cooperative, reciprocal fashion in order to supply material wants, meet social needs such as companionship and status, and establish an individual identity in a larger society. For a psychologist, trust is an expectation of benign or favorable intent by another actor based on previous experiences with parents, siblings, and peers.

While the economic, sociological, and psychological literature is replete with discussions of trust, trust remains an elusive academic quarry, not easily defined or explained. On the other hand, we think that most people have an intuitive, common-sense notion tied to honesty, reciprocity, and reputation. Trust involves predictability, consistency, and forgiveness, too. Genuine trust allows room for mistakes. Trust is that which allows couples to hold joint checking accounts, parents to let children borrow the car, and business-persons to conclude an agreement with a handshake.

We think a simple aphorism can go a long way toward building and maintaining trust. The Mad Hatter said to Alice, "Say what you mean, and mean what you say." Met Ed had trouble with this simple formula. Rather than admitting that radiation readings above background level had been re-corded, the company chose to say that no "significant" readings had been taken. This second statement did not convey what the company knew to be the truth. The company sought to decide for the public how it should in-terpret the facts. Contrary to Met Ed's hopes, the media and the public inter-preted the company's statement, not as an assurance of safety, but as an effort to whitewash the situation. Met Ed also failed to mean what they said. "No further releases are expected," Met Ed told the public, only to release radia-tion later into the air and water. Statements followed by contradictions made Met Ed out to be a poor forecaster at best and a liar at worst.

The simple fact is that concealing pertinent information is too diffi-cult. A policy of cautious concealment rarely works. On Friday morning of the crisis, Met Ed failed to notify the public of its "planned release," yet it immediately revealed the 1,200 millirems of radiation measured from the release. Consequently, the press and government officials used that one piece of information to attack the company for another action that was not fully disclosed until later. The "planned" release, as Herbein termed it, looked like a cover-up to the press. Later investigations proved this assumption erro-neous, but, as one investigation pointed out, "The press believed that Met Ed knew the plant inside and out and thus must have known exactly what was going on at any time with respect to the accident."[43] Leaks of information are far more likely to happen than leaks of radiation. Even if contradictions are only a reflection of confusion or uncertainty within an organization, the public may very well interpret such contradictions as malicious and willful.

Prescription 2: Say what you mean and mean what you say.

In addition to saying what you mean, and meaning what you say, the mutual-gains approach offers another prescription that can go a long way toward building trust: Acknowledge the concerns of the other side. The press and the public were already skeptical of Met Ed. Of course, the public would suspect Met Ed of downplaying the seriousness of the problem and concealing the bad news to protect its multimillion dollar investment. But by focusing primarily on the "successful" containment of disaster by the plant's safety systems, and by emphasizing the "control" Met Ed had over the situation, the company only played into the public's suspicion of its bias.

In contrast, public officials were particularly adept at acknowledging the concerns of the public. Take for instance President Carter's speech to the residents of the stricken area: "The primary and overriding concerns for all of us are the health and the safety of the people in this entire area . . . ." The President pointedly empathized with the concerns of the public. He emphasized caution, concern, and worry. This emphasis was also shared by the two spokesmen who proved to be most effective throughout the crisis: Harold Denton of the NRC and Governor Richard Thornburgh. In contrast, rather than acknowledge the concerns of the other side, the company worked very hard to minimize and downplay the public's fears. Met Ed's assurances had precisely the opposite effect: People became more worried and more distrustful.

While the mutual-gains approach encourages organizations to share information with the public, we are not suggesting a naive revelation of every fact, assumption, and bit of speculation. Too much information, poorly stated and issued at inopportune moments, will not gain the public's trust either. Take the NRC's revelation that a meltdown was possible. Though the spokesperson for the NRC was being honest, he did not help the press or the public put the relevant risks in context. Did "ultimate" mean "inevitable" or did it mean "possible"? If it meant "possible," how "possible" was it? The NRC, in this case, was too willing to speculate on the worst possible outcome of the accident. Too often, the NRC barely knew enough about what was actually happening to assess the situation accurately, let alone to estimate what might transpire in the future. The NRC ignored its own internal policy: Avoid speculation.

Prescription 3: Acknowledge the concerns of others.

Select a Capable Spokesperson

An organization must establish trust through the words and actions of its representatives. Although thorough contingency planning, explicit corporate communication policies, and staff training can go a long way toward preparing an organization for a crisis, when the crisis breaks someone has to slide out from behind their desk, step onto the stage, and address the public directly. Building trust requires a trustworthy spokesperson.

Soon after the reactor tripped, Met Ed's Jack Herbein courageously stepped up to bat. While he was a capable engineer and manager, a comparison of the NRC's Denton, Governor Thornburgh, and Herbein offers some important lessons for selecting an effective spokesperson.

Herbein faced a monumental task. He was forced to deal, under the public's worried eyes, with an accident that was not supposed to happen. He had to address complex technical problems with too little accurate information and at the same time address hundreds of reporters ready to relay his words to millions. As a station manager, Herbein was apparently highly skilled. One NRC official remarked later, "I have a high regard for him as a station superintendent. He's conscientious, honest, straight, hard working . . . "[44] But Herbein had to move from the highly technical and insulated world of plant operations to a world of nonexperts in which every action and word was exposed, reported, scrutinized, and analyzed. At the plant, Herbein was in charge. His workmates were familiar with the technical language he used, and his employees were comfortable in a situation mediated through gauges, meters, and elaborate display panels. His customer was a vague "Everyman" who turned on his lights each morning as oblivious to Met Ed employees as they were to him. But overnight Herbein was forced to meet his customers and their stand-in, the press, face to face. It was as if Herbein had been instantly transported from the back technical-operations office to the front sales office. The public needed everything that Herbein took for granted explained. This was more than he could handle.

The same NRC official who expressed his high regard for Herbein also remarked that "Jack has a very tough, condescending attitude. He's a very sharp man himself. And he's the sort . . . you would want to avoid, a very strong-willed, assertive expert who has little patience with ignorance or with slow understanding."[45] As the fateful conference in the lieutenant governor's office on that first day proved, Herbein's manner was a liability. Herbein's withholding of information as well as the way in which he conveyed information was problematic. One state official at that meeting gave his impression of Herbein's presentation: "It was over, and, 'Ha, ha, ha.' And, 'I don't know what you people are interested for, and we ought to be down at the plant making sure things are going smoothly.'"[46] Herbein's lowest moment came, when, tired and frustrated, he exclaimed: "I don't know why we need to tell you each and every thing we do."[47] He was unwilling to lay all the facts on the table, to acknowledge the concerns of others, and to explain rather than defend his actions.

In contrast, Harold Denton was a successful spokesperson. What did he do right? His manner proved reassuring to the press. He spoke easily, smoothly, and conveyed honesty. He did not deal abruptly with people or treat them condescendingly. The *New York Times* applauded his "friendly, jowly grin and confident, calming voice" and his ability to speak in a "measured, clear and straightforward" manner.[48] This is not to say Denton was perfect. One *Chicago Tribune* reporter said, "Denton was the hero of Harrisburg because he was the only one talking, but he should learn to talk English like the rest of us."[49]

Denton was both formally and informally forthcoming about information. Not only did he engage the press in formal briefings, he was also available at other times and provided information to reporters when they asked for it. Denton also had the support of high-level government leaders. President Carter selected him. Governor Thornburgh liked and trusted him. Denton's association with high-ranking officials gave him the credibility Herbein did not have, and could not get—in part because the NRC refused to hold press conferences together with Met Ed. Finally, Denton had experience working in complex public settings. Like Herbein, he was an engineer. But unlike Herbein, Denton had gained valuable experience appearing before Congress and serving on Capitol Hill as director of the NRC's nuclear-reactor regulations. Denton said of his experience on the Hill: "I'm a scientist. But I found since I've become responsible for overseeing reactor regulations that you have to do a lot of explaining, . . . "[50]

Prescription 4: Select an informed, experienced, clear-spoken spokesperson who is not condescending to the public.

Republican Governor Richard Thornburgh, new in office, was also successful at earning the public's trust. He had run on a platform of honesty after a major government scandal. Thornburgh was both an engineer and a lawyer. Like Denton, he had a great deal of experience operating in public settings. He was able to demonstrate concern and, when the crisis eased, a good sense of humor. As he described the situation, "You have to go before the cameras and microphones and tell them what you know and what you don't. You have to stop the rumors. And, of course, you have to make decisions."[51] In addition, the governor had help; he had a staff person whose prime objective was to preserve Dick Thornburgh's credibility.

Paul Critchlow, the governor's press secretary, had one overriding goal: Protect the credibility of his boss if it became necessary to order an evacuation. In the fateful meeting where Herbein angered state officials, Critchlow recalled thinking, "I have deep suspicions about Herbein and I'm not going to associate the lieutenant governor with him. I'm not going to give him credibility. I wanted to preserve the governor and the lieutenant governor's credibility."[52] Credibility had an advocate in the governor's office. While Critchlow made many mistakes, including shutting out the BRP from decision making and shutting off the BRP's contact with the public, his intense dedication to the governor's perceived trustworthiness helped ensure his success. Met Ed desperately needed such a credible advocate, but they did not have one.

What makes a spokesperson credible? While every crisis has unique contextual features, we think the attributes of a credible spokesperson are almost always obvious. In a crisis situation it is best to have someone who

- is likable, affable, and straightforward;
- has a reputation for honesty, internally within a company or agency as well as externally with others;
- has a reputation for collaboration rather than confrontation;
- is familiar with the technical subject and can explain it in a clear fashion;
- already has experience in public settings;
- has a strong internal advocate whose primary objective is to preserve the spokeperson's credibility;
- has or can gain the support of high-ranking government leaders.

   Prescription 5: Find an advocate who can defend and promote the company's or the agency's credibility from inside.

Enlist Support on the Outside

Met Ed made an attempt to enlist the support of government leaders. On at least three separate occasions during the first three days of the crisis, Met Ed sought to present a united front with NRC and state officials. Unfortunately, those officials were not willing to cooperate.

Part of Met Ed's lack of success in engaging the regulators can in part be blamed on Herbein's manner during that first day. But, NRC officials made it their policy to have little or no public contact with Met Ed. Karl Abraham, Public Affairs Officer, Region I NRC, and Joe Fouchard did not believe that the NRC should take information from anyone but their own people. Fouchard said, "I don't think it [the information function] can be a cooperative effort. In other words, we are the regulatory agency. Let us face it. There are some actions we're going to have to take which the utility won't like."[53] Met Ed was also queasy about a close association with the NRC. Herbein opposed cross-checking information with the NRC because it "could be viewed by some as collusion and we certainly aren't going to be party to that."[54] One of many negative outcomes of this "arm's-length" relationship was that at least seven separate information centers were established during the crisis by the state, the NRC, and Met Ed, leading to a mass of often contradictory information.

An arm's-length relationship, while helping to maintain autonomy and oversight, tends to get in the way of problem-solving, especially during a crisis when rapid, honest, and complete communication is necessary. We have some advice, particularly for government officials.

Government and Business Should, Can, and Do Cooperate

To government officials, we say that collaborative, cooperative government–business relationships are not only possible but already exist. Furthermore, the more government officials can cooperate and work with, not against, private industry—within the bounds of the law—the more likely government is to achieve its stated goals, at a lower cost, as well as to achieve voluntary compliance. First let's look at a simple case. During the 1980s, the U.S. Army Corps of Engineers reassessed its management of construction contracts. With an annual budget of $11 billion, the Corps found that legal claims associated with construction contracts were increasing, that quality in construction was suffering, and that the Corps was spending too much money fighting with contractors who were hired to build dams, erect levies, and construct military installations. In response, the Corps implemented a program known as "partnering." Using workshops, team-building exercises, and the setting of mutual goals, Corps staff and private contractors developed a sense of themselves as partners rather than enemies. The Corps wasn't merely a watchdog, but rather a partner with joint responsibility for finishing projects on time and within budget. Since 1988, when it was begun, partnering has swept through 35 districts of the 40,000-employee organization. Safety records are better, quality has improved, and outstanding claims have dropped dramatically. The public–private partnership has saved money, reduced costly conflict, and helped to improve the final product.[55]

Now a more complicated case. The NRC, the EPA, and many other government agencies must regulate industries and not just work with them to accomplish federal objectives. In the United States, we have relied mostly on enforced compliance to ensure that government regulations are followed. This approach punishes those who break the rules by applying sanctions and penalties. The problem with this method is that there is no evidence that escalating penalties and fines significantly increase compliance. Moreover, this approach to enforcement is expensive, discourages innovation, and leads those regulated to hide information and act defensively. This approach has also clogged the courts, perversely diminishing the probability that violators will actually be prosecuted and penalized.

In other countries, and increasingly at the state and local levels in this country, government is trying another model, often called the "interactive compliance" model. Regulatory agencies work *with* regulated firms to achieve the best possible compliance at the lowest possible cost to the regulatee. In this model, government focuses on educating firms and helping them stay within the rules. These agencies are *not* serving as promoters of industry like the NRC's precursor, the Atomic Energy Agency. Rather, they are promoting a broader set of public goals, but in a spirit of cooperation. Great Britain, not necessarily known historically for its lack of excess government intervention in the marketplace, has utilized this model frequently to achieve environmental compliance. The result? Compliance is strong, and when firms don't comply, the government acts as a consultant to help them make the necessary adjustments, rather than as a constable to impose punishment. One British pollution control inspector described it this way. "'We look upon our jobs as educating industry, persuading it, cajoling it. We achieve far more this way."[56]

In the United States, the Corps of Engineers has tried this method to enforce compliance with permits issued to protect wetlands in Florida. When a permittee is found in violation of permit conditions, before the case is sent to litigation, Corps management sit down with the purported violator. In a "low-key and amicable" atmosphere, as one Corps official described it, the two parties meet to discuss the problem. The permittee offers its side of the story, then the Corps presents its case to the permittee, without a judge and often without attorneys. After considering the arguments on both sides, the Corps issues a set of stipulations for the permittee to follow. If the permittee agrees to these stipulations, a consent decree is issued, and the litigation is dropped. In fact, litigation has dropped drastically, freeing up staff attorneys to pursue the worst and most flagrant violators. Because permittees know the Corps is serious about enforcement, compliance levels are up throughout the Florida District. Last but not least, the stipulations that the Corps imposes provide for the direct mitigation and restoration of Florida's wetlands. No longer does a distant judge impose a general fine that enters the nation's coffers without improving or protecting even a dollar's worth of wetlands.

To conclude our advice to government officials, consider again the case of Three Mile Island. While the NRC saw its "information function" as separate, an arm's-length relationship, in practice, only served to increase confusion, to encourage the utility to conceal information from NRC officials and to frighten the public. Given the history of the Atomic Energy Commission's overzealous promotion of nuclear power, it is understandable that the NRC and Met Ed were both concerned about perceptions of collusion in the charged public atmosphere surrounding the accident. But, as other countries and agencies have demonstrated, good governance does not require a separate, distant, and uncommunicative relationships that gets in the way of effective action. Joseph DiMento, a professor at the University of California, Irvine, puts it this way: "Tactics which involve actors in the compliance framework hold considerable promise for improving the communicability of, respect for, and ultimately the enforceability of law."[57]

Prescription 6: For government: Seek voluntary rather than enforced compliance.

The Exxon Valdez*: When Paying Out Doesn't Pay Off*

What should a company or a government agency do in the aftermath of an accident, when injured parties must be compensated? How can the way money is spent after an accident bring the taxpayers or a company the best value for its dollar? How can a company or an agency use a crisis situation to increase, rather than diminish, its credibility? The *Exxon Valdez* oil spill offers a clear picture of what can go wrong when an angry public is not approached effectively after an accident. In the second part of this chapter, we explore how the mutual-gains approach might have been used to rebuild credibility.

In the early morning hours of March 24, 1989, the weather calm and clear, third mate Gregory Cousins piloted the 978-foot tanker *Exxon Valdez,* loaded with million gallons of oil, through Prince William Sound, 25 miles south of the port of Valdez, Alaska. In the dark, Cousins could not see the tree-lined shores, the rock pinnacles of the Sound jutting out of the water, or the abundant seals, sea lions, and birds resting on shore. In order to avoid icebergs from the Columbia glacier, Cousins was authorized to steer out of one southbound channel and into another. Three miles through that second channel, the steel from the single hull met a shallow underwater rock known as Bligh Reef (named for the notorious captain of the H.M.S. *Bounty,* who sailed the same waters with Captain Cook in 1778). Metal ripped. For a few seconds, a glowing aura surrounded the bow. The second mate, asleep until awakened by the crash, saw a plume of oil spurt seventy feet into the air. Over 11 million gallons of Alaska crude began spewing into Prince William Sound, one of the most biologically rich waters in the world. Six to eight large holes had been torn in the hull of the vessel. Captain Joseph J. Hazelwood, who was not at the helm at the time of the accident, radioed the Coast guard: "[E]vidently we're leaking some oil. And we're going to be here awhile."[58] So began the largest oil spill in U.S. history.

The spill eventually contained over 270,000 barrels of oil, or over 11 million gallons, covering 3,000 square miles of Prince William Sound and blackening 1,300 miles of shoreline. The spill occurred at a time when the pink salmon migrate from the coast to the ocean in what is believed to be the second largest wild run of salmon in the world; the herring move toward shore to spawn in the kelp beds; whales, dolphins, seals, and sea lions begin to migrate back to this major feeding ground for the summer months. What began as metal tearing and screeching against an underwater rock, propelled by millions of pounds of steel and crude oil, became an environmental, corporate, and public-relations disaster.

Cleaning Up

As oil spread across the water of Prince William Sound's numerous bays and inlets, Exxon Shipping Company president Frank Iarossi assured the public that Exxon would accept full financial responsibility. Iarossi said in a press conference: "At this point, I don't have any assessment of the costs. That's somebody's worry, but it's not mine. There is no reason for me to even be concerned about that right now. There's no monetary limit on what I can do to help. It's going to be a helluva bill, but right now I'm not stopping to count."[59]

By mid-May, almost two months after the spill, Exxon had spent $115 million on the cleanup. In a May, 1989 *Fortune* magazine interview, when he was asked, "What are the cleanups and the lawsuits going to cost Exxon?" Lawrence G. Rawl, chairman of the board of Exxon, stated, "We're not talking billions, but I don't know what we're talking."[60] By the fall of 1992, Exxon certainly knew. The company had spent $2.1 billion on cleanup efforts. Ten thousand workers, 1,000 water craft, 70 airplanes and helicopters, and 134 aquatic biologists and toxicologists had been called in to help.

In addition to cleanup payments, in October 1992, Exxon agreed to settle with the state of Alaska and the federal government for $1.3 billion to be paid over 10 years. This settlement included repayment to the state and federal governments for cleanup costs and for restoration of the Sound and the Gulf of Alaska, as well as fines for four violations of environmental law and restitution for damages. In July of 1993, Alyeska Corporation, a consortium of six oil companies including Exxon that owns the Trans-Alaska Pipeline, settled with fishermen and other Alaskans for $98 million. In July of 1994, Exxon agreed to pay $20 million in damages to 3,500 Alaskan villagers who said that the oil spill had ruined their food supply. In the next month, a federal jury ordered Exxon to pay $287 million in compensatory damages to 10,000 fishermen and $5 billion in punitive damages to 34,000 fishermen, natives, and citizens, the largest punitive damages ever awarded in a pollution case![61]

If nothing else, the spill certainly emptied a deluge of funds into the Alaska economy, from within hours after the spill until today. By midsummer of 1989, Valdez's population had swelled to 12,000 people, some five times more than usual. The City of Cordova, a fishing town some 70 miles by air from Valdez, saw its sales tax revenues increase by 22 percent. Money flowed into Valdez, spawning what the locals dubbed "spillionaires." A young skipper supposedly leased his skiff and skills to Exxon for the summer and left with $700,000. Some of Cordova's fishing fleet was chartered for up to $6,000 per boat per day. Rents rose by as much as $500 a month. In contrast, Valdez's small public radio station refused the $32,283 grant offered by Exxon and squeaked by on small donations.[62] The money also spawned opportunism, crime, and community disintegration. Kelly Weaverling, an

Alaska resident who directed the wildlife-rescue boats, said, "'Most of these hard-luck cases pouring into Valdez don't care about restoring the sound, they just want the bucks. . . . They're toasting Joe Hazelwood for bringing easy money. If they don't get jobs, they steal. They vandalize. They break and enter. The crime rate is out of control."[63] When it came time to manage the flow of funds into Alaska, Exxon, much like its ship, ran aground.

A Modest Proposal

Early in the crisis, Exxon Corporation received a proposal from a reputable provider of dispute resolution and conflict management services. In its proposal, the firm stated, "In sum, the *Exxon Valdez* oil spill has and will continue to spawn a large number of difficult, interrelated disputes. Some will be complex, multiissue, multiparty disputes. Some will turn on difficult scientific and technological matters. Some will involve governmental authorities directly; others will pit Exxon against various private individuals and groups. Most will generate strong emotions and all will be subject to public scrutiny and the interest of public entities. . . . It is in the interest of all parties to seek out and apply the best current knowledge about dispute resolution and management, both to the process of negotiating over spill-related cleanup matters and to the settlement of claims and litigation."[64]

The firm outlined an initial two-phase work plan, including four weeks of fact-finding and diagnosis followed by 12 weeks of developing an ad hoc dispute-handling forum. Not only would the forum serve the many parties who would come forward, but the development of the forum would include consensus-building discussions among the many different groups involved. The proposal suggested that such a process would expedite the resolution of disputes, achieve more creative and technically sound solutions, reduce transaction costs for all parties, and achieve fairer results.[65]

Exxon rejected this proposal. What, instead, did Exxon do? What was Exxon's response to the claims it faced regarding mitigation and compensation, especially for irreparable harm?

Exxon's Response

Within three months of the spill, Exxon reportedly paid out $5.5 million on more than 500 claims filed by private and commercial interests. By mid-April 1989, the Cordova District Fishermen United had received $250,000 from

Exxon. In June of 1989, Exxon paid the Sound's fishery, the Prince William Sound Aquaculture Company, (PWSAC) $8 million. As of early 1990, Exxon had paid out some $180 million to compensate private parties. By June of 1990, the City of Cordova had received $740,000 in Exxon grants.

Even before the cleanup crews were on location, Exxon opened a claims office in Cordova. Exxon President Bill Stevens said: "It's our very strong desire to settle all of the damage claims . . . without resorting to lawsuits."[66] Stevens reported before the House Committee on Internal and Insular Affairs, "In addition to our efforts to contain and clean up the spill, we have mobilized to mitigate the economic impact on the communities affected by the spill. We currently have 50 people handling claims, and we have opened claims offices in Valdez, Cordova, Homer, Kodiak, and Seward. We have worked with hatcheries, canneries, fishermen's groups, city and borough governments, and many individuals to assure their financial viability while claims are being processed."[67] Further testimony reported that Exxon provided loans to damaged parties while their claims were processed. According to a policy report prepared for the House committee, Exxon had resisted the use of federal troops in spill cleanup in favor of hiring local residents. Local compensation involved payments to residents who participated in the cleanup and payments to residents who suffered damages. Exxon, under supervision of government agencies, paid into a 311(k) fund for compensation for expenses resulting from the cleanup.

Mitigation Efforts

Residents in towns on the Sound went into action early in the crisis without Exxon's request or approval. One woman prepared a list of suppliers, outlets, and fishermen willing to help fight the spill. In 48 hours, she had 100 boats signed up. Within weeks, her database included "storage tanks, hydroblasters, shovels, five-gallon buckets, people, showers, skiffs, airplanes, and 800 boats."[68] Because of the lack of commercial booms, locals established a log boom project. Volunteers designed, built, and operated the booms. Volunteers set up bird and otter rescue centers.

But all this locally-inspired activity was frustrated when Veco, Exxon's contractor overseeing the cleanup efforts, entered the scene. As soon as Veco began to direct the log boom business, chain saws disappeared and ordered groceries were not delivered. One partner in a local fishing fleet said of Veco's efforts, "'The people running the operations are good supervisors from

Texas, but they don't know a thing about our beaches."[69] The woman who had established the database raised concerns to Veco about her own exposure to liability when fishermen she had "recruited" went out to sea in a storm. They replied, according to her: "You shut up. You do what we want you to do, and say what we want you to say."[70] When one fisherman offered Veco his services, they responded that his size of boat was no longer needed. He was then told his boat was not insured, therefore not eligible to enlist in the cleanup effort. Then he was told that Veco had hiring priorities. The fisherman claimed he discovered that many of the Veco-enlisted boats were also uninsured. About the hiring priorities, he said: "They lied about that, too."[71]

Local residents expressed concern about how their participation in the cleanup was constrained by Exxon's efforts to limit its corporate liability. Fishermen said they had to sign gag orders in order to participate in and be paid for mitigation efforts. During a follow-up public hearing in Alaska, Representative Owens asked if people involved in the cleanup were being prohibited from speaking. Mr. Kopchack, a fisherman, responded: "That is correct. Individuals under contract were instructed that as part of their contract, they were not to have discussions or to provide access for press."[72]

Compensation for Damages

The Legal Framework Prior to the Spill

At the time of the *Exxon Valdez* spill, numerous federal statutes as well as state common law offered several possible, though by no means certain, legal guidelines regarding compensation. The Trans-Alaska Pipeline Authorization Act (TAPAA) required action by the owner and operator of the vessel as well as the Trans-Alaska Pipeline Fund (TAPAA fund) in the case of accidents involving the transport of oil after loading from the pipeline. Under the Transport section of TAPAA, the TAPAA fund allowed for a strict liability limit of $100 million for: (1) cleanup by state and federal agencies; (2) private party injuries; (3) damages to the ecosystem not restored through cleanup. The extent to which the three separate kinds of compensations could be kept under the $100 million limit was not entirely clear. The legislation had not been tested in court.[73]

Under a separate section of TAPAA involving the liability of pipeline right-of-way holders for spills, cleanup costs were not included in the strict liability limits, and the statute explicitly stated that all costs and duties imposed by the cleanup and removal of the spill would be borne by the responsible party. This section of TAPAA also laid out clear responsibilities toward native Alaskans, including immediate subsistence aid if necessary. However, the transport statute in the same Act lacked specific language as to whether damages would include only physical damage to a proprietary interest, or more comprehensive damages such as secondary economic impacts and social upheaval. In addition, the transport section made no mention of subsistence aid.

In addition to TAPAA, the Federal Water Pollution Control Act (FWPCA) came into play in the aftermath of the spill. Though the FWPCA lacked clear enforcement provisions (requiring the federal government to quickly and effectively force cleanup efforts by recalcitrant companies), it did require a payment of $150 per gross ton of the carrying vessel. In the *Exxon Valdez* case, this amounted to $31 million. Only if the government could prove willful negligence or misconduct could this compensation limit be overcome. Since the FWCPA did not address compensation to private parties, private claims would have to be brought under other federal or state laws.

At least immediately after the spill, it was not necessarily clear how different statutes such as FWPCA and TAPAA might interact, or even how conflicting parts of TAPAA such as the right-of-way-holder and transport sections might play out. In addition to such federal statutes, claimants also had access to maritime tort law under common law. This body of law raised questions regarding liability limits and the ability of private parties to obtain compensation for indirect economic losses. Within this uncertain legal framework, Exxon was left to wrestle with the best way of mitigating the disaster and compensating those parties adversely affected.[74]

How Exxon Managed Claims for Compensation During the Spill

Compensation claims for damages were handled differently from payment for locals' cleanup efforts. In order to process compensation claims, residents were separated into primary, secondary, and tertiary categories. Primary claimants were those affected directly by the spill, primarily fishermen. Secondary claimants were those who had some kind of direct claim, such as tour operators. Tertiary claimants, including businesses such as restaurants, hotels, and hardware stores, were affected more indirectly. Exxon indicated early on that they would compensate primary individuals and perhaps secondary claimants. There was little hope that tertiary claimants would be compensated.

The compensation issue raised concerns throughout the local community and the state. Exxon's handling of compensation raised a variety of criticisms surrounding the size of the payments, purported dubious contingencies attached to offers, fairness to differing claimants, and timeliness of company response. Mayor John Devens of Valdez expressed two concerns about the economic compensation fund. First, the fund might be restricted to the $100 million available under TAPAA, thus compelling individuals to litigate in order to receive compensation. He noted that compensation in the *Amoco Cadiz* case took some 11 years to be litigated, awarded, and paid. Second, the mayor expressed concern about the waivers individuals might have to sign in order to collect their compensation. As with aiding the mitigation effort, the mayor expressed concern that those receiving compensation for damages would be asked to sign dubious contracts waiving future rights. The City of Kodiak responded by asking that the City Attorney review all contracts and that all boat operators and fishermen should have the same kind of contracts.[75]

Exxon was accused of moving slowly in providing the proper claim forms. A herring fisherman claimed in testimony that while Exxon was putting money forward in "good faith" so "we would not have to lose our homes, our boats, et cetera, so our lives would not be further disrupted by this tragedy," disagreement over the proper contract forms caused over a month's delay in filing claims.[76] One disagreement, for example, involved Exxon's request that fishermen sign off rights to the 1989 fishing season. The same herring fisherman reported, "Here we have the simplest, the most clear-cut case, and yet it was, what, Day 41 before they could have the proper form in place. I think not only are we going to have a problem, but it is going to be a huge problem in getting any money from Exxon to help us out here. . . "[77]

Regardless of how Exxon handled payments, or the amount of the payments it made, many locals would not have been satisfied. Mr. Kopchack, a fisherman, reported to the oversight committee that he had put 260 hours of time into the oil spill in 35 days, would miss the fishing opening, and could find no one to work with him on his boat. He asked, "How can you say I am owed this much money because I could not go fishing on the day the fishing season opened? The merchants have other nightmare stories. How do you get compensated for that? There is no fair way that works."[78] For Native

Americans, the compensation claims could not begin to address the harm to them. Representative George Miller said, "I went to Chugach . . . when we talked to the residents there, and . . . explained to them not to eat anything that had come in contact with the water in Sawmill Bay and watched the faces and the reaction of the people who say that is their way of life, that is how they ate."[79]

As for tertiary claimants, they could only express their indignation at not receiving any compensation whatsoever. Many of Cordova's small-business owners mentioned that they had already purchased inventories in anticipation of the fishing season. "When these things do not happen, our inventories pile up, and there is no way to stop them when they are in process," said Jim Rankin, a retail businessman. "We were at that point fearful of what was going to happen in Cordova. The fishermen who they admitted were impacted are having difficulties dealing with this. We were not admitted to being taken care of. If they are having problems, we are having a real serious problem."[80]

While many were suffering from the effects of the slow or nonexistent payment of compensation moneys, others in the town were being what might be called entrepreneurial. A professional business consultant, a graduate of Yale University and Harvard Business School, was hired to head the Cordova Oil Spill Disaster Relief Office (COSDRO). The consultant saw the spill as an opportunity to widen the economic base of a town that could not go back to the way it was before the disaster. He said, "'This city is trying to recover from an economic disaster, and I don't see anything wrong with trying to mount a deeper keel to stabilize the city."[81] Cordova, he reasoned, could utilize compensation funds not only to fund the science center that arose after the spill, but perhaps to construct a deep-water port and a road to Anchorage and Fairbanks. The head of COSDRO reasoned, "Twenty-nine families have left town because they made so much money on the cleanup that they had no reason to stay. It's what's called a pattern dislocation in our economy, and Cordova will be feeling it for years."[82]

The Aftermath

However sincere, Exxon's efforts at providing timely and fair compensation to those affected by the disaster left many residents of towns such as Valdez and Cordova feeling angry yet again.

The community was ripped apart by the money flowing into the settlements of the Sound. While many fishermen could not wait to help clean up their own backyard, in doing so, they had to choose whether or not to accept funds from the very company that had damaged their livelihood. Neighbors would wonder if cleanup participants had sold out. Others would feel left out because they did not benefit from the bounty. One part-time fisherman angrily remarked, "Some of my neighbors made a half a million dollars. All I got was a lost month and a half of work and the frustration."[83] As Representative Miller noted at the hearings," . . . this is not just about polluted water and otters and birds and deer and bear. This is about communities, families, businesses, and social fabric."[84] The money flowing into the community threatened the social fabric perhaps as much as the ecological destruction of the Sound.

Anchorage attorney Paul Davis counseled, "I think it is counterproductive for a fisherman, processor, or cafe owner to initiate litigation without trying negotiation first. Suing one of the world's largest corporations won't ever be a picnic. . . . "[85] But lawyers quickly descended on the stricken communities. Exxon's Stevens was quick to confirm the rumor that a "slick of lawyers" had spilled across the Sound right behind the oil.[86]

Mayor Devens of Valdez responded to Exxon's compensation efforts by saying, "It's insulting to me to have to go to Exxon for everything this community needs. We're experiencing a lot of social problems related to the spill—fights, depression, divorces. We asked for a counselor, but Exxon turned us down and then gave the $20,000 we requested to Seward to enhance its summer celebration. A community shouldn't have to come begging to a company, and it bothers me that we are getting their handouts. . . . Exxon treats us like a child: 'No, son, we don't think you need that, but we'll give you this.'"[87]

One participant in the cleanup efforts remarked: "I didn't believe it at first, but now I think Exxon is using its money to divide and conquer these communities. At least, that's the effect of its actions." He continued, "Exxon goes into a town where everybody is mad and says, 'We're going to give you $5,000 per day for a boat.' And people start thinking, 'Well, we're mad, but give us some of that money and we won't be quite as mad.' . . . They put out big bucks to get everybody to shut up for a while."[88]

The impression that Exxon was simply buying people off was reinforced when Exxon paid $4 million to the Alaska Visitors Association with the encouragement of the state tourism division. The Association hired Alyeska's very own P.R. firm. The result? An ad campaign featuring Marilyn Monroe without the small mole on her cheek. As noted earlier, the campaign announced, "Unless you look long and hard, you probably won't notice her beauty mark is missing."[89] Not only was the ad in bad taste at best and an outright lie at worst, it lent support to the critics who saw compensation payments as merely a public-relations trick without sincere intent. Exxon would just buy the state off, critics argued. One Alaska Audubon official said, "Oil means jobs. It's money. The industry is staging expensive television programs saying that we shouldn't do anything to hurt oil, and they're getting their message across."[90]

Doing It Differently: The Mutual-Gains Approach

Although Exxon initially accepted responsibility, it failed to convince the public that it understood the reasons for the accident and would, over time, take the steps necessary to avoid a repeat of the tragedy. They also failed to establish clear lines of communication, making few efforts to engage the victims of the spill in face-to-face dialogue. Compensation preceded rather than followed efforts to mitigate the adverse impacts of the oil spill. Moreover, the basis for allocating compensation payments was not clear, sending the message that compensation was primarily a means of silencing potential litigants. Exxon failed to create an effective forum for joint problem-solving, and because of this probably triggered a harsher overall reaction to the spill—and its efforts to respond—than might otherwise have been the case. It is important to examine each of Exxon's errors in dealing with an angry public in the aftermath of the spill.

The Company's Failure to Accept Responsibility

First, and foremost, a company that has caused harm, regardless of why it has caused that harm, must accept responsibility for the hurt attributed to its employees, products, or services. While bearing the brunt of people's anger is unpleasant, and even frightening, denying responsibility will only exacerbate, not soothe, the public's anger.

At first, Exxon seemed to accept responsibility. Within a day and a half of the spill, Exxon Shipping Company president Frank Iarossi assured the public that Exxon would accept full financial responsibility for the spill.

However, as the initial shock wore off, the company began pointing the finger at others. When it came to the light that a Coast Guard officer had smelled alcohol on the tanker captain's breath only hours after the accident, William Stevens, president of Exxon USA, claimed: "This incident should never have happened. In my view, it was a human failure that it did happen." When the oil spread while Exxon waited for approval from the state and the Coast Guard to spray dispersant, Exxon later said, "We were ready on Saturday," but " . . . we couldn't get authority to do anything until 6:45 P.M. Sunday. . . . I don't want to point fingers, but the facts are we're getting a bad rap on that delay."[91] "It was the state and the Coast Guard that really wouldn't give us the go-ahead to load those planes, fly those sorties, and get on with it."[92] Alaska's Lieutenant Governor Stephen MacAlpine fired back at Exxon's finger-pointing: "I would suggest it's Exxon's tanker that ran up on the rocks. Trying to shift the burden of the blame in this situation is something that just cannot and should not be done."[93]

Even when company officials admitted their mistake, their rhetoric showed an unwillingness to adhere to President Truman's old adage, "The buck stops here." Exxon chairman Rawl, virtually silent during the first days of the crisis, later remarked: "We feel very badly about the damage to the environment."[94] Ten days after the spill, the company ran an apology in newspapers nationwide, but as the *New York Times* reported, "To some readers the ad seemed platitudinous and failed to address the many pointed questions raised about Exxon's conduct."[95] In a May interview with *Fortune* magazine, Rawl acknowledged responsibility for the spill while hedging against taking blame for having caused it: "It's our problem the ship was on the rock. It's our problem the oil was spilled."[96] In the eyes of the public, "our problem" and "our fault" are not the same thing. A problem is something you solve. A fault is something you admit, then attempt to correct. The impact of the spill was, in a sense, everybody's problem. The cause of the spill was not, however, everybody's fault. Exxon needed to accept responsibility for its actions. All company spokespeople needed to be quite clear on this point. Exxon's ship ran aground; Exxon's oil was spewing into Prince William Sound; Exxon caused the spill; and Exxon was to blame, whether they admitted it or not.

The Company's Failure to Establish Clear Lines of Communication

In an accident such as the *Exxon Valdez* spill, the company (or companies) involved must meet the difficult challenge of communicating clearly and consistently with the public. Equally importantly, the public must have some means of communicating back to the company. Much like the ideal market, where supply and demand continually interact in a dynamic process that results in the most efficient production of goods, ideal communication requires both suppliers of information and consumers who need and respond. The ideal involves not merely information-giving, but dialogic communication, a dynamic process of gathering and disseminating information, listening for feedback, and responding accordingly. Good communication does not simply mean press releases, news flashes, and press conferences. Good communication should not be confused with technical wizards spouting explanations in confusing and opaque jargon, or reassuring but disingenuous spin doctors attempting to soothe the public. Corporations, governments, groups, and alliances do not communicate; only people do. Consequently, good communication requires direct, face-to-face dialogue between company officials and representatives of the public.

In cleaning up the spill, Exxon was not able to establish clear and legitimate lines of communication with local fishermen, business leaders, Native Americans, affected municipalities, or the state. Exxon had no legitimate public forum in which to conduct a conversation about who could best help in the cleanup efforts, how those efforts should be directed, how the services should be contracted, and how those helping should be paid for their services. Veco's services were rendered behind closed doors, offers were not made publicly, and ultimately, the cleanup excluded many of the local residents most severely affected by the spill.

But even clear communication would not have been sufficient. The mutual-gains approach requires those who have caused accidents to share power. Not only did Exxon not communicate as effectively as it might have, but it failed to share decision-making power with the injured parties. Exxon did set up claim centers and, to its credit, began considering claims even before personal-injury lawyers had flooded coastal Alaska. But what Exxon failed to realize was that taking active steps to provide compensation is not enough; these steps must be taken openly and jointly with affected stakeholders. Riders on compensation agreements, seemingly pell-mell or autocratic payments to different constituencies, and the difficulties of finding a counterbalance to the losses experienced by subsistence-living Native Americans, all created the appearance of a paternalistic, distant, unfair multinational corporation paying money only as it saw fit. Exxon had no means to test various compensation formulas, or to have an organized and inclusive discussion about how compensation should be handled to best meet the needs of those directly affected. Exxon desperately needed to establish a forum where open, honest, face-to-face dialogue could take place. Furthermore, Exxon needed to find a way to share decision-making power with the stakeholders affected by the spill.

How could Exxon have done this? Through the help of a neutral, Exxon could have been aided in identifying all the relevant stakeholder groups, locating respected and widely accepted leaders of those groups and assessing the major concerns and worries of the parties. That neutral might have been a professional private or not-for-profit provider of facilitation services, a respected association of dispute-resolution professionals such as the Society for Professionals in Dispute Resolution, or, if the accident had occurred off the coast of Oregon, for example, an established state office of dispute resolution.

Furthermore, had Exxon prepared a more thorough contingency plan to begin with, the company could have identified ahead of time indigenous groups and individuals who could represent the interests of their communities. These individuals might have been town mayors, heads of chambers of commerce, presidents of fishermen's associations, heads of fishermen's wives' associations, and tribal leaders of native peoples. Even immediately after the spill, clearly capable local leaders arose who could have worked alongside, instead of against, Exxon to solve the problems at hand. As de-Tocqueville remarked over 150 years ago, the strength of American democracy lies not so much in large, federal institutions such as Congress but in the local associations of trade, profession, philosophy, and religion that dominate local American life. Exxon could have tapped these powerful local institutions to serve as partners in addressing the problems it faced.

Such a public forum would certainly have been difficult to organize in a hurry. It would also have been quite contentious and difficult to manage. Feelings were running high along Prince William Sound. A professional, neutral facilitation team trained in high-visibility and emotionally charged situations could have helped all parties to harness their energy and explore mutual interests. Parties certainly would have pounded their fists on tables, shouted at times, and expressed their anger in other ways; but, through clear ground rules, active participation by high-level company officials, and a neutral facilitator to help everyone address their anger head on, a real and useful dialogue could have taken place.

The Company's Failure to First Mitigate, Then Compensate
(and Ultimately Leave People Better Off)

Such an open and public forum would have helped solve another problem that beset Exxon: how to mitigate the spill and fairly compensate those parties who were injured. Instead Exxon, sparing no expense, made payments to selected fishermen willing to help with the cleanup and to some of the groups who were harmed. Unfortunately, these payments looked mostly like payoffs aimed at buying goodwill and fending off future litigation.

To understand how Exxon could have done better in addressing the community's suffering in the months after the spill, the meaning of "mitigation" and "compensation" must be made clear. Mitigation involves actions that minimize or reduce the severity of the harm done. For example, by erecting oil booms, scooping up oil, and washing off beaches, Exxon and its contractors were attempting to minimize the damage done by the spill. Mitigation is an attempt to reduce hurt. Compensation, in contrast, is about making amends for damages caused that can no longer be reduced or minimized. *Webster's New World Dictionary* defines compensation as, "To make up for, counterbalance; to pay, to make amends." For example, compensation after the spill included Exxon's attempts to pay fishermen for days lost at sea and tour operators for lost business.

In most industrial accidents, mitigation and compensation are mandated by law. For example, the Federal Water Pollution Control Act (FWPCA) authorizes the president of the United States to remove the oil and prevent further releases. While cleanup moneys, under the Act, are to be drawn from a government fund, the responsible operators and owners must repay the government. State law at the time of the spill imposed strict liability on Exxon. Recoverable damages included injury or loss to persons, property, income, means of producing income, and economic benefit.[97] Under state law, Exxon was responsible for compensating all individuals injured. In many other situations, such as Three Mile Island, mitigation and compensation requirements are not prescribed by law, or the law is too vague to determine the levels that are appropriate.

After any accident, companies and agencies face a difficult decision. Companies may choose to do nothing that will not ultimately be required by law. This might be deemed the "wait and see" approach. Companies might, on the other hand, choose to mitigate the effects of an accident and/or offer compensation to those harmed, before litigation ensues and settlements are hashed out in pre-Court conferences or imposed by a judge or jury. Of course, estimates of what the law will require may vary widely from group to group. Finally, there is the option of offering to make people better off than they were before an accident. Why should they be satisfied with a level of compensation that only brings them back to where they were before their lives were disrupted? This option will be examined in much more detail in Chapter V.

Exxon had at least three options. They could have held tight to the purse strings and allowed the courts to make the final decision about what compensation would be appropriate. They could have offered money or other forms of assistance to help minimize the problems they had created, before things got worse. Along these lines, they could have tried to forestall any further harm *immediately* and waited to offer compensation until *after* the wronged parties had had a chance to sort out their losses and Exxon had had a chance to meet with the various stakeholders to see if an equitable, adequate, and fair overall standard for compensation could be worked out.

To their credit, Exxon did not exercise the first option. Companies may choose to hold off taking expensive actions, but this only increases distrust and anger. Consider these two seemingly disparate events that took place in late 1994: the release of the Pentium chip and the sale by L. L. Bean of mail-order Christmas trees. For two weeks, Intel, not exactly a seasoned veteran of direct mass marketing to consumers, found itself in the hot seat with a potentially flawed chip. The company did not, at first, agree to replace its chip. The company stated that only those customers who could prove to Intel that they might be affected by the defect would be given new chips. The result? Two weeks later Intel was forced to change its policy—forced by the actions of its biggest corporate customer, IBM. In the short time the company remained reluctant, 15 suits in three states were brought against the chip maker, including allegations ranging from securities fraud to product liability to false advertising. The chip maker not only paid for the recall, but paid for its initial reluctance with a sizable piece of its reputation. It took a $475 million hit to its fourth-quarter earnings too.[98] At almost the same time, L. L. Bean discovered that its mail-order Christmas trees were not arriving on time. With the Christmas season upon them, the Maine company quickly reimbursed any and all who had ordered trees, no questions asked. The company announced: "If your tree doesn't arrive on time, you're instantly reimbursed. But when the tree shows up a few days later, we ask that you donate it to the charity of your choice."[99] L. L. Bean, with its old-fashioned policy—"the customer is always right"—responded promptly to customer complaints, winning favorable press notices and perhaps some new customers in the process.

Exxon exercised the second choice. Almost immediately it began paying money to individuals who could help in the cleanup efforts, and later established claim centers to compensate victims. However, in enlisting local fishermen, Veco, the cleanup contractor, required that the boat owners agree to suspend all criticism of Exxon. Decisions about where compensation moneys ought to go were made unilaterally by the company. When municipalities pointed out specific needs, they were often ignored. A substantial amount of money went into an advertising campaign that offended a great many people locally. These funds were not used to mitigate or compensate for the direct effects of the spill. The pell-mell distribution of funds did a lot more to create "spillionaires" than to create good will among those adversely affected.

When the party that has caused harm tries to decide on its own what the appropriate response should be, the wronged parties are likely to balk. Only when compensation is seen as appropriate and fair in the eyes of those who feel harmed will the need for further bloodletting subside. This brings us to the third option, not exercised by Exxon: Seek to derive agreed-upon community standards that can guide the payment of moneys to wronged or injured parties. Compensation must represent value equivalent to the loss in the eyes of those who have been harmed. Furthermore, while money may serve as a measure of the compensation owed, the best and most significant offers are usually framed in terms of equivalent value. There must be a connection between the compensation offered and the hurt experienced by the parties, and often money will be insufficient and inappropriate to achieving that balance.

For example, L. L. Bean successfully compensated its customers, and not merely by stating, "We'll pay you $54 for each undelivered tree." Instead, L. L. Bean's actions conveyed several messages at once. First, the company acknowledged the concerns of its customers. Second, the company did not place blame; instead, it took responsibility. The delivery service would have been a likely scapegoat, but L. L. Bean did not point a finger in that or any other direction. Third, the company compensated its customers in kind by offering a full rebate immediately for goods not delivered on time; it did not offer a twenty-dollar gift certificate or a pair of free wool socks. Fourth, in a perhaps homespun but brilliant addition, the company suggested donating the trees to charity when they finally arrived. Thus, the company created additional goodwill by acting in the spirit of the holidays.

The Company's Failure to Convene an Effective Problem-Solving Forum

Had Exxon helped convene an appropriate public forum, it would have had a setting in which to seek advice on the difficult question of how to calculate fair compensation. Once such a forum is established—and has been given the power to influence decision making—it can be used for mutual problem-solving on any number of issues. Below are the questions we are typically asked when people hear our prescriptions regarding the creation of such problem-solving forums.

> *How can we establish a useful dialogue when people are legitimately angry because a terrible tragedy has occurred? They are going to be furious because a wrong has been done to them. How will it be possible to have a reasoned dialogue in such a context?*

The key to establishing a useful forum for dialogue, even in an emotionally charged environment, is the involvement of a professional neutral. Shortly after the *Exxon Valdez* accident, a firm composed of experts trained in negotiation, law, public policy, and business management contacted Exxon about designing just such a forum in Alaska. The firm had already made arrangements with a national foundation for the latter to accept funds from Exxon to support the neutral forum. (It was absolutely crucial that the neutrals not be paid directly by "the guilty party.") The neutrals suggested that they interview all the stakeholding groups to hear their concerns. It is important for those who have been hurt that an uninvolved but responsive party listen to their plight. The neutrals would then have assembled caucuses of the various stakeholders to select a manageable number (i.e., 40–50) of stakeholder representatives to join the forum. They would also have helped the group draft ground rules to govern their regular meetings as well as interactions with the press. Exxon chose not to go this route, but there are numerous examples of conflicts that have been mediated in this fashion.[100] This process works even when the parties are feeling quite hostile toward each other. The presence of a professional neutral and the development of shared ground rules make it possible to structure a helpful dialogue—even when the parties are very upset.

> *Who do we include in this forum? What if we leave out an important stakeholder? Isn't it true that some groups are so irresponsible that they ought not be included?*

While all stakeholder groups should be represented, it is not absolutely essential that they all be on board at the outset. It is possible, for example, to begin with the most obvious stakeholders and add others as the agenda of the group becomes clear (and the relevant parties realize that they want to participate). As long as the neutral facilitator is both sensitive to the need to involve all relevant stakeholders and available to brief newcomers about the ground rules—as well as the past accomplishments of the group—it is possible to add players over time. Thus there need be no fear of leaving out a group at the outset. Groups unwilling to live by the ground rules (which stress civility in interpersonal interactions) should not be able to participate. All others should be included. The facilitator may have to play the role of referee from time to time, but the ground rules usually create a sufficient foundation to ensure useful conversation.

> *How can we let others dictate the amount of money we should spend? We have fiduciary responsibilities that must be met.*

All stakeholders must have a conversation about *how* decisions will be made (i.e., they must adopt ground rules for group decision making). Stakeholders, and not just a company in Exxon's position, must have a significant role to play, lest the advantage of creating a problem-solving forum be lost. In a crisis situation, when the company, its consultants, and others are trying to make rapid decisions (e.g., what dispersant at what concentration in what areas will best minimize the spread of the oil slick?), it will seem almost irrelevant to have a discussion about group decision making, but that is when it needs to be done. Concerns about power, trust, communication style, and personalities can become hopelessly tangled in substantive matters, but the creation of a useful forum for collaborative problem solving requires that all the stakeholders agree on the design and operation of the forum.

In the Exxon case, to help determine compensation for lost fishing days, the stakeholders might have decided that a fisherman's panel should be established. Representatives from fishermen's organizations, the National Marine Fisheries Service, and Exxon might have been designated by the forum to sit on the panel. The panel could have brought in consultants to describe different ways of determining how losses should be quantified, and what mechanisms might best be used to expedite the claims of the fishermen. The panel could have reviewed options and presented alternatives to the full forum for consideration.

It may be that the ground rules of the group would give them only advisory powers on certain issues. Thus Exxon, or others called upon to spend money, would not have delegated away their right to make such decisions. On other matters, the group might have decided to operate by consensus. Thus, Exxon would have had the equivalent of a veto over any recommendation of the forum.

> *What do we do when someone initiates litigation even after we have created an ad hoc forum? We'll have to pull out of the forum to keep information confidential, won't we?*

One key goal of creating a joint problem-solving forum is to avoid litigation. Of course, that may not be possible. There is no need to dismantle the forum if litigation is initiated. In some instances, the forum may be the context in which a settlement is generated that resolves a lawsuit. In other instances, courts have taken a keen interest in the consensus-building initiated by companies or agencies responsible for accidents. The commitment to such a forum can alter the Court's posture toward such defendants.

Even if litigation is filed against a participant in a forum, they do not necessarily have to pull out of the discussions. They may want to have counsel present to be certain that they do not hurt their case in court, but counsel may also find the dialogue helpful in preparing for court should a case actually go forward.

Conclusion

Exxon had an opportunity to enlist the support of local interests in designing a compensation fund. They could have engaged the energies of the local fishing community in the cleanup effort by treating them as equal partners rather than as subservient contractors. Exxon could have helped sway the opinions of the anxious American public through sincere, organized, and inclusive efforts at paying out compensation, if they had had a credible formula that explained what they were doing. But Exxon missed the opportunity.

Money did pour into the communities of the Sound after the spill. But the confusing, bureaucratic, and, at times, autocratic distribution of funds, the uncertainties of who would be compensated and when, the contingencies attached to payments, and the general perception of the payments as a public-relations gimmick, a payoff, or an attempt to fracture communities and regional solidarity severely limited the value of the payments. Though Exxon was constrained by an uncertain legal framework, a heightened level of post-disaster confusion, and a damned-if-you-do/damned-if-you-don't reaction, the company exacerbated its problems by the approach it chose. All of Exxon's money could not put the communities of the Sound back together again. If anything is to be learned from the aftermath of the *Exxon Valdez* spill, hopefully this one lesson is clear: it's not how much you spend, it's how you spend it.

CHAPTER V

Risky Business

The public can get just as angry about what it thinks *might* happen as it can about an accident that has already happened. Proposed policies, projects, or activities can generate harsh and defensive reactions even though nothing has yet transpired. To deal effectively with this second type of anger, corporations and public agencies need to respond to *perceived* levels of risk and to do everything they can to minimize or manage risk. Unfortunately, promises about the management of risk will be no more credible than efforts to mitigate or compensate the impacts of accidents if they are developed unilaterally by policy or project proponents. Too often, agencies and especially corporations promise that they will reduce risks to zero when in fact that is not possible. Furthermore, it is rarely, if ever, preferable to deny the risks that are likely; so it is not appropriate to suppress information to win support for a proposed product, project or policy. Corporations and agencies should seek to share forecasts; and they ought to engage all relevant stakeholders in making risky decisions through the creation of consensus-building forums. Whatever the assessment of potential risks, there is almost always something that can be done to reduce or manage them. When risks are uncertain, it is still possible to offer contingent promises of risk reduction. To begin, it is necessary to distinguish risk perception and risk assessment from strategies for risk reduction.

What Is Risk?

As we define it, risk includes the likelihood of a hazard occurring multiplied by the impact that such an event might have if it does occur. Thus, risk is about the chance of encountering a negative consequence or incurring a cost—whether it is measured in terms of dollars, health impacts, or lives lost. Societal (as opposed to individual) risk can be summed up in a single equation:

Risk = Probability of a hazard occurring x Impact of the hazard

The case of silicone breast implants—and the hazards associated with implant rupture—will help to explain what we mean and make clear the connection between risk and the problems of dealing with various kinds of angry publics. Applying the general formula to breast implants we find

- *Hazard:* Among the hazards imposed by surgical implantation of a mammographic implant device, as they are called, is the possible rupture of the elastomer, the outside silicone envelope that contains the silicone gel, causing an infusion of silicone into the body.
- *Probability:* The probability of this hazard actually occurring ranges from .2 percent to 35 percent, depending on who you believe. In 1977 four plastic surgeons estimated rupture rates from 11 percent to 32 percent.[1] In clinical trials involving some 1,000 individuals, the reported rupture rate was 1.1 percent.[2] From the number of ruptures reported back to Dow Corning, a major manufacturer of the implants, divided by the total number of implants sold, the company estimated in 1992 that the rupture rate was between .2 percent and .5 percent.[3]
- *Impact:* Supposing that the implant did rupture, several consequences might result. For one, the patient would, at the least, face the immediate risk of further surgery; general medical practice suggests that free silicone should be removed from the body. The rupture could also result in disfigurement of the breast. The introduction of silicone into the body could also lead to ulceration, burning sensations and pain, enlarged lymph nodes, and even respiratory distress. The introduction of silicone into the human body, some suspect or even assert, could lead to rare autoimmune diseases and possibly even cancer—though this theory is surrounded by far more controversy.

To sum up the risk, then, a breast implant may rupture (the hazard) in anywhere from .2 percent to 32 percent of the relevant cases (the probability) resulting in numerous possible consequences including the uncertain possibility of an autoimmune disorder (the impact of the hazard).

Assessing Risk

While the equation is not terribly complicated, the calculation of the probability and the impact are not as simple as our equation suggests. The determination of risk, in the case of silicone breast implants, requires numerous inputs from engineers, physicians, epidemiologists, biologists, chemists, statisticians, and computer programmers. Numerous bench tests of the product outside the human body, as well as animal, clinical, and epidemiological studies would have to be conducted to calculate the risk accurately. Ultimately, to achieve a meaningful risk assessment, millions of dollars and years of study would be required. Given the complex interaction of players and techniques, it should come as no surprise that the determination of risk can generate enormous public controversy. As *Business Week* reported when the debate over the mandatory use of risk assessment heated up in Congress in the early spring of 1995: "In its rush to base all regulations on risk assessment, Congress is forgetting the method's dirty little secret: It doesn't give very good answers."[4] We highlight below five reasons why this is true.

• *Differing Assumptions*: Risk assessments require experts to make a number of nonobjective judgments. One public-policy analyst estimated that some fifty opportunities for discretionary judgments exist in typical risk-assessment procedures.[5] These choices can lead to very different results. Often, there is no scientific consensus on the best way to proceed. Because of different data sets or missing data, different models of analysis, and different assumptions used to produce the final forecasts, two respectable scientists might examine the same situation and arrive at two very different estimated levels of risk. For example, in the study of the risks of PCE, a solvent used in dry cleaning, choices about the type of test animal to use (mice or rats), the methodology for extrapolating to humans (by body surface or by weight), and the selection of one dose-response model over another (linear or quadratic) could change the resulting risk assessment by a factor of as much as 35,000.[6]

• *Errors of Omission*: Errors in risk assessment are often the result of innocent omissions. If the risk assessor fails to consider certain consequences of the hazard in question, the assessor will fail to accurately assess the risk. For instance, for many years the safety of chemicals was determined only on the basis of their acute (immediate) toxic effects. More chronic hazards such as cancer, birth defects, or sterility were not considered. In fact, less than 10 percent of the chemicals used in commerce have been tested for chronic effects such as cancer or mutagenicity.[7] In another example, when the International Institute of Applied Systems Analysis reviewed a series of studies on the risks associated with the use of liquefied natural gas (LNG) facilities, they found that none of the studies had figured in deliberate sabotage, despite the real threat of terrorism in many parts of the world.[8]

• *Unknown Latent Effects*: The difficulties of risk assessment are also compounded by the latent effects of exposure to toxic substances. It might take years, if not decades, for the consequences of exposure to a certain hazard to arise. Whereas the visible impacts of an oil spill are immediately obvious, the long-term effects on the lives of salmon, seals, otters, and whales are not. We now know that asbestos is highly carcinogenic. Among those highly exposed to it, 20 percent to 25 percent will die of lung cancer. But its deadly impact came to light long after its introduction in the workplace, because the cancers it induces arose only after 15 to 40 years.[9]

• *Animal Studies versus Human Effects*: The animal toxicology tests used to determine the potential risks to humans are also controversial. Because most controlled human studies (to test the effects of chemicals or devices on humans) would be unethical, scientists often rely on animal studies to assess risk. Researchers are required to use high doses of the substances in question to induce effects that are detectable. Then these results must be extrapolated to humans. There are a host of problems associated with this method. First, there is no assurance that the high doses of the substance would bring about the same effects in humans at much lower doses. Second, there is not necessarily a direct correlation between effects on humans and effects on other species. Even similar organisms can react and adapt to exposures in very different ways. For instance, dioxin is 5,000 times more toxic to guinea pigs than to hamsters.[10] Third, as mentioned previously, extrapolating the effects to humans can be error-laden, depending on the characteristics used (e.g., body weight versus surface area) to compare the two.

• *Subjective Bias*: The "objective" assessment of risk can also be compromised by the biases of researchers who undertake assessments. While well-established methodological guidelines and ethical practices can help minimize subjective bias, given the numerous assumptions and choices required of risk assessors, even the best of scientists will be influenced by their personal and political beliefs as well as their institutional affiliations and loyalties. In a 1986 study of 136 occupational physicians and industrial hygienists, researchers explored the participants' opinions about standards for regulating carcinogens proposed by the federal Occupational Safety and Health Administration (OSHA).[11] The study found that scientists employed by industry were more likely than government scientists to favor assumptions about risks that decreased the likelihood that the hazards in question would adversely affect human health. This bias can play both ways. In a dispute over a proposed municipal waste-incineration plant in Brooklyn, New York, one report commissioned by environmental groups estimated that 1,430 cancer deaths per million would result from exposure to the potential dioxin emissions from the incinerator. The authorizing government agency, however, estimated that only 6 deaths per million would occur.[12] It is not so much that the environmental group's estimate was "wrong," but that it utilized a worst-case scenario supporting its sponsors' point of view.

Perceiving Risk

If professional risk assessment were not problematic enough, the "unscientific" assessment of risk by the public may diverge significantly from the assessments made by experts. In a now-famous study, four different groups of individuals were asked to rank the risks associated with thirty activities including smoking, drinking, hunting, using a power mower, and living next to a nuclear power plant. While college students and members of the League of Women Voters believed that the nuclear power plant was the most risky to human health, the expert group rated it only twentieth. However, when it came to swimming, college students rated it dead last, while experts rated it tenth on their list.[13]

In another report issued by the EPA in 1987, entitled *Unfinished Business: A Comparative Assessment of Environmental Problems*, an EPA work group ranked worker exposure to industrial chemicals, indoor radon, and pesticide residue on foods as the three environmental hazards with the greatest cancer risk. A summary of public-opinion data collected in the previous two years by the Roper Organization revealed that the public was, in contrast, more worried about chemical-waste disposal, water pollution, and chemical-plant accidents. (Radon did not appear in the Roper polls, either because of an oversight by the poll's sponsors or because no one was even concerned enough to bother measuring the public's concern about it.) While the EPA ranked non-radon indoor air pollution as tied for fourth in cancer risk, and classified it as high risk for noncancer health risks, the public considered it a low risk: 10th out of 15 categories.[14] If these studies are any indication, the experts and the public do not seem to agree.

What might account for the wide discrepancy between publicly perceived and expert-assessed risk? Certainly the general public is not well informed about many issues. If a high-school student in California is surprised to learn that her school was named after President Grover Cleveland, and not after "that city in Canada," it is no wonder that the public has a tough time accurately assessing risk. Many expert risk assessors believe that if only the public were better educated, or if only more technical and accurate data about risk were reported by the media, the discrepancy would go away. However, we think that this discrepancy has deeper roots than simple ignorance or miscommunication.

• *Research versus Real Life*: The esoteric world of risk assessment and the day-to-day life of most citizens are quite separate. Hearings about government regulations are often crowded with citizens who decry the scientists' distance from the "real world." New England fishermen, overwhelmed by diminishing stocks and severe fishing restrictions, often complain to National Marine Fisheries Scientists, "You go out once a year and do an annual survey. Then you come back and plug that data into your fancy model telling me there are no fish. I'm out on the water everyday, all year long. Don't tell me what is and isn't out there." The fact is, scientists and the rest of the public often live in quite different worlds, with vastly different educations and with exposure to very different sources of information. Just to cite one example, when a Pesticide Advisory Committee in Britain attempted to assert that there was no evidence of harm caused by the pesticide 2,4,5-T, farm workers and foresters assailed the results.[15] The Committee reviewed the problem again and arrived at the same conclusion with the qualification that it was safe "so long as it was produced and used under the proper conditions." The problem was, workers using the pesticide concluded that the "proper conditions" did not exist. What were "proper conditions" to the scientists were "improbable conditions" to the farmers.

• *Weighing Consequences Differently*: Individuals value the consequences of a hazard very differently, even when they agree on the probability of it occurring. Proponents of nuclear power consistently point to the extremely low risk of a nuclear meltdown. But for many, minuscule probabilities pale in comparison to people's visions of nuclear disaster stimulated by Nagasaki and Hiroshima. Individuals may prefer one form of injury over another, even if the probability of the greater injury is far less. Underlying such judgments is the notion of personal choice and control. People would rather have the choice about whether or not to take a risk. Individuals, particularly in a democratic, rights-based society such as ours, value personal autonomy in decision making. Thus, because of widely held values about personal control, the same individual who is happy to ride a motorcycle without a helmet may vehemently oppose nuclear power. This helps explain why students rank swimming low on their list while experts rank it far higher. Swimming is a risky activity we choose; nuclear power carries a risk imposed on us by someone else.

• *Exposure versus Harm*: Researchers have found that risk assessors are trained to worry about the number of potential casualties a hazard might cause. The public, on the other hand, is often more worried about the number of people exposed to a hazard than the scope of the injuries that would occur.[16] While the leak at Three Mile Island caused only minimal radiation exposure, the fact that millions were potentially at risk increased the public's sense of the danger. Had the accident only exposed a few Met Ed workers, even fatally, the public would probably have perceived the risk as minimal.

• *Allocation of Benefits and Costs*: The benefits and costs of hazards as borne by individuals, not populations, may vary considerably. Thus, the risk of living next to a nuclear power plant may be far less than that of taking a 100-mile journey in a car, but the people living near Three Mile Island would find that small consolation. While an entire region would undoubtedly benefit from a waste-to-energy plant—from both inexpensive electricity and efficient garbage disposal—a small number of families living near the plant would bear most of the risk associated with plant emissions. While the distributed benefits might well outweigh the localized costs, each individual would view the calculation quite differently. It also works the other way. Individuals may partake in risky behavior precisely because they do not bear the full cost of their actions. If an individual's health insurance rates do not reflect that person's propensity to partake of risky activities like rock climbing, bungee jumping, or parachuting, others in their workplace or insurance pool will have to bear the costs of their risk-taking. Perceptions about risk often vary simply because the costs and benefits of risks are allocated differently across clusters of individuals.

Two policy scientists from Canada, William Leiss and Christina Cho-ciolko, have discovered that many individuals have an interest in underesti-mating risks so as to maximize net benefits [or minimize net losses] for themselves.[17] If they are right, individuals and institutions have an incentive to maximize the benefits of undertaking risky behavior, while at the same time off-loading the risk onto as many other people as possible.[18] Proponents of power plants, new waste storage sites, or new products extol their benefits but downplay or ignore the risks that may be imposed on a small segment of society. At the same time, individuals who engage in risky behavior, from driving drunk to smoking, either ignore the obvious consequences of their actions or naively assume, like children, that "it won't happen to them." Those who undertake "objective" risk assessment should acknowledge that they are likely to view our complex, risk-laden, and uncertain world in a way that benefits them.

• *Lack of Trust*: There is one more reason why the public is often skeptical of expert risk assessments. Both government and business have, in the past, imposed undisclosed risks upon unsuspecting citizens. In the 1950s the U.S. government allowed citizens to be exposed to high levels of radioactive fall-out without their knowledge or consent. In the 1970s the Ford Motor Company sold millions of Pinto automobiles while concealing the risks of the gasoline tank exploding from rear-end collisions. A. H. Robins marketed the Dalkon Shield intrauterine contraceptive device while aware of at least some of its damaging effects on women's health. The mishandling of risk by major institutions has shaken the public's faith.

Communicating Risk

If assessing risk and perceiving risk were not problematic enough, the link between the two—risk communication—is also fraught with difficulty. As both the Three Mile Island and breast implant cases indicate, company of-ficials are often in too much of a rush to reassure the public that a risk is neg-ligible, whereas the already anxious public is far more interested in knowing what the company is doing to alleviate the threat. Officials offer detailed nu-merical estimates of risk, while the public—more comfortable with personal accounts than statistical tables—seeks personal accountability from the risk makers. The fact is that risk communication is rarely performed well. When the National Research Council's committee on risk communication tried to develop a handbook detailing successful examples of risk communication, the committee discovered, to its frustration and surprise, only one good example.[19] If economics is a dismal science, risk communication is apparently a failed one. The National Research Council has identified several areas where risk communicators usually stumble.

• *Lack of Credibility*: Lack of credibility interferes with successful risk communication. If the public feels that communicators are advocating rather than communicating, they will discount the information provided. If the public believes that a communicator has engaged in deceit or misrepresentation, they will question the "facts." If messages contradict one another, either because the communicator has changed positions, or because various sources contradict each other, public distrust will grow. The Three Mile Island case highlights these pitfalls. Once Met Ed's credibility was lost, no one believed them even when they told the truth.

• *Confusing Language*: Arcane scientific language interferes with effective risk communication. Since risk is based on probabilistic estimates, the public can be confused by something as simple as the statement that there is a 70 percent chance of rain. To some, this means it will rain 70 percent of the time, or, over 70 percent of the reported area. How numerical risks are communicated is crucial. At Chernobyl, the same cancer risk could have been conveyed in the following ways: 131 cancers expected in the lifetimes of the 24,000 people within 15 kilometers of the plant; a 2.6 percent increase in cancer over that exposed population; or, an increase in cancer of only .0047 percent over the population of the 75 million people exposed in Ukraine and Byelorussia.[20] Though all these values express the same risk, they convey very different degrees of seriousness.

• *Access*: Risk communication can fail if the public has difficulty obtaining access to information. Decision making, particularly in the private sector, can be done without the public knowing what is going on. In turn, the public often assume the worst. Authorities, out of indifference, incompetence, or naiveté, may ignore or respond ineffectively to the public's request for information. As was the case at Three Mile Island, access to accurate information, because of simple logistics, may be limited. Lastly, the information requested is sometimes not available. Either scientists have not generated the right studies, monitoring is incomplete, or a sudden crisis has made it impossible to open the necessary channels of communication.

Risky Business

In 1989, the EPA announced that over a 70-year period five of 100,000 persons exposed to Alar, the trade name for a chemical formerly used to treat apples, would get cancer. Even higher risks were projected for children who ate and drank apple products. Yet, the EPA announced, the chemical would not be banned because studies did not show an imminent hazard. Uniroyal, the product's manufacturer, quickly refuted the EPA's warning, stating that Alar posed no significant risk to public health. Soon after EPA's ambiguous announcement, the Natural Resources Defense Council (NRDC) reported in an ominous-sounding publication, entitled *Intolerable Risk*, that five of every 20,000 children might eventually get cancer prior to their sixth birthday because of exposure to Alar. Ed Bradley introduced the results of this report on a segment of *60 Minutes* with a skull and crossbones overlaying an apple. Meryl Streep, the actress and a mother of four, signed on as a spokesperson for the NRDC. Soon everyone from consumer groups to apple growers were testing for the presence of Alar in apple products. "Am I killing my children by feeding them applesauce?" became the preeminent question in parents' minds. Within months, despite protests from apple growers, Uniroyal withdrew Alar from the market.

While the specifics of this scenario are peculiar to Alar, the resulting battle between various interest groups was not. A government agency released an ambiguous statement about the risk of a product. The product's manufacturer and other businesses who stood to profit from the product quickly stepped in to extol the product's benefits. Environmental and consumer groups jumped in, highlighting the worst possible impacts of the hazard while brushing aside the benefits of the product. The media announced it all: statistics, compelling personal stories of injury, the potential economic losses if the product was discontinued—statements by vociferous defenders and attackers alike. The public is typically left in an anxious state. The average citizen feels like the patron of a restaurant that suddenly smells of smoke. At the kitchen end, some poor dishwasher yells, "Fire! Run for your lives!" while the manager, in a shirt and tie, calmly stands in the middle of the dining room telling everyone not to panic. Who should we believe?

There have been suggestions that risk assessors should be isolated, free from politics and influence, disturbed only by the hum of their computers. If trained technicians are left alone with their complex mathematical models, there is a hope (albeit false) that they will find the "truth." Others suggest that whatever the technicians discover, it should be our legislative bodies that determine levels of acceptable risk and the appropriate risk–benefit trade-offs.

We suggest that there is a way for government agencies and private interests to approach risk that depends neither on independent experts alone nor on final legislative decision making. While both elected government and technically trained experts are important players, neither is sufficient. Decision making about acceptable levels and the distribution of risks should involve all the stakeholders who will bear both the benefits and costs of the risky decisions that must be made. Effective management of risk must actively involve the public. We will highlight our recommendations for doing this using the controversy surrounding silicone breast implants.

The Breast Implant Controversy

The Story Unfolds

In 1962, two Houston plastic surgeons, unhappy with the products available for breast implants, approached Dow Corning of Midland, Michigan, a subsidiary of Dow Chemical, about developing an alternative device. The silicone breast implant was born, an envelope of flexible silicone elastomer filled with silicone gel. Since then, an estimated 1 to 2 million women in the United States have had one or two of the devices surgically implanted in their breasts.[21] The annual market for surgery was estimated in the early 1990s at between 300 and 450 million dollars.[22] Though no exact figures were available, the manufacturers estimated that 80 percent of the women who had the device implanted did so for "cosmetic reasons," while 20 percent received the implants after undergoing surgery for breast cancer. Over the years, the device was improved to increase the strength of the envelope, to reduce a peculiar property of the implants known as "bleed," and to minimize a painful condition known as capsular contraction: the unintended contracture of the implant caused by the naturally occurring fibrous capsule that the human body forms around any implanted material.

In 1976, when the U.S. Food and Drug Administration (FDA) was given regulatory authority over medical devices, the device was grandfathered in without the requisite studies required of newer products. In 1978 and 1982, the FDA reviewed the devices and sanctioned their continued use. But in 1984, the court cases began. A San Francisco federal jury awarded a Nevada woman $1.5 million in punitive damages, holding that the company had committed fraud in marketing the device as safe. But after Dow appealed the case, and settled for an undisclosed sum, the file was put under protective order at the request of the company. Thus there was very little media coverage. Dow Corning did alter its product literature and included warnings of immune-system sensitivity and potential migration of silicone following rupture.

In 1988 things began to heat up for Dow Corning and the other manufacturers of implants. The FDA mandated premarket approval (PMA) applications from all manufacturers. Dow Corning, in response, eventually submitted over 115 volumes totaling some 33,000 pages to the FDA. A group known as Public Citizen Health Research Group, associated with consumer advocate Ralph Nader, petitioned the FDA to take the implants off the market. They believed the devices increased women's risk of cancer. Prior to 1990, the major complaints against the devices included capsular contracture, interference with standard mammographic X-ray techniques used to detect breast cancer, and actual cancer-causing potential.

The growing controversy hit the major media in late 1990 and early 1991. In March of 1991, a New York jury awarded $4.5 million to a woman who asserted that an implant with a polyurethane-foam shell (not Dow Corning's implant) had caused her breast cancer. *Business Week* ran an article suggesting that Dow Corning knew of the potential risks of their devices even in the 1970s. Cancer was no longer the only worry. Instead, women grew fearful of such diseases as lupus, chronic arthritis, scleroderma, and Sjogren's Syndrome. Distraught women appeared on television and in numerous news magazines, blaming the implants for painful and rare "autoimmune" and connective-tissue diseases.

To address the rising tide of concern, the FDA convened an advisory panel on medical devices. This panel first met in November 1991. After three days of presentations and discussions, the panel, composed of plastic surgeons and other medical experts, as well as one representative each of manufacturers and consumers, concluded that the data submitted in the company PMA applications were not sufficient to support a finding of safety and effectiveness. In January, FDA responded by calling for a temporary moratorium on selling the devices because the agency could not assure their safety. Corning's stock immediately fell $2, from its previous value of $77.

By the end of January, Corning's stock was valued at only $61. The American Society of Plastic and Reconstructive Surgery said it promised to abide by the FDA's decision, but the Society's president warned: "[it] sends a very negative message to patients that there is something wrong with these implants."[23] A member of the American Medical Society was less circumspect. Dr. Mitchell Karlan told the *New York Times*: "There will be absolute hysteria among women."[24]

Individuals from all sides of the debate headed to Washington to express their views. The American Society of Plastic and Reconstructive Surgeons levied a $1,050 fee per member to be paid over three years to sponsor activities such as educational teleconferences for concerned implant recipients. Plaintiffs' lawyers fed the press horror stories and gathered evidence against Dow Corning. Women, from recovering breast cancer victims to patients with agonizing connective-tissue disorders, told their painful and personal stories of both suffering and disfigurement. Most implant recipients were left in a muddle. As one representative of an organization known as Y-Me said, "It is easy for administrators and scientists to take their time reviewing the data. It is a different story for us on the emotional firing line, and it must stop now."[25]

In February of 1992 the panel reconvened to make further recommendations to the FDA. At the end of its three-day meeting, the panel recommended that the FDA should not ban implants altogether but should severely restrict their use. It also recommended that the FDA should require that all implant patients participate in clinical trials and should limit access to implants for those seeking breast augmentation. Mastectomy patients, the panel argued, should still have access to the implants. According to the *New York Times*, the Panel concluded that "there was insufficient evidence that the implants were safe and effective."[26] According to the *Wall Street Journal*, the panel had determined that there was "no evidence of harm, but more research would help."[27]

What had happened? Breast implants were restricted but not banned? Implants weren't safe, but they caused no harm? Even before FDA issued its final ruling in April, Dow Corning announced in mid-March that "it would stop making and selling silicone gel breast implants."[28] In April, the company announced that its first-quarter profits had dropped by 16 percent (mostly because of legal fees). In July, second-quarter reported earnings dropped 84 percent, in part because of a pretax charge for dropping the implant business.

The Story Is Retold

We skip ahead two years. In the midst of negotiations over a $4.25 billion settlement among nearly 60 companies to compensate women worldwide who said implants had caused them harm, a new study appeared in the June 1994 *New England Journal of Medicine*. Researchers at the respected Mayo Clinic in Rochester, Minnesota found, after following 749 women for an average period of 7.8 years ". . . no association between breast implants and the connective-tissue diseases and other disorders that were studied."[29] In an accompanying editorial, the journal argued that "scientific conclusions cannot be based on argument and opinion" as they had been in the breast-implant case, but "like other scientific questions, must await the marshaling of a sufficient amount of carefully gathered and critically analyzed data."[30]

On June 17th, following the publication of the Mayo Clinic study, the *Wall Street Journal* entitled an editorial "The $4.3 Billion Mistake," and railed, "Too bad, though, that in our era the scientific method can't compete anymore with lawyers marauding after some $1 billion in contingency fees, politically correct mind-sets in the media, or Dr. Kessler's Food and Drug Administration."[31] The *Journal* turned the case into proof that contingency fees for lawyers should be eliminated, that Vice President Quayle's "significant reform" of the FDA had been stymied, and that the "loser pays" rule ought to be adopted by the courts.

The *New York Times* drew a quite different conclusion, pointing out that while the Mayo Clinic study was "encouraging news," it was too small to detect double and triple increases in connective-tissue diseases. The editorial concluded, "The FDA banned the implants not on the grounds that they were unsafe but that the manufacturers, despite decades of selling the devices, had failed to conduct the studies needed to show their safety and effectiveness. The fact that scientists are still scurrying today to measure those effects is proof that the agency's judgment was right."[32] For the *Times*, the FDA had been right after all. Thus, three respectable national publications all reached different conclusions.

What Should the Company Do?

A device as seemingly simple as an implant had become a focal point for American political and cultural debate. In part, it became a story about the vanity of American women, who would do anything to look and feel better. It was also a story about ravaged cancer patients who had been helped to feel whole again; corporate America once again concealing information from the public; voracious lawyers out to build a reputation; and, finally, either a reluctant or an overly ambitious regulatory agency out to hamstring American business.

Despite the almost mythical quality of this story, there are several things the company could have done to gain more control over its own destiny.

Implant Rupture

Putting aside the debate about the potential ill effects of ruptured or leaking breast implants, one seemingly simple point worrying physicians was how frequently the implants could be expected to rupture in the first place. It appeared that the company had never estimated the life of these devices. The rupture rate, given an implant's age and manufacturer, was undetermined. As the *Times* reported, "It is not known how often implants rupture. Most panel members who spoke said they did not accept assertions by manufacturers and plastic surgeons that the frequency was less than one in 100."[33]

As the story unfolded at both the November and February panel discussions, a great deal of contradictory information came to light. As early as 1971, doctors implanting the devices had reported ruptures of the implants. In 1973 Dow Corning asked its sales force to return ruptured implants so that the company could determine the rate of envelope rupture. Even though a new model was available by 1975, rupture continued to be a problem. Indeed, in 1976, during the taping of augmentation surgery for a trade show, two of the implants broke on camera. Internal memos reported that one company investigator, estimating a rupture rate at 5 percent, repeatedly expressed concern. A 1983 "company document" indicated that since ruptures did occur, the safety of the gel could not be based on containment in the envelope. Although the company pointed out the improved durability of their newer models, even in 1987 one physician reported, "The original silastic [silicone] implant that was removed from a patient that you observed, had gel which literally ran to the floor. We all observed it. It was far from cohesive, having the consistency of 50 weight motor oil."[34]

On the other hand, the panel was presented with mechanical and clinical studies supporting the strength and durability of the devices. The company submitted numerous studies indicating that their devices met or exceeded the standards published by the American Society of Testing and Materials (ASTM). The company also made note in the November panel that out of 1,000 patients covered in their clinical evaluations, only 11 patients, or 1.1 percent, were listed as having implants that "lost shell integrity."[35] Given the number of ruptures reported back to Dow Corning, divided by the total number of implants sold, the company estimated in 1992 that the rupture rate was only between .2 and .5 percent.[36]

Two studies attempted to clear up the muddle by identifying the incidence of rupture through mammography. One study done by researchers from the Washington University School of Medicine in St. Louis found that 17 percent of 350 women with implants had some form of herniation of the implant, while 4.6 percent showed evidence of implant rupture.[37] The researchers noted that, at times, the distinction between a herniation and rupture was difficult to make, and therefore, they might have underestimated the actual rupture rate.[38] Furthermore, since the study was not longitudinal, they had no way of knowing how many herniations might later become ruptures.[39] Another study done at the University of Pittsburgh Medical School found that 3 percent of 424 implants examined via ultrasound had leaks. This implied a rupture rate of 6.6 percent out of 212 women.[40] The researchers also noted that through cross-comparison with later surgery and other diagnostic techniques they had discovered that physical exams had only detected half the ruptures, mammograms had missed four, but sonograms had missed only one leak. Consequently, the study suggested that the rates of rupture reported in mammographic or physical-examination studies might have been underestimated. The researchers also noted that they were able to determine the age of the implants in only 80 percent of the cases and that they did not identify the implants' manufacturer. Thus, it was impossible to correlate the age and the manufacturer of implants with rupture rates.[41]

Drawing Conclusions in the Face of Uncertainty

Given this array of anecdotal, clinical, and statistical findings, what might a respected scientist conclude? John Lynch, M.D., a consultant to the panel and chairman of plastic surgery at Vanderbilt University Medical Center, stated, "I think the best we can say at the moment is that based on these two large series here, of older implants of unknown types and probably quite a diverse, mixed bag, that the failure rate over a long period of time has been low, and that's about all we can say."[42] So much for scientific certainty.

What did the FDA conclude? On January 7, 1992, the head of the FDA, Dr. David Kessler, said at a news conference, "We still do not know how often the implants leak; and when they do, we do not know exactly what materials get into the body. We still do not know how often the implants break, or how long they last."[43] As the November panel had impressed upon Dow Corning, for a product that had been on the market for thirty years and that was implanted in millions of customers, it was worrisome that the company had no real estimate of the lifetime of the product. One panel member asked a Dow Corning official, "Is it true that there are no data [regarding] the flex life or fatigue life of an implant under any physiological condition or after exposure to body fluids or adsorption or absorption of biological compounds? Is that true?"[44] The company responded, "That is correct."

Given all the uncertainty, what did Dow Corning do? Through their Product Replacement Expense Program, the company guaranteed to pay for removal or replacement of their product "due to loss of product shell integrity within five years of implantation."[45] The panel was quick to ask, since the company reported particularly low rupture rates for almost thirty years, why was the [five-year] warranty so short? One Dow Corning official responded, "The five years was to acknowledge for the patient that indeed, not because it's at six years it is going to disintegrate or that there's some problem at a given time, the five years was a reasonable time to be able to provide the patient with some support in the event of a loss of shell integrity."[46]

Knowing Your Product and Presenting It Truthfully: The Mutual-Gains Approach

Dow Corning's warranty established two important anchor points in the ongoing disagreement over the implant's risk. First, the warranty established an implicit standard of performance: implants will likely not rupture for at least five years. Second, the warranty unintentionally placed the company at odds with itself in that it guaranteed that the life of the product was only five years, but the company's own data suggested that its implants, even after ten or more years, ruptured less than 1 percent of the time. This five-year guarantee, in the context of the hearings, suggested several unsavory conclusions. Did the company doubt its own forecasts? If rupture rates were so low, why would the company limit the warranty so dramatically? Couldn't the company afford to correct whatever defects were involved? Either the company was not telling the public about the real risk of rupture, or they were incredibly tight-fisted.

Set Clear Performance Standards

The first lesson we draw from the implant controversy is that a company or an agency must establish and state clear and believable standards of performance if the public is worried about risk. For example, a power company might say to residents living under a transmission line who are worried about the potential adverse impacts of electric and magnetic fields, "Beyond one hundred meters from our high-power transmission lines, you can take an appropriate instrument, and you will find an electric field of less than 1 kV per meter."

Such standard setting is not easy. With regard to just the one issue about implants—rupture rate—numerous experts had a difficult time ascertaining the performance level the manufacturers were achieving. To complicate matters, there was little evidence to indicate how different manufacturers or different models compared. Part of the problem was, while the company had implicitly set a rupture-rate standard for its implants by citing low return rates, nobody believed them. Mammographic studies suggested a failure rate of 1 to 5 percent, not tenths of 1 percent. A plastic surgeon representing one of the implant manufacturers told the panel that he inflated the manufacturer's reported rate when speaking with his patients.[47]

Dow Corning's response to the panel's questions suggested that the five-year warranty was arbitrary. "We're not saying at six years the implant will rupture, though we don't really know when it will," the company responded. The panel and the public were left with many questions. How did Dow Corning's rupture rate compare to other companies'? How did it compare to other medical devices? When, precisely, was the risk for rupture the greatest—right after surgery or years later? How did the company explain the wide variation in reported rupture rates?

The lesson is this: There ought to be some explainable basis for proposed performance standards. The public will not accept goals that cannot be backed up. Objective and agreed-upon criteria, however, are not always easy to come by. A rather frank Florida plastic surgeon explained to the panel just how he communicated the risk of rupture to his patients: "I warn them that 1.5 to 3 percent, as reported by the manufacturer, will deflate during the lifetime of the implant, and require re-operation for reimplantation; and, that

I found that it's going to be higher than that. I tell them to consider 6 to 10 percent, and that way they're not going to be disappointed."[48] This doctor, testifying for an implant manufacturer, made his living from implant surgery, and could easily have been seen as biased. But, given that he built in a margin of error, he could also be seen as believable. He took the lowest estimate available, compared it to his actual experience, and added a measure of comfort. Dow Corning, by contrast, not only repeated the lowest possible figure, but used an estimate (i.e., returns of ruptured implants to the company) that they knew was probably not accurate.

While setting clear and believable performance standards is not sufficient to ease all the public worry about potential risks, without such standards, the undertaking will probably fail. Setting a believable standard based on clear evidence will not solve the problem in its entirety, especially if there is not consensus among the stakeholders, but Dow Corning failed even to do this.

Prescription 1: Set clear and believable performance standards.

Minimize the Risk, Not the Concerns of Others

In November, Dow Corning offered its case to the panel. Dr. Bailey Lipscomb, Director of Clinical and Regulatory Affairs, presented the company's application. His argument is worth a closer look. "I want to state up-front and categorically that Dow Corning Wright believes in the safety of our products," he began.[49] Dr. Lipscomb presented a thorough, methodical, and well-documented defense of the company's PMA application. He noted the company's 30 years of experience with implants and its expenditure of millions of dollars on physical and clinical studies. He catalogued the 11 preclinical studies that uncovered no evidence of elevated immune rates or immune suppression. He mentioned that no clinical studies showed any evidence of linkage to cancer. He noted that basic research in progress in silicone antigen and blood chemistry had not detected any adverse consequences. Dr. Lipscomb emphasized, "We certainly sympathize with anyone who is suffering from health problems, whatever the cause. However, these issues must be resolved with valid scientific evidence."[50] Lipscomb took pains to mention that, according to company studies: "Overall, more than 95 percent of the women indicated satisfaction with their surgical procedure. . . [there were] similar rates of surgeon satisfaction."[51] (The chief psychiatrist of Memorial Sloan-

Kettering Hospital in New York City catalogued the psychological benefits of implants. Where problems had arisen, such as with capsular contraction, the doctor noted that the company had been aggressive in reporting these complications.) To end his presentation, Dr. Lipscomb stated, "My remarks so far have provided only a brief overview of the safety and efficacy data included in our PMA applications. We submitted an abundance of data that show these products are safe, effective, and of high quality."[52]

Dr. Lipscomb's argument was not convincing either to the FDA or to the press. The doctor, with the best of intentions, set about to defend the company rather than to acknowledge the concerns of an angry public. His defense was perceived as merely stonewalling. "He's not addressing the problem, he's protecting the company," according to the angriest observers. Dr. Lipscomb did not talk about what the company would do; he only talked only about what the company had already done. His remarks made little mention of the scientific uncertainty surrounding the issue. He focused only on the numerous benefits of the product, minimizing the potential costs.

Dr. Lipscomb's defense was hardly Dow Corning's only attempt to minimize rather than address the concerns of its customers. As the debate heated up during the summer of 1991, Dow Corning set up a telephone hot line for women with questions about the implants. Advertisements in major newspapers announced, "If you want accurate information about breast implants . . . instead of innuendo and half truths . . . call the Dow Corning Implant Information Center. . . . "[53] When the FDA's special assistant to the Commissioner on Women's Health called the hot line in late 1991, pretending to be a college student, the telephone worker told her that "scientific data and research show that they [implants] are 100 percent safe . . . . We have done lengthy studies as have thousands of plastic surgeons to show they are safe."[54] When the FDA sent the company a warning letter pointing out that such claims were inaccurate, the hot-line operators became far more cautious. But when written information, as requested, was mailed out to callers, the articles, written by others outside the company, still made the same overconfident claims. Dow Corning seemed far more willing to claim that their device was safe than to prove it. In the final analysis, the company seemed more invested in minimizing the concerns of its critics than in reducing the risks associated with its product.

What else might the company have done? Interestingly enough, though too late in many respects, Dow Corning's new C.E.O. as of February 1992,

Keith R. McKennon, a veteran of Dow's dioxin and Agent Orange controversies, offered a new and far more sophisticated approach. One panel
member deemed McKennon's new approach a "new spirit of cooperativity,
and, to borrow a term, 'Glasnost.'"[55] McKennon told the press such uncon-
ventional things as, "For me and Dow Corning, the overriding responsibility
is to the women who have mammary implants. . . . If it hasn't been clear
until now, we are going to cooperate absolutely with the Food and Drug Administration, and that means we're going to quit complaining about who is
on the advisory panel and all that."[56]

When McKennon appeared before the FDA Panel in February, only a few
months after Dr. Lipscomb, the company's tone had shifted. McKennon
began his presentation by stating, "I believe my and Dow Corning's overriding responsibility in this issue is to women who are using our implant devices."[57] After putting safety first, instead of trying to defend the company,
McKennon offered a plan for addressing the concerns of its customers. The
company's tack had changed: Dow Corning was no longer minimizing concern; instead, they were seeking to minimize risk.

Although the company would continue to seek protective orders in court,
as advised by counsel, this long-time company policy would be limited in
two important respects: Dow Corning would not use such orders to with-
hold information from the FDA; and if the FDA wanted to make such information public, Dow Corning would work to assure that such requests
were met. McKennon outlined an integrated research plan of 30 studies to
investigate the uncertainties raised by various individuals and groups. He
made a commitment to track implants with the help of physicians, patients,
the FDA, and other manufacturers, while at the same time protecting the
privacy of breast implant recipients. McKennon said that the company
would make sure women were informed about their "options and the risks
and benefits of implants prior to surgery."[58] Finally, Dow Corning would establish a women's council for dialogue on issues of concern.

McKennon was no longer offering bland assurances of safety. He was offering concrete actions to prove Dow Corning's good faith. He had legiti-
mized women's fears and concerns. While protecting the company's legal
position, McKennon had set out to be as forthcoming with the regulatory
agency as possible. He did not merely announce the company's disclosure
policy, he explained it. He actively set forth a scientific agenda to help explore remaining uncertainties. The company did not merely suggest that
they would take care of things; in addition, they set up a comprehensive

multi-stakeholder monitoring and tracking system as well as a forum for the company–customer interaction.

Peter Sandman, a researcher at Rutgers University, has articulated several principles suggesting that companies and agencies are better off communicating concrete and purposeful action rather than merely attempting to "educate" the public about risk. Three of his principles are especially important:

1. The amount of coverage accorded an environmental risk is unrelated to the seriousness of the risk in health terms. Instead, it is based on traditional journalistic criteria like timeliness and human interest.
2. Within individual risk stories, most of the coverage isn't about the risk. It is about blame, fear, anger, and other nontechnical issues.
3. When technical information about risk is provided in news stories, it has little if any impact on the audience.

In short, the public is generally not interested in being educated. Rather, the public is interested in action. As Sandman argues,

> . . . the most impactful statements an industry spokesperson can make to the media are aimed at reducing outrage: acknowledging problems, apologizing for misbehaviors, offering to share control, explaining what the source is doing and what the audience can do to mitigate the risk . . . "[59]

Dow Corning's McKennon had, intentionally or not, adopted a strategy much more in keeping with the mutual-gains approach. He was taking responsibility; addressing people's concerns, not minimizing or ignoring their fears; and proposing ways of minimizing the risk. He set out a policy that was more than mere information and argument; it was action oriented. To address the public's concern, decision makers must invest in risk reduction: whether through improved manufacturing procedures, increased information, improved products, or ultimately, product recall when the situation warrants it. Efforts to minimizing risk usually pay off.

Prescription 2: Minimize the risks, not the concerns of others.

Make Commitments You Can Keep

Unfortunately, at least part of McKennon's strategy failed in practice. The company's commitment to honor FDA requests for information was broken several months later. In late 1991, the company had hired former attorney general Griffin Bell to undertake an "independent" and "objective" investigation of its implant business in late 1991. When he completed his work in late 1992, the company refused to turn over the results to the FDA, citing attorney-client privilege. Bell's investigation had mysteriously been transformed from an independent, outside look to a confidential insider analysis. Just what did Bell find that Dow Corning felt compelled to hide?

When he came on board in February of 1992, McKennon told the *Wall Street Journal* that the company had "got itself in a terrible pickle" by insisting on keeping so many documents sealed under court order.[60] (Nevertheless, something or someone had changed his mind. While Dow Corning might have been protecting its privilege, it certainly undermined its already damaged reputation. Even the *Wall Street Journal*, a strong sympathizer, reacted negatively. "Dow Corning refused to turn over to the Food and Drug Administration an outside counsel's report on the company's breast implants, despite a self-proclaimed policy of openness."[61] One senior FDA aide complained, "Dow Corning has tried to create the public impression that they're cooperating fully with us . . . . While they have sent us hundreds of thousands of documents that were reviewed for the report, they are not organized in any useful order."[62]

McKennon's earlier words expressing concern for women with implants rang hollow after the refusal to turn over Bell's report. Assuming the report did contain information affecting women's safety, yet again women would be the last to know. The lesson is simple: Only make commitments you intend to keep. Back up your concern with believable promises. Giving, then taking away a commitment, only fuels public anger and reinforces the worst possible interpretation of agency or company motives.

Prescription 3: Make commitments you intend to keep, and then keep them.

Seek to Know, Not to Hide

As the controversy wore on, scrutiny of the company's past actions increased. Whatever the scientific merits of Dow Corning's case, the appearance of past impropriety heightened the alarm surrounding implant safety. It was not so much what the company did not know and resisted finding out as what they did know and would not reveal that fueled public concern. One panel member, who had changed her mind between the two meetings and had come to favor more restricted access to the devices, said, "When we came in November, we were faced with a list of the benefits of implants, and the sufficiency of the data to support those benefits was asserted. We've come back in February, and the focus has been on the risks of implants and on the astonishing paucity of data."[63] The *Journal of the American Medical Association* reported, "There is, however, no rigorous record of safety and efficacy compiled on the basis of clinical trials for any of the implants—because there were no clinical trials. Epidemiological evidence for or against associated disorders is lacking, as is the type of detail available only from long-term follow-up studies."[64]

What did the industry strive not to know? What did the company and others not do to ensure the safety of implants? One consultant to the panel was particularly harsh on Dow Corning for never conducting animal studies approximating the implant of silicone devices in or near mammalian breasts. In 10,000 pages of data, the consultant noted, only two to three pages dealt with silicone in or near its anatomic site of use. He said to company officials, "I think that is inscribed in my words as a peculiar phenomenon; unheard of in device regulation. . . . [W]e're talking about a silicone gel prosthesis put in or near the breast that you and I both admit bleeds and ruptures. The only good data that I can find on the consequence for the female breast is from human data."[65]

Instead of seeking more knowledge through animal studies, the company was more than willing to gather data from the field, that is, from unsuspecting implant patients. A plastic surgeon pointed out that it was customary practice for manufacturers to modify implants based on suggestions from surgeons, and then to allow doctors to try out the modified implants in new patients (without any animal studies). This doctor deemed these actions "seemingly unethical."[66] One staff member of the House committee concluded that this practice was best described as "the use of patients as guinea pigs in research."[67]

Internal memos later uncovered in lawsuits and finally offered by Dow Corning suggested that at least some company personnel were extremely worried about the purported safety of the product. One 1975 internal memo to the company's Mammary Task Force stated, "A question not yet answered is whether or not there is an excessive bleed of the gel through the envelope. We must address ourselves to this problem immediately. The stakes are too high if a wrong decision is made."[68] Nevertheless, additional studies were not conducted. In 1976, a senior clinical research specialist at Dow Corning wrote to his colleagues, "I have proposed again and again that we must begin an in-depth study of our gel, envelope, and bleed phenomenon. Capsule contraction isn't the only problem. Time is going to run out for us if we don't get under way."[69] Another internal memorandum, dated 1983, stated, "Only inferential data exist to substantiate the long-term safety of these gels for human implant application. I must strongly urge that Bill's group be given an approval to design and conduct the necessary work to validate that these gels are safe."[70] In 1985, when Dow Corning found out that the FDA might require lifetime animal safety studies, one employee described the request as "ominous."[71] Such lifetime studies would require seven-year dog studies, but the company had based its claims on only two-year studies.

The entire industry also resisted creating a nationwide registry, as finally recommended by McKennon, that would provide more information on implant recipients' well-being. A former chair of the FDA panel reminded the later panel, as well as the implant companies, that the American Society of Plastic and Reconstructive Surgery (ASPRS) committed in 1988 to work with the FDA to form a patient registry. However, within 48 hours of that meeting, the ASPRS rescinded the offer. The ASPRS was not alone in dropping the ball. While the panel had made the registry one of its four chief recommendations, the FDA, too, had abandoned the idea because it might be too expensive.[72]

What did the industry know and not tell? In addition to avoiding information gathering that might be helpful, manufacturers and surgeons resisted fully informing women of all the risks of implants, even when others tried to do so. Joan Pitkin, a Maryland state legislator, told the panel in February that she had been stymied in her attempt to introduce legislation mandating that brochures be distributed to those women seeking implants in Maryland. She added that, despite opposition by manufacturers and surgeons, such a law was finally passed in 1987.

Despite the fact that the 1988 panel had recommended a mandatory program to inform the public of the potential risks of breast implants, the program never got off the ground. The FDA quickly decided that opposition from manufacturers and surgeons would be too great, so they proposed a voluntary program instead. However, despite a 1989 attempt to develop a brochure and videotape for voluntarily distribution, the sponsoring group, which included consumers, manufacturers, and health professionals, failed to come to an agreement on the materials. Mistakenly, each representative was given the power to veto the entire group's decision. The American Society of Plastic and Reconstructive Surgeons did just that by threatening to veto the brochure if the names of any consumer support groups were included in the Resources section of the brochure. The FDA finally gave up, and instead asked manufacturers to include a package insert of their own.

Dow Corning also worked hard to suppress information coming out of the courts. The company defended its position by stating simply, "We don't want to be overeducating plaintiffs' lawyers."[73] Internal documents dating from 1960 to 1987 were placed under court seal. After the 1984 San Francisco federal-court decision awarded a Nevada woman $1.5 million in punitive damages, despite deeming the case "a highly-charged, emotional piece of litigation," the company still sought, following an appeal and a settlement for an undisclosed amount, a protective order covering most of the case files.[74] In a post-trial ruling, the judge argued that the company's own studies "cast considerable doubt on the safety of the product that was not disclosed to patients."[75] In a 1991 $7.3 million settlement, another San Francisco federal jury concluded that Dow Corning had concealed evidence linking ruptured implants to immune-system disorders.

Even if Dow Corning did not lie, and even if the company never intended to jeopardize the health of its customers, its actions made people very angry. One consumer representative, speaking before the February 1992 panel, stated, "In the past several years, three major drug companies have pleaded guilty to criminal charges of withholding data from the FDA. There have also been investigations into possible criminal behavior on the part of Upjohn for Halcion; Roche for Versed; Pfizer for the Bjork-Shiley heart valve; and, hopefully, Dow Corning and other manufacturers of silicone gel breast implants for what they have withheld. . . . The question is: Why should we trust these organizations who have lied repeatedly to us over the years?"[76] Dow Corning's attempts to protect itself in the courtroom mobilized public opinion against the company. This is not to say that the FDA, consumer groups, and product liability plaintiff lawyers didn't also come under attack, but Dow Corning's attempts to suppress information stimulated a great deal of unwanted attention.

Leiss and Chociolko, in their book *Risk and Responsibility* (1994) have this to say about such actions:

> From the standpoint of the public interest, playing elaborate games with uncertainties in the science of risk assessment, with or without the additional layers of obstructionism that lawyers can supply, is intolerable. Such tactics,

however tempting for the risk manager, fuel the fears of the unknown felt by many non-expert stakeholders and cause them to harden their view that, in the face of a substantial range of unknown factors, many of which appear to stem only from the risk-promoter's evident wish not to find out whether there might be any bad news in the missing data, the only prudent course of action is to be extremely risk adverse.[77]

We agree. The breast-implant case suggests that playing hide-and-seek with relevant information is not fruitful. It may deflect some courtroom losses (although in this case, that is doubtful), but it certainly breeds mistrust and anger.

> *Prescription 4: Seek to know, not to hide information about your product or policy.*

The Company Appeals to Science

Numerous critics of the panel, the FDA, and previous court decisions favoring plaintiffs appealed to science during the course of the implant controversy. They complained bitterly that the law was running roughshod over reason. Dow Corning repeatedly called for a return to science. Dr. Lipscomb, speaking for Dow Corning, said, "We certainly sympathize with anyone who is suffering from health problems, whatever the cause. However, these issues must be resolved with valid scientific evidence."[78] Robert T. Rylee, director of the health care companies for Dow Corning, told the press, when confronted with internal memorandums that suggested Dow Corning employees were worried about the lack of adequate tests: "'Internal memos are not science . . . They are a printed record of one side of a two-way conversation. The real question is, what does the science say?"[79]

Outside the company, others urged a return to science, as opposed to the "speculation" and "hysteria" that seemed to engulf the case. One plastic surgeon who testified before the November panel said, in reference to the critics of implants, "They have generated silicone phobia in this country by taking bits of true science and distorting it."[80] Congresswoman Marilyn Lloyd of Tennessee, an adamant critic of the FDA's breast-implant approval process, argued at the February meeting, "This decision cannot be based on a biased FDA evaluation; an FDA that has demonstrated today an inability to deal with this issue on a scientific basis without clear scientific evidence [that] the implants are unsafe for women."[81] A *Wall Street Journal* editorial said of Dr. Kessler's 45–day moratorium on the implants, "At this point, David Kessler, J.D., M.D., suspended the apparatus of science and invoked the apparatus of the courtroom. Peer review and randomized studies, we see so clearly, can easily be trumped by discovery and the adversarial process."[82]

While this call for a greater reliance on science is understandable, we also think it is insufficient. This is not to say that science and technical experts should not play an active role in making risky decisions, but science, particularly in debates over risk, cannot always supply easy answers. As the debate over rupture rates—only one of the many scientific debates surrounding implants—suggests, the data available on implants were inconclusive and contradictory. It was precisely because the studies were insufficient to generate a scientific consensus and because a great deal of science had, in fact, been left undone that the debate arose. It was at least a little ironic that many of the very critics calling for better science tended to downplay or ignore the fact that Dow Corning had not employed a particularly scientific approach to ensuring the effectiveness of its product in the first place.[83]

Sources of Scientific Disagreement

In debates over risk, scientists are sure to disagree. Connie Ozawa, in her book *Recasting Science* (1991), highlights several reasons why such disagreements arise. First, simple miscommunication errors often occur among scientists. During the rupture-rate debate, while one mammographic study measured the percentage of ruptures *per woman* (the Washington University study), another study reported findings in ruptures *per implant* (the University of Pittsburgh study). The two figures, measuring the rate of rupture in different terms, needed to be carefully compared. One respected plastic surgeon compared the 4.6 percent rate per woman and the 3 percent rate per implant as if they measured the same thing.

Second, differences in research design can produce different data or disagreements over data. For instance, the Washington study drew from a sample of women without any symptoms of breast cancer who had obtained mammograms in a large-scale, on-site mobile screening program. In the other study, the women were drawn not from a similar population, but instead from women either referred by a doctor or referred by themselves. In addition, some patients in the Pittsburgh study reported symptoms, such as a palpable mass in their breast, as their reason for coming for testing. Because the samples were gathered in different ways, this could have influenced the conclusions of the investigations. If these differences in design are not made transparent, sharp lines of disagreement and contradiction may be drawn that obscure the more likely source of disagreement.

Third, scientists may disagree on the choice of analytic methods. One researcher in the Washington study stated that detecting a leak by ultrasound was *not* "easy." Dr. Judy Destouet said: "But I must caution you. Dr. Harris has made it sound quite easy to find a leak with ultrasound."[84] Another researcher, a consultant to the FDA, later refuted Destouet's challenge by noting that his results matched well with the success of using ultrasound to detect silicone outside the envelope.

Of course, even if the findings are well understood, accurately compared, and the methods agreed upon, different conclusions might still be drawn. Dr. E. James Potchen, a radiologist on the FDA panel, was quick to point out that while the mammographic studies were "interesting," the results were not statistically inferential and that people should not think the findings had "major clinical impact."[85] However, Dr. Destouet pointed out the importance of the finding that not all ruptures were detected, as it turned out, by physical examination alone. The two experts spoke from the same data, but emphasized different conclusions based on different concerns. The panel member wanted to be sure that these findings did not result in more panic in implant recipients. The researcher wanted to be sure the panel understood that she had arrived at a noteworthy clinical finding about detection of leaks in breast implants through mammography.

When experts must make concrete decisions from mixed-data sources, interpretations become even more convoluted, uncertain, and unscientific. As Ozawa (1991) points out, there is a great distance between the discrete findings, statistics, methods, and narrow conclusions that can be drawn from particular studies, and the final broad policy decisions that agencies such as the FDA must make. It is no wonder that from the same numerous and complex data intelligent, well-trained, highly-skilled professionals can draw different conclusions. When it comes to risky decisions, choices are often based on informed human judgment, not scientific fact. As the editor of the *New England Journal of Medicine* said in June of 1992, "David Kessler has been a remarkably effective commissioner, and it is easy to sympathize with the view that he had no choice but to remove breast implants from the market in view of the FDA's finding that their safety and effectiveness have not been demonstrated. And it is also easy to sympathize with irritation that the manufacturers have not been more responsible. But the fact is that Kessler had the discretion to decide either way. The decision was a matter of judgment that he himself acknowledges was 'especially difficult.'"[86] Dr. Alexander Baumgarten, a professor of laboratory medicine at Yale University Medical School, arrived at the same conclusion: "The issue of what is a safe and effective device in the absence of hard data, is obviously a judgment call."[87]

Risky Decisions Require Human Judgments

Controversies over risk arise, not because most scientists have reached a consensus and a few are unwilling to go along, but because science has not yet arrived at a clear understanding of the situation. In the space between "safe" and "unproven," the politics of risk assessment unfold. As Leiss and Chociolko (1994) report, this is not peculiar to the breast implant controversy.

> All the risk controversy cases analyzed in the literature with which we are familiar have a common feature: at the point when the controversy erupted, some risk-assessment data that was regarded as indispensable from the standpoint of at least one key stakeholder was unavailable.[88]

Science alone cannot always offer a clear path. Decision makers must make ideologically informed, interest-based decisions and choices about what is and isn't acceptable. As one of the FDA panel members, Dr. Sheryl Ruzek, an associate professor of health education at Temple University, pointed out,

> One of the things that is most troubling to this panel is that, by law, we are to make some statement about safety, and safety is always a normative judgment. It's a statement about the acceptability of a reasonably well-known level of risk, because nothing is ever totally safe or probably totally risky, and people have a great variation in the amount of risk that they consider acceptable.[89]

As it turns out, the courtroom is a particularly ineffective forum for settling science-intensive policy disputes. As numerous articles in both the *New York Times* and the *Wall Street Journal* pointed out, the objectives of science and the law are quite different, if not contradictory. The adversarial process, through which information is often concealed, positional arguments prevail, and cagey legal maneuvering wins the day, is not likely to ensure that important information is shared with those at risk or that the sources of uncertainty are clearly understood. The courtroom battles over implants may have been valuable for the injured parties and their attorneys, but they did not help the millions of other women who were at risk. Unfortunately, the legal mentality—not the scientific mentality—shapes the way many organizations do business long before they appear in court.

In America, we have collectively turned to a hoped-for, independent and objective arbiter—science. Consumers expect the FDA to rely on science to ensure product safety. Businesses, threatened by the din of an angry public, appeal to well-credentialed scientists to protect them. Consumer representatives and environmentalists find scientific advocates to argue their side of the story. "Let's turn to science," each says, as if it offered a monolithic view of the world. No one bothers to ask, "Which scientists and which scientific interpretations should we trust?"

Out of frustration with the inexactitude of science, we turn to the courts. Perhaps there, we hope, someone will deliver a conclusive finding. There, too, we are disappointed. Court decisions turn on due process, eyewitnesses, and expert testimony, but not on scientific consensus nor on the rules of scientific method. In personal-injury cases, complex and sometimes contradictory scientific findings are appropriated by legal experts. When agency decisions come before the courts, the courts are unable and usually unwilling to do more than analyze the process by which the agency went about meeting its statutory obligations and authority. Thus, the courts adjudicate the process, not the substance, of the risk-assessment and risk-management debate.

If traditional scientific discourse is insufficient, regulatory agencies are not in a position to make objective decisions, and the courts operate along other lines, how should debates over acceptable levels of risk be settled? Fortunately, there is another way, a way that has been tried before and does work. It is a way that appeals both to the impulse for collective decision-making and to a growing desire for less bureaucratic and less intrusive governmental intervention. It is, in some respects, conservative in its reliance on self-determination and liberal in its concern for fairness. This third way is direct face-to-face negotiations among the actual parties who must bear both the benefits and costs of risky decisions.

Voices Heard and Unheard

We return to the breast implant case. As one FDA panelist noted, the individuals involved displayed great variation in the amount of risk they considered acceptable. In the course of the hearings, many "voices" were heard: Women who had survived breast cancer; women who had contracted rare forms of connective-tissue disorders; plastic surgeons; consumer watchdogs; experts in radiology, immunology, and oncology. Each approached risk in a different way. Each stood to benefit depending on how the FDA ruled. It is not clear which voices should have been given the greatest weight.

If the product were banned, breast-cancer survivors would lose a reconstruction option. Women who wished to obtain the implants for cosmetic reasons would be denied. Manufacturers and plastic surgeons would lose business. On the other hand, if the implants were not banned, more women might be exposed to increased risks of connective-tissue disorders. Scores of healthy women seeking implants for cosmetic reasons might be exposed to painful capsular contracture and a greater risk of undetected breast cancer. The FDA's reputation and credibility were on the line, as were the reputations and market shares of the manufacturers and plastic surgeons.

Marilyn Lloyd, the congresswoman from Tennessee, had survived breast cancer. Because of the 45-day moratorium imposed by the FDA in January of 1992, she was unable to undergo elective surgery to counteract the disfiguring effects of her mastectomy. "A ban, even temporary, is absolutely unwarranted," she told the panel.[90] Ms. Lloyd was not alone in her view. Barbara Quinn, a member of the American Cancer Society's Bosom Buddies, told the panel, "The cancer diagnosis was one trauma to deal with, but the second emotional stress of losing my breasts was mentally unmanageable. The grief of a body part dying is unbearable . . . . Why is the FDA denying cancer-maimed women the use of this device to make their bodies whole again and to keep their emotional well-being intact? Why should women be paraded in front of the media and society to defend their psychological reasons for wanting implants?"[91] Rosemary Locke, testifying for the Y-Me National Organization for Breast Cancer Information and Support, told an April 30th, 1992 hearing sponsored by Congresswoman Lloyd, "Raped by a disease which invades and threatens and a treatment that mutilates, breast reconstruction can help restore a sense of well-being even when one's life span is uncertain."[92] Supreme Court Justice Sandra Day O'Connor, too, remarked on just how important reconstructive surgery had been in her own recovery from breast cancer.

On the other hand, there were women who believed that their implants had caused them great harm. These women expressed regret that these devices had ever been implanted. There was the former plastic-surgery nurse who had worked for the Texas surgeon who had invented the implants. She received implants, and later contracted a connective-tissue disease and cancer that was detected late, partially because her implants interfered with mammography. When she left her job in 1981, she said she had never been informed about the risks of immunological disorders or the barriers to mammography. When she attempted to report her concerns to Dow Corning, she was told the company did not accept reports from patients.

Sybil Goldrich, cofounder of Command Trust Network, also a survivor of breast cancer, reported: ". . . even though I am a doctor's wife, had ample health insurance to take care of the costs, and did what we then believed was quite a bit of research on the subject. None of this saved me from enduring operations to variously insert and remove four different sets of implants, each of which caused me great physical pain (not to mention the effect on my family) . . . "[93] Janet Van Winkle, a breast-cancer victim with an organization called As-Is, testified before the FDA Panel, "My choice of silicone implants has today left me in complete and total financial ruin and devastatingly poor health."[94] As a counterpoint in some respects to Congresswoman Lloyd, Maryland state legislator Joan Pitkin testified before the February panel about her difficulties in making laws requiring mandated brochures about breast reconstruction and augmentation in her state owing to pressures coming from manufacturers and the medical community. She concluded, "A crime has been perpetrated on these women, and now the manufacturers' cynical lack of concern for today's victims is something you must address."[95]

Women and their affiliated organizations lined up on both sides of the debate. One group urged a full moratorium or substantial restrictions while the other urged more informed choice. Ralph Nader's Public Citizen Health Research Group, the American Academy of Cosmetic Surgery, the American College of Reconstructive and Cosmetic Surgery, the American Medical Society, the American College of Radiology, and the American College of Surgeons also joined in the exchange of views.

Needless to say, the interested parties to this debate were diverse and plentiful. However, one interest group, for the most part, was noticeably absent: the 800,000 or more women who had received implants solely for cosmetic reasons. No organization was present, if one even existed, to represent these women. Of the numerous individuals who testified before both panels, most were cancer patients. They were well organized, well funded, and represented by numerous professional lobbyists. While some women who had received breast implants for "cosmetic" reasons spoke before the panels, many of those who had received such cosmetic implants had been disfigured at birth or had experienced major changes in their breasts after pregnancy and nursing. Few of the 80 percent of women who had received implants solely for "self-improvement" had a voice in the debate.

This is not surprising, given that these women were frequently maligned and subtly castigated for having given in, out of vanity and insecurity, to the buxom Playboy image of the ideal woman. One panel member concluded her statement at the end-of-February meeting by explaining that a woman without breasts was as much a woman as a man without hair was a man. This quixotic and not particularly compassionate conclusion certainly did not address the fact that all implant recipients, regardless of their reasons for undergoing this surgery, faced increased anxiety because of the controversy. These 800,000 women, as consumers of a product and as patients with legitimate concerns and fears, deserved a voice in the debate.

Engage Stakeholders in Making Risky Decisions

Unfortunately, given the structure of public debate, even the women who did speak were relegated to pleading their case before an FDA panel. In return, the FDA made its decisions behind closed doors. The stakeholders most directly affected by the outcome of the FDA's decision had little real say. In our view, the expert panel, the public hearing, and the media circus did not serve the stakeholders well.

Plastic surgeons maligned doctors of patients inflicted with rare connective-tissue disorders for engaging in "junk science." Yet, in the previous few years, they had effectively stymied FDA-sponsored efforts to complete a seemingly simple information pamphlet for prospective implant patients. Consumer advocates assailed Dow Corning as a perfidious, greedy, reckless, and callous corporation while ignoring the numerous studies that did not link implants in any significant way to connective-tissue diseases. Breast cancer survivors assailed the FDA while ignoring the concerns of other women in the same situation who doubted the safety and efficacy of the implants.[96] Most of the women who had received implants for cosmetic reasons were never heard. The FDA pleased almost no one, and certainly infuriated many.

Both the FDA and the manufacturers of implants might have called for a joint consensus-building forum. Rather than a formal panel operating under the spotlight of the Washington press corps, self-selected representatives of all the stakeholding groups could have met in a problem-solving context away from the hubbub of the nation's capital. Imagine that a woman suffering from a painful condition, such as scleroderma, had an opportunity to meet a woman whose implant had helped her recover from disfiguring breast surgery. Imagine that these two women had a chance to speak to the chief executive and the director of clinical and regulatory affairs for Dow Corning. Imagine if someone had helped bring women who had received implants for cosmetic reasons more directly into the debate. What might they have said? Imagine if plastic surgeons with different views on implants had a chance to talk in an unofficial setting. What if a consumer advocate and a cosmetic-implant recipient happy with her implants had met? With the help of a professional neutral to soothe tempers and ensure that basic ground rules were followed, what kind of dialogue might have occurred? What if representatives of all these different parties had actually been compelled to sit in a room together and hash through policy recommendations with the FDA?

Unfortunately, we will never know. But we do know that such stakeholder forums are possible and have worked in other instances. While government agencies have been more inclined to call for such forums, we advise companies to encourage such ventures long before they become embroiled in painful and highly public conflicts. With support from the Chemical Manufacturers Association, such companies as Rhone-Poulenc and Dow have already established community advisory panels to directly advise plant managers on the best ways of handling wastewater treatment, incineration, and emergency planning. As the chemical industry learned from the painful Bhopal incident, it is better to engage stakeholders early in company decision making, rather than later when the public is inflamed over damage or losses. Public involvement turns out to be good for business. Community advisory panels have helped to remind plant managers of the community's needs, raising questions about safety, odor, and emissions that otherwise might have gone neglected and erupted later into full-blown, costly disputes.

Forums for Consensus Building

What should consensus-building forums look like? We suggest three different models.

A limited forum might involve nothing more than a conference at which a neutral and respected body in the debate, such as the American Medical Association, would organize a non-decision-making gathering at which scientific experts from many different fields meet publicly to "walk through" a science-intensive policy question. The chief purpose of such a session would be to highlight the extent of the scientific consensus already existing as well as the reasons why technical experts disagree. A professional facilitator would have to help all the groups involved to select a credible panel of experts, establish an agenda and ground rules, and manage the flow, but not the content, of the conversation. Unlike the formal FDA panel, the participants would not be expected to make recommendations. Such a conference would attempt to give all credible scientific viewpoints a chance to debate the question, avoiding the narrowness that occurs when only the consulting members of government-selected panels meet in front of the press. Just such a facilitated consensus-finding conference was sponsored by the New York Academy of Sciences to help explore differences in the assessment of the risks associated with a trash-to-energy plant proposed for the Brooklyn Navy Yard in New York City in the mid-1980s.[97]

The forum might also be shaped as a "policy dialogue" to help hammer out one or two specific policy options. For instance, a forum of breast-implant stakeholders might have been convened to develop an informed-consent procedure or to find ways of minimizing the risks of mammographic interference. Representatives of cancer patients, plastic surgeons, consumer groups, and others could have been called together to work for several months, with the support of a team of professional neutrals, to develop policy options. Rather than a short one- or two-day conference, a policy dialogue would have required multiple meetings, input from technical advisors, joint fact finding, the generation of policy options, and the careful packaging of proposals to take account of the different preferences of the parties. Despite its complexity, with the good faith of the participants and the help of a seasoned neutral, such a forum could produce a small set of policy options and move the contending interests into a collaborative problem-solving mode.

Such forums have worked in other situations. The Regulatory Branch of the U.S. Army Corps of Engineers used a "policy dialogue" to develop conditions of issue for a general wetlands permit that had earlier caused acrimonious debate between environmentalists wanting to protect national wildlife refuges and gas and oil drillers eager to explore new fields. The dialogue resulted in a 1987 permit acceptable to all. When its renewal was considered in 1992, there were no complaints about reissuing the general permit.

If the FDA had wanted to convene an official consensus-building (as opposed to a public participation) process, it could have done so. Such a forum might have been organized as a "negotiated rule-making" or "reg neg." This is a process through which stakeholders are brought together in face-to-face negotiations, generally aided by an experienced facilitator, to hammer out full-fledged regulations (not just recommendations) that become the subject of formal agency rule-making. Unlike consensus-finding conferences or policy dialogues, the outcomes of full-dress negotiated rule-making are formally enacted by an agency. They are not just recommendations; they become the actual rules. The process, while entailing many of the complexities of a policy dialogue, may, because of the scope of work, be even more intensive. Despite its complexity (and cost), such rule-making has occurred in numerous instances, including EPA's development of wood-burning stove emissions rules in 1986, Agriculture Canada's development of regulations for anti-sap-stain chemicals used in controlling mold on freshly sawn or stored lumber in 1990, and the U.S. Coast Guard's 1992 development of tank-vessel oil-spill response plans in accordance with the Oil Pollution Act of 1990 passed in the wake of the *Exxon Valdez* accident. Indeed, more than a dozen federal agencies in the United States and Canada have used negotiated rule-making procedures successfully.[98]

We cannot guarantee that any of these processes, had they been employed in the breast implant controversy, would have avoided litigation. As the failure of the attempt to produce even a simple pamphlet for prospective implant patients attests, gathering stakeholders together can be slow, labor intensive, and ultimately unsuccessful. Consensus building with stakeholders, like anything else, can be done well or done poorly. Stakeholders who believe they will gain more by impeding the process will do just that. Stakeholders committed to entrenched positions, extreme position taking, and fighting rather than negotiating may feel hopelessly ineffective in a joint problem-solving setting. A poorly-designed process, such as the one used to develop the pamphlet, with only lukewarm support from the FDA and a unanimous-vote rule, is not likely to produce consensus.

In the following section, we try to illustrate that even in a highly contentious public controversy, consensus-building forums not only help soothe inflamed tempers but also help the parties to work toward a mutually agreeable solution to their common problem.

The New Bedford Harbor Superfund Forum

In 1982, New Bedford Harbor—once Melville's launching point for Ishmael and Captain Ahab's hunt for the great white whale—was placed on the

Environmental Protection Agency's Superfund cleanup list. For over a quarter of a century, companies manufacturing electrical equipment had dumped carcinogenic PCBs into the harbor. After seven years of study and consideration of some fifty different alternative remediation strategies, the EPA announced that it would dredge sediments from the most polluted portions of the harbor and incinerate them on-site. "On-site," as it turned out, was an old soccer field adjacent to working-class homes and small businesses. Within a one-mile radius of the planned incineration site were six schools. Within three miles over 100,000 people, mainly poor and working-class Portuguese immigrants, resided.

Despite the fact that the EPA had attempted to integrate community concerns into the decision making, protest erupted. In 1990, grassroots groups formed to fight the proposed incineration. They feared that carcinogenic airborne pollutants, such as dioxin, would be released into their neighborhood. In a November of 1991 city-wide referendum, 87 percent of the voters opposed the plan. In 1992, an article in the *National Law Journal* on the slower pace of EPA cleanup in poor and minority communities cited New Bedford as a prime example of "environmental injustice." By the summer of 1993, the dispute had widened. The City Council passed an ordinance banning incineration equipment from city streets. The city refused to grant the federal government the permits required to hook up to city water services. In retaliation, the EPA threatened to slap a $25,000 per day fine on the city for obstructing the cleanup. The regional head of the EPA told one of the local papers, "We can't adjust and change and be jerked around . . . . We want to do something good here . . . If I thought that this is going to be harmful to people, I wouldn't have picked it. . . . We're the only ones who can help New Bedford."[99]

By October, opposition groups had filed a suit against the city for not holding public health hearings on the proposed incineration. The same groups had also garnered the support of state representatives as well the district's powerful Washington legislators, Representative Barney Frank and Senator Ted Kennedy. In an interview with the *New York Times* an EPA spokesperson said, "We're not looking for confrontation here; we're trying to do our job . . . . New Bedford would be a very bad precedent if we had to stop in the middle after all the years of work and the studies that have been done."[100]

With the city in an uproar and powerful elected officials hounding the EPA, the agency relented; it agreed to reopen the public discussion. The agency also agreed to a panel, as proposed by Massachusetts Senators Kerry and Kennedy, to review alternative technologies. With the help of the Massachusetts Office of Dispute Resolution, the EPA and a cross-section of community representatives selected a facilitator to assist in reviewing cleanup technologies. While the community activists were extremely concerned that the facilitator might not be neutral, the state office convinced them to interview two candidates. To everyone's surprise, one of the finalists was chosen with everyone's, including the community's, glowing endorsement. Even before the forum officially met, the local press exclaimed with relief, "At last, someone in the agency has realized that poor communications and public relations have caused a breakdown of public confidence with EPA, which often acts as though it cares nothing for local decision-making and its impact on the public."[101] In a new spirit of cooperation, the EPA opened a cleanup headquarters to provide guided tours of the area.

The final composition of the forum included representatives from three community groups, three municipalities, the New Bedford mayor's office, the state legislator, the state's environmental agency, and the EPA. At the outset, the facilitator told the parties: "I'm not asking you people to love each other, but to suspend disbelief."[102] In the first meeting, the parties struck their first interim agreement. The EPA would delay dredging the harbor for 30 days while the community activists delayed their lawsuit for the same length of time. Despite this positive turn of events, many citizens remained skeptical. "It's difficult to be optimistic," one advocate told the local press, "the EPA has opted for incineration, and I personally see no way of turning it around."[103]

Several things helped the parties improve communication. First, the forum insisted that its members communicate not only with one another, but with all the citizens of the affected area as well. All meetings of the forum were open to the public, as well as broadcast on a local cable channel, to keep everyone informed. Minutes of its meetings were also available. Second, the forum enlisted all the stakeholders in decision making. Many vendors of cleanup technologies were given a chance to make presentations. Community groups, as well as government agencies, were forced to consider difficult trade-offs between competing cleanup technologies. Third, the parties developed a common evaluation procedure to ensure that all interests were being met. To help the representatives ask the right questions and evaluate the technologies correctly, the group developed a score card that included criteria not only required by federal and state law, but reflecting the concerns of the community as well.

Fourth, the less technically skilled parties—the community groups— needed technical help to evaluate the options before them. When forum presentations were highly technical, the community groups, using EPA money, hired additional consulting help. The community groups received legal advice from a legal advocacy group called Alternatives for Community and the Environment (ACE), three young attorneys committed to promoting environmental justice in poor and underserved neighborhoods. Environmental advocacy groups are sometimes seen as promoters of conflict and impediments to consensus building, but, as this case proved, they can help to even the playing field by providing technical and/or legal assistance to community groups who need it.

After almost a year of hard work, the forum arrived at an agreement to proceed with the cleanup. All parties supported a remedy that avoided on-site incineration. They also agreed to find a technology that destroyed, and did not merely contain, the PCBs. Finally, once the results of treatability studies were available, all parties agreed to work toward consensus on the choice of a preferred and a back-up cleanup remedy. While the final selection of a cleanup technology will take several more years, the forum managed to transform a painful confrontation into a joint problem-solving process.

This process was not without its travails. The companies that had already settled with the EPA over the cleanup costs were worried that this mid-course change would add to their bills. One company from South Carolina enlisted that state's senators, Strom Thurmond and Ernest Hollings, to pressure the EPA to closely monitor the costs of the forum and any proposals that it made. Despite serious community concern that dredging the contaminated sediments would stir up more contaminants, the EPA decided to proceed anyway. The forum ultimately did grant reluctant approval, but only in a session at which the attendance was severely limited by a heavy winter storm. When the EPA indicated, several months into the forum, that it might consider dropping the incineration option, conflicting statements from different EPA officials baffled and angered community activists. Despite these problems, the forum members worked their way toward agreement. Everyday citizens, with the support of technical advisors they trusted, were able to tackle complex environmental issues. In the midst of a local and loud debate that had gained national attention, a consensus-building forum helped the stakeholders find common ground while offering the EPA a chance to redeem itself as a protector of public health.

Prescription 5: Engage stakeholders in making risky decisions through consensus-building forums.

Make Contingent Commitments

Imagine, for a moment, that years previous to the fiasco Dow Corning and other manufacturers had undertaken what CEO Keith McKennon finally recommended to the 1992 FDA panel. Imagine, also, that an integrated research plan of 30 studies was well underway; that a national registry of implant recipients was established; that better informed-consent documents, brochures, and pamphlets were available; that a women's council was working closely with companies to review ongoing concerns; and that Dow Corning and others had truly instituted the mutual-gains approach.

Even after all this, there might still be injured or angry individuals claiming that Dow Corning, or another manufacturer, had caused them to contract rare connective-tissue disorders. Their personal stories of pain, suffering, and perhaps healing after implants were removed, would continue. With enough organization and motivation, they might capture the media's attention even though they had no conclusive scientific evidence to justify their claims. What should Dow Corning and the other "defendants" do?

The mutual-gains approach emphasizes the importance of contingent commitments. This means providing a guarantee that will alter perceived risks; for example, insurance guarantees that alleviate customer anxieties. In our imagined version of the breast-implant controversy, the company might have offered a contingent commitment to ease its customers' worst fears. In part, a guarantee to help women pay for explantation (i.e., surgical removal of the implant) who would otherwise not have been able to afford it, would have been a good example of a contingent commitment. Even this did not address the concerns of a vocal minority who believed they had suffered impacts far greater than mere discomfort. For this group the company might have been forced to offer compensation *without* acknowledging blame or fault.

The manufacturers might have said: If you contract these particular medically identifiable diseases, we will help to ease your suffering. When weighed against the cost of public fury, sliding stock values, legal expenses, and lost credibility, that cost could be small, especially since the specified disorders occur so rarely. We advise: Before litigation is filed, consider the benefits of offering to compensate individuals who are worried they might be injured by something you have done or are proposing to do. Once numerous suits accumulate, sympathetic juries award individuals compensatory and punitive damages, and plaintiff's attorneys have become heavily invested in winning class action suits, the value of contingent commitments will be lost.

What form should contingent commitments take? In the case of breast implants, an insurance policy of sorts might have been offered to offset future health-care costs for anyone injured. To cover the losses associated with "autoimmune" and connective-tissue disorders, the manufacturers could have invested in a pooled health policy. How might such a compensation scheme have worked? To begin, the companies would probably have had to establish what is called a claims facility to review and approve individual claims.[104] Numerous models for establishing such facilities exist. They have been successful, as a senior scientist at Rand's Institute for Civil Justice has noted, in situations where substantial proof of liability has been established (as in asbestos claims) and even in situations where there is less certain proof of liability (as in claims concerning Agent Orange and DDT).[105]

Successful claims facilities must balance several objectives simultaneously.[106] They must identify legitimate claimants and reject illegitimate claims. They must be perceived as fair by all sides. They have to compensate those who deserve it, in proportion to the injury incurred, *and* provide due process in terms of deliberative, objective, and thorough reviews that treat claimants with dignity. They must also be cost-effective, minimizing transaction costs in order to maximize the amount available for compensation payments. They must be widely accessible so that all who have legitimate claims understand the options available to them. Ultimately, they must be tailored to the specifics of the situation: the hazard, the potential impacts, the severity of impacts, the players, and the alternatives available outside such a scheme.

One such claims facility was established by 32 producers of asbestos and 16 insurers in 1985.[107] It was later reorganized because of disagreements among its member organizations over how financial responsibility should be calculated and how the facility should be governed, but in its three years of operation it achieved several notable results. First, it settled numerous claims. In the ten years previous, only 6,000 claims had been settled. The facility, or Joint Center as it was called, settled 18,500 claims in three years. Second, the facility established a registry for victims who had been exposed to asbestos but showed no symptoms. This registry will facilitate settlements if claims arise in the future. Third, transaction costs were reduced. By minimizing the number of law firms involved (a reduction from 1,100 firms to just 55 of them), the facility achieved substantial cost savings. Last, in those cases that did go to trial, the defendants prevailed in 65 percent of the cases, rather than in the 28 percent of cases before the Joint Center was created. The average award to plaintiffs fell from $600,000 to $330,000. These outcomes do not include the gains in improved company reputation and increased shareholder confidence that such an effort can engender.

When companies consider compensation schemes and other contingent commitments to be made in cases where harm or injury could occur, several points must be kept in mind. Companies ought to do everything they can to mitigate potential impacts and minimize risk before considering compensation schemes. The best risk-management strategies address the public's concerns by minimizing the chances that a hazard will occur, not simply paying someone to incur it. Of course, companies must carefully weigh the costs and benefits of such offers. We encourage executives engaged in this calculus to go beyond a narrow comparison of expected litigation costs versus compensation expenses to consider the potential value of maintaining—indeed improving—relationships with current and potential customers as well as enhancing the company's reputation.

When contingent commitments imply a determination of blame or liability, companies must be very careful to develop an explanation for why compensation is being offered that does not compromise their legal situation. The mutual-gains approach argues that companies and agencies should accept responsibility, but it does not suggest that companies ought to assume blame indiscriminately. We have focused on financial compensation, but countless other contingent commitments are possible. For instance, implant manufacturers might have worked closely with the American Cancer Society to improve mammographic techniques, and then to offer free access to improved screening for implant patients concerned about the possibility of breast cancer. In the Agent Orange case, in addition to financial compensation, the litigants were offered a referral network to provide information on available settlement and other governmental benefits, services for children with birth defects, outreach programs for homeless veterans, and genetic counseling. In many land-development conflicts, both for-profit corporations and nonprofit institutions such as hospitals have established escrow accounts from which they promise to compensate owners who suffer property value losses as a result of new construction. Builders have also promised to construct artificial wetlands if the projects they have in mind adversely affect existing wetlands.

It is crucial that the nexus between compensation or contingent offers and the injury or harm being addressed be made explicit. The better the compensation fits the cost or suffering in question, the more likely the outcome will be perceived as fair by the public, and the more likely the company or agency will be to regain its credibility. In other words, patients suffering from connective-tissue disorders would most appropriately be helped through payment of medical expenses. The more the compensation veers from the complaint, the more it will be seen as a payoff or bribe. To ensure an acceptable nexus, the structure of compensation agreements can best be worked out in a stakeholder forum.

In some instances, offering to compensate an injured party, or offering a contingent commitment to hold a person harmless if a hazard does occur, will not be sufficient to win their support. Why should a promise of being "made whole" justify the imposition of additional risk or worry? In some instances it may be necessary to make someone "even better off." In the case of communities anxious about risky facilities such as incinerators, unless the residents stand to become better off than they will be without such facilities, why should they agree to accept the risks involved? Even a contingent promise to clean up, pay medical expenses, or cover the loss of property values won't be enough, especially if the community is relatively well off. Even if the community is not well off, recent emphasis on environmental justice suggests that poor and minority communities, just like everybody else, do not want to bear undue and unfair risks. The only way to site such facilities successfully is to promise the community something valuable—something that they define as "worth the risk." The mechanics of such negotiations are quite complicated and have been described elsewhere.[108] However, the concept is straightforward: Contingent commitments need to be sufficient to convince an angry public that prospective risks are worth taking.

Prescription 6: Offer contingent commitments to alleviate worry and reduce uncertainty. Be certain that the basis for these offers is credible.

CHAPTER VI

When Values Collide

In the early 1990s, a Massachusetts water supply agency called the Metropolitan District Commission (MDC) granted hunters the right to shoot deer in the 48,000-acre protected watershed of the Quabbin Reservoir, metropolitan Boston's chief water supply. A half-century prohibition against hunting in the reservation and a dearth of natural predators had caused the deer population to explode. As a result of heavy browsing by the plentiful deer, the forest surrounding the reservoir was not regenerating. Seeds would sprout, but their shoots would quickly be gobbled up.

To the casual passerby, the shadowed floor of the Quabbin forest, blanketed only by tall, graceful ferns, looked perfect. To knowledgeable foresters, however, it was a forest without a future. If a hurricane were to level the surrounding forest (and just such a hurricane is expected every 100 years), no new seedlings would be in place to regenerate the forest. With most new vegetation unable to develop, erosion would increase, nutrients would leach from the soil, and the quality of the water in the reservoir would decline. Reducing the deer population seemed the logical step toward protecting the drinking water for 2.4 million people in the greater Boston area and, at the same time, preserving the future of the forest.

Despite careful planning, research, and public education, the agency's decision to stage a controlled hunt erupted into controversy. Local animal-rights activists chained themselves to a radiator at the agency's Boston headquarters.[1] Protesters marched down a highway adjacent to the reservoir. Their signs exclaimed "Stop the Slaughter!" and "Bald Eagles and Shotgun Blasts Don't Mix!" A lawsuit was filed. At public meetings, angry citizens derided the agency manager. "Your past forest management practices have

152

failed!" some exclaimed. Others declared, "This is just a front. Your hidden agenda is to log the forest and let everyone use it as they please." "It's the agency, stupid, not the deer," the MDC's critics asserted. The agency moved ahead, but the protest continued.

After the first hunt, animal-rights activists held a vigil for the 576 deer killed. One of the activist leaders told those gathered: "Two weeks ago, I lost 576 of my closest friends. Another activist said: "This decision to kill the Quabbin deer was a betrayal. War was waged against the deer."[2] In turn, local hunters, wildlife experts, and other supporters of the hunt wrote to the local papers defending the agency's actions. One hunter said, after observing the stunted growth of the Quabbin deer, "The healthiest creature I saw during my three-day hunt was the CEASE [animal rights group] member dressed like a deer, running through the woods prior to arrest."[3] In response to these comments, opponents wrote back denouncing hunters as "idiots," "rednecks," and "killers."

A public agency had on its hands, not a dispute over an accident, or a fight about uncertain risks (though uncertainty surely played a role in the debate), but a dispute about what is right and what is good. Deeply held values were at stake. The very meaning of life was at issue. How could these contending forces possibly find common ground? To one group, deer were innocent creatures that should be left alone; to the other, they were an impediment to protecting the integrity of the public water supply. While activists insisted on the deers' right "to be," public officials emphasized that the deer were a public resource. To kill or not to kill? To toy with mother nature or to leave her alone—this was the gist of the Quabbin deer-hunt debate. How might such fundamental differences in values be bridged?

There are a great many disputes, ranging from the use of animals in medical experimentation to the sale of infant formula in developing countries to the development of massive public-works projects on the untouched land of indigenous peoples, that are primarily disputes over values. When values collide, all sides tend to wrap themselves in the rhetoric of moral right and moral outrage. The other side is portrayed as ignorant at best and as inhuman at worst. Each side views itself as righteous, and, above all, as eminently reasonable, while it views the other side as unreasonable and even evil. Though these disputes are the most difficult of all to address, the mutual-gains approach to dealing with an angry public can help in these situations as well.

What Are Values?

In the preceding chapters, the concept of "interests" has been central to our arguments. "Interests," as William Ury, an anthropologist and mediator explains, are "needs, desires, concerns, or fears—the things one cares about or wants. They underlie people's positions—the tangible items they say they want."[4] Interests explain the positions that people take in any negotiation. In the siting of a risky facility, for example, opponents state in no uncertain terms: "We refuse to allow a cancer-causing incinerator to be located in our back yard!" While this statement outlines their position, several interests are likely to motivate or explain it. Such interests might include a basic concern for health, safety, and welfare; an interest in fairness; the desire to maintain their property values; and the right to make, or at least influence, decisions about their own neighborhood.

When conflicts revolve around interests, numerous solutions are possible. Since individuals and groups usually have numerous interests, it is usually possible with creativity and hard work to find a deal that satisfies many, if not all, of the interests involved. Mutual-gains negotiation, or integrative bargaining as it is called in the theoretical literature, is about advancing self-interest through the invention of "packages" that meet interests on all sides. However, interests are not always the only thing at stake. Fundamental values may be involved as well. For instance, the opponents of an incinerator may be concerned about more than their own safety or local autonomy. They may believe that incinerators are inherently wrong.

An argument based on fundamental values might sound something like this: "Incinerators are emblematic of a deeper and more disturbing problem—Americans consume too much, and they waste too much. They pollute the natural world and use up a disproportionate share of the world's natural resources. This is morally wrong. If Americans consumed less and recycled more, incinerators and all their dreadful impacts would not exist in the first place." It is not merely that incinerator opponents have economic or environmental interests at stake. As mediator Christopher Moore explains: "Values disputes focus on such issues as guilt and innocence, what norms should prevail in a social relationship, what facts should be considered valid, what beliefs are correct, who merits what, or what principles should guide decision-making."[5] Values involve strongly held personal beliefs, moral and ethical principles, basic legal rights, and, more generally, idealized views of the world. While interests are about what we want, values are about what we care about and what we stand for.

Thinking back to the agency manager involved in the controversy over the deer hunting, we can see more clearly what he was up against. He was trying to convince the public that the excess deer should be killed so that the forest, and ultimately the drinking water for Boston, could be protected. His opponents believed that the lives of deer have a status equivalent to those of human beings. No additional information about forest management or improvements in communication will defuse the stand-off: two world views are in conflict.

Why Are Value Conflicts So Difficult to Resolve?

We believe that the public is especially angry when its beliefs have been ignored or ridiculed, because basic notions of self-worth are at stake. Values are not only about what we hold dear, but fundamentally about who we are. In the words of social psychologist Terrell Northrup, "Identity is defined as an abiding sense of the self and of the relationship of the self to the world. It is a system of beliefs or a way of construing the world that makes life predictable rather than random."[6] Debates involving values are not only about what we want, but also who we think we are and who we think "they" are in relation to us. Debates involving values upset our view of the world and ourselves.

In value-laden debates, to compromise or to accommodate neither advances one's self-interest nor increases joint gains. Compromise, in its most pejorative sense, means abandoning deeply held beliefs, values, or ideals. To negotiate away values is to risk giving up one's identity. Thus, such conflicts are intense.

Northrup details several stages through which value disputes move toward intractability. Intense conflict begins when individuals feel threatened. The threat is perceived as an awful trade-off: either you survive or I do. For example, in the Israeli-Palestinian conflict, both groups associate their national and religious identity with Jerusalem. For one to have control of the city is to desecrate a primary symbol of the other's national and religious identity. Once threatened, according to Northrup, distortion almost automatically occurs. For example, if a racist WASP father discovers that his son is marrying an African-American woman, he may feel threatened because "the other" is about to become part of his family, or part of him. In response, in order to maintain his belief system in the face of this perceived threat, the father distorts the situation. He might deny that the woman is African-American—arguing to himself and others that she is really Spanish because her parents were born in Cuba. He may make an exception to his strict belief—she is all right because she has a college degree and is a white-collar worker and she talks the way I do. Or the father may ostracize the future daughter-in-law, refusing to attend the marriage, or he may even disown his son.

After the perceived threat and subsequent distortion have occurred, over time individuals, groups, or even nations begin to develop increasingly rigid explanations of their own actions and the actions of others. In order to maintain the integrity of our beliefs and our sense of self, we increasingly rely on stereotypes of others. Furthermore, as numerous psychologists have pointed out, behaviors that we find disgusting or distasteful in ourselves are projected onto our "enemies." As this process continues, the enemy becomes dehumanized and is seen not merely as different, but as subhuman or inhuman. This process is most often seen in wartime: Germans become "Huns," Japanese become "Japs," and North Vietnamese become "Gooks." As this rigidification and stereotyping occurs, the capacity to justify violence increases. Extremists can rationalize as follows: "If those who commit abortions are murdering unborn babies, then perhaps they are nothing more than butchers. If they are nothing more than callous, unfeeling, morally degenerate butchers, then they are nothing more, really, than savage beasts. If they are savage beasts that threaten life, then it is perfectly sensible to stop them, with all means possible, before they kill again." Such reasoning, carried to its radical end, justifies and supports violent behavior.

In Northrup's final stage, maintaining the conflict becomes central to each party's identity. To maintain their own values, the groups in the conflict must keep the conflict alive. Ironically, this creates an implicit and often tragic agreement among the parties that Northrup labels "collusion." Over time, groups, cultures, and nations institutionalize behaviors and beliefs which maintain long-standing conflicts. For example, in certain conflicts between nations, the "hawks" on both sides tend, intentionally or not, to support one other's cause. An explosion in a crowded market placed by an extreme left-wing group leads the right-wing group on the other side to call for more law and order. Increased law and order is seen as further evidence of oppression in the eyes of the left, justifying more terrorist acts. By continuing the conflict, each side encourages behavior in their adversaries that provides further evidence for continuing the conflict, and consequently, for maintaining the identities that have now become enmeshed in the ongoing feud.

As the examples above suggest, the identity of an individual is not merely bound up with personal tastes, likes, and dislikes, but with fundamental identification. Individual identities are almost always intertwined with ethnicity, race, religion, or nationality. Those attempting to protect their social identity can act in violent or extreme ways that they would never feel were justified if they were being attacked solely as individuals. To make an obvious point, murder, except in self-defense, is rarely sanctioned in a "civilized" society, but killing during war is not only acceptable, but compulsory. When individuals feel their social identity is being threatened, they can react with extraordinary force. As political philosopher Stephen Holmes pointed out, "It is manifestly easier to be cruel when you act in the name of others, or in the name of an ideal, or even for the benefit of your victim, than when you act for your own sake."[7]

As Northrup indicates, the cohesiveness of a group is often less well-maintained by shared preferences than it is by a common threat. Indeed, a common enemy can shore up divisiveness at home and compel individuals to work together. Thus, when an individual in a threatened group notes that someone from the "other side" has a valid point or a legitimate concern, that individual is often portrayed as a traitor, or sell-out. People's need to collectively protect their social identity (at times, even at the expense of their own lives) can undermine even the best-intentioned efforts to resolve disagreements peacefully.

When conflict has been going on for some time, it may become difficult to pinpoint what started the feud. Anthony Oberschall, in his book *Social Movements*, notes that the original issues at stake—animal rights versus human rights, or anti-abortion versus pro-choice—become entangled in "derivative issues." Derivative issues concern the way that institutions and their critics handle escalating conflict. Did the authorities ignore the critics' initial concerns, discounting them, and, thus adding insult to injury? Did the opponents, feeling slighted, resort to tactics such as demonstrations or outrageous acts rather than civil discussion? Did the authorities, in response, use rough tactics to quell dissent? Did the opponents, in retaliation, resort to violence—bombings, break-ins, and vandalism? Action, reaction, and retaliation, along with blame, are all knotted together.[8]

At this stage, as Vamik Volkan, a psychoanalyst, says, "Aggression bonds enemies together so that tensions recreating and perpetuating themselves become a source of dynamic energy."[9] Unfortunately, efforts to de-escalate such conflicts are all too often thwarted by this dynamic energy and the mutual hostility that has come to define the identities of the parties. Volkan argues that at this point not merely rage is operating, but hatred. Rage is focused on the thing (be it a person or object) that frustrates a person from obtaining what he wants. (In the words of object relations, the ego's desire for an object is thwarted.) Hatred is bound up not only with the external thing, but with the psyche of the person doing the hating. A mental image of the hated is formed, internalized, and becomes, strangely enough, a part of the person who then must confront and combat this image, even in the absence of the enemy. The conflict becomes internal as well as external. Volkan concludes: "Hatred may become an essential element from which one derives a sense of self-sameness and upon which one formulates one's identity."[10]

At worst, then, value conflicts become intricately bound up with *who* people perceive themselves to be. The very thought of meeting with the other side becomes impossible because any acknowledgment of the other gives the enemy recognition and legitimacy and, at the same time, might shatter one's own painfully won sense of self. Honor and respect are reserved for one's own, not one's enemies. This, of course, makes dialogue, a mainstay of the mutual-gains approach, difficult if not impossible. Original issues become mixed with derivative issues, hopelessly complicating matters. Trust breaks down completely, and extremists take charge.

A Model for Deescalating Intractable Conflicts

Given the intensity of these intractable conflicts, what, if anything, can be done? Northrup suggests that there are three levels at which conflicts involving fundamental values and identities can be addressed. At the *first level*, the disputants may agree on peripheral changes that do not eliminate the ongoing hostilities but alleviate specific problems. For example, in the wake of the killing of two employees at a Planned Parenthood clinic in Brookline, Massachusetts, Bernard Cardinal Law of Boston called for a temporary moratorium on sidewalk demonstrations and asked protesters to move their vigils inside churches. The Catholic Church has worked, in other instances, with pro-choice groups to ensure the protection of those who elect to utilize and work in family-planning clinics. At this level, both sides hold fast to their basic principles. Pro-life Catholics continue to oppose abortion and support demonstrations. Pro-choice groups continue to support a woman's right to choose abortion. However, when they focus on the goal of minimizing violence, it is possible to reach agreement on specific steps that can be taken. Unfortunately, such agreements have little effect on the basic conflict.

Second-level changes alter some aspects of the ongoing relationship, but fundamental values are not challenged or transformed, at least in the short run. Agreements reached at this level focus on how the parties will relate to one another over time, as opposed to merely how one specific situation or problem will be solved. For instance, in Missouri, the director of an abortion clinic, an attorney opposing abortion, and a board member of a Missouri right-to-life group agreed to meet to discuss adoption, foster care, and abstinence for teenagers. Surprisingly, these groups agreed to support legislation to pay for the treatment of pregnant drug addicts. They also established an ongoing dialogue that transformed the way they dealt with each other. For instance, they began to meet individually, on a personal basis, to work on problems they had in common.

Third-level change is far more difficult. This kind of change involves shifts in the identities that people hold dear. Not only are working relationships changed at this level, but the way people view themselves is altered. Northrup uses the example of psychotherapy to illustrate his point. In psychotherapy, an individual's core constructs are examined, faulty constructs are discarded, and the individual develops a transformed sense of self over time. On a far broader scale, the civil rights movement in the United States accomplished something similar on a societal level. Through the initiation of discrimination cases over many years, the exercise of leadership from Rosa Parks to Martin Luther King, Jr., and the peaceful mass protest of millions of Americans, white and black, the way both groups saw themselves was transformed. Blacks rose to power as mayors of major cities. African-Americans began to fill the ranks of corporate middle and even sometimes upper management. While racism and prejudice are hardly eradicated here, millions of Americans today do see themselves and others in a fundamentally different and more common light.

In the practical world of day-to-day management, we do not think it is likely that any one institution, be it a corporation or a government agency, can bring changes at the third level. These must be accomplished over a long period of time by numerous individuals, organizations, and institutions working together. It is important to note, though, that changes at the first and second levels frequently set the stage for third-level changes. The mutual-gains approach can help to prevent (or help to transform) protracted conflict over clashing values by encouraging leaders to acknowledge the concerns of the other side and to solve immediate problems that get in the way of relationship building. The mutual-gains approach encourages leaders to respect differences, listen to people's concerns, and make decisions openly. While third-level changes may be hard to achieve, the mutual-gains approach can help institutions to avoid the distraction of derivative issues by forestalling behaviors, tempting though they may be, that exacerbate disagreement and animosity. Two cases—the story of hydroelectric development at James Bay in Quebec and the animal-rights debate—pinpoint the pitfalls of values disputes and the possible alternatives to traditional ways of handling them.

Hydro-Quebec and the Cree: Clashing Cultures

The people at the mouth of the Great Whale River, the Crees and the Inuit, have built Odeyak, half canoe and half kayak, to make a journey. . . . Odeyak will symbolize the flood that is about to come again over our land. Odeyak will symbolize our own journey through life. We will carry our message: we are the victims of environmental racism. *Statement made to the Grand Council of the Crees of Quebec before the launching of the Odeyak.*

On Earth Day in April 1990, a group of Cree, one of the two indigenous peoples of the James Bay peninsula of northern Quebec, paddled down the Hudson River in a native vessel called an *odeyak*. They had portaged the craft across the winter snows of northern Quebec to Montreal. For six weeks they paddled, until they reached New York City. That trip plus follow-up public relations efforts over the next several months garnered support from more than 100 organizations including the Sierra Club, Greenpeace, and the National Audubon Society. Why did the Cree journey 1,500 miles from their homeland in the low-lying blueberry bogs and scraggly black spruce forest to the concrete-clad streets of New York?

Hailed as the "project of the century" by then Quebec provincial leader Robert Bourassa, the James Bay (Phase I) Hydroelectric Project was begun in 1973. After 12 years, 14 billion Canadian dollars, 150 million person-hours of labor, over 447,343 tons of cement and 262,400,000 tons of earthen fill, Hydro-Quebec completed the five major reservoirs of the LaGrande River complex. In March 1989, with the massive $14-billion undertaking complete, the world's fourth largest hydroelectric utility, Hydro-Quebec, announced Phase II of the project. This $12.7-billion (Canadian) project included plans to dam eight more rivers north of the LaGrande River, including the Great Whale River, to generate 3,212 megawatts of electricity from 3,400 square kilometers of flooded land.

For the Quebecois, the entire James Bay project has been a source of national pride. The Quebecois value dearly their French language, their French customs, and their cultural distinctness from the rest of Canada. The James Bay project proved to the world that Quebec was technologically sophisticated, economically developed, and capable of energy (and presumably political) independence. In a book authored in 1985 entitled *Power from the North*, Bourassa wrote: "[Northern Quebec] is a vast hydroelectric project-in-the-bud and every day millions of potential kilowatt hours flow downhill and out to the sea. What a waste!" Lysiane Gagnon, a Quebecois columnist, wrote: "Northern waters are to Quebec what oil is to Alberta: an invaluable natural resource, a precious source of energy, a tremendous economic asset."[11] With a painful recession and unemployment hovering above 11 percent, the project's undertaking gained even greater urgency. Organized labor, major business organizations, and the major political parties in Quebec backed the project.

For the Cree, the massive damming of their hunting and fishing territories, along with the influx of the modern world, has not been a blessing. The first phase of the James Bay project brought harmful and unexpected change to the northern native communities. The influx of organic material caused by flooding altered the insoluble mercury that naturally occurred in the region's rocks and soil, changing it into soluble methyl mercury, a substance ten times as toxic. Because methyl mercury is assimilated into nerve and muscle tissue, fish can contain concentrations 100 million times greater than surrounding waters. By 1984, nine years after the project began, two-thirds of the Cree living in the village of Chisasibi were found to have mercury levels exceeding the World Health Organization's exposure standard. Ten percent of Cree sampled in 1985 had mercury levels high enough to put them at risk of developing neurological symptoms. In response, the Cree were told to restrict their intake of fish, a mainstay of the native diet. As the General Secretary of the utility said: "All they have to do is change some of their fishing habits for a while."[12]

Other physical and social diseases also followed from the development. Obesity, heart disease, and diabetes, previously almost unknown in this population, increased dramatically. Alcohol and drug abuse, spouse abuse, unemployment, and teenage suicide increased. As many as three suicide attempts a week were recorded. As *Amicus Journal* pointed out, it was as if 3,500 people a week made attempts in a city of one million.[13] Violet Pachanos, elected chief of the Chisasibi band council, said, "What we have said is that yes, our life is in many ways much easier now than it used to be. But we are also prey to all the social diseases of the south. We are no longer in control of our lives."[14] The former mayor of the Inuit in Great Whale perhaps summed it up most poignantly. He said of the region's newfound progress, "Well, my children can choose from six different kinds of potato chips. . . . I suppose that is a kind of progress."[15]

The canoe journey to New York brought the Cree's plight to the attention of major American environmental groups and the media. Soon, a flurry of organizing, letter writing, and media advertising began. The New York Power Authority, considering the purchase of power from Hydro-Quebec, informed the company that they disapproved of a split environmental review allowing the construction of roads (to the project site) prior to the completion of a full environmental review. Within the year, New York City's Mayor David Dinkins requested that the Authority delay any contract for one year to reconsider whether the power was really needed. Nine Vermont municipalities considered power purchases from Quebec, but later on four, including Burlington, the state's largest city, voted against such power contracts. In New York City, a "Ban the Dam Jam for James Bay" was held with numerous famous rock acts including Jackson Browne and David Byrne. Several environmental advocacy groups took out a full-page ad in the *New York Times* calling the James Bay project "the most destructive energy project ever in North America." The Cree's plight came before the United Nations Commission on Human Rights. The Cree also presented their case before the International Water Tribunal Foundation in Amsterdam.

Hydro-Quebec's Response to the Cree

How did Hydro-Quebec respond to the Cree's public-relations campaign? In response to the ad in the *New York Times*, Robert Bourassa asked, "How can you seriously consider those ads in the *New York Times*?"[16] He was also reported to have said, "Seven million Quebecois can't be wrong." One Cree chief countered, "The premier seems to have suggested that it doesn't matter if you kill 1,000 people—there are seven million people who need this. Is he God?"[17] The Minister of Energy, Lise Bacon, responded to the U.S. environmental ad campaign by stating: "I find this article insulting to Quebecois, beneath the dignity of a Cree nation that wants to be respected." She also said, "I'll ask him [Mercredi, Chief of the Assembly of First Nations in Canada] perhaps to get a better hold on his Quebec troops. If they want to insult us, they can do it at the bargaining table. I don't negotiate with them in public."[18]

Of course, Bacon's "I don't negotiate in public" remark had particular resonance in the public debate. During the Vermont referenda, it had been revealed that Hydro-Quebec had struck secret "sweetheart" deals with multinational aluminum-smelting plants. The plants received subsidies without the knowledge of the Canadian or American public. In one deal, Hydro-Quebec had agreed to sell power that cost 2.4 cents per kilowatt-hour to produce at a price of 1.5 cents per kWh. To make matters worse, the province had supported the company in forbidding the Quebec press to make mention of these favorable contracts. The Cree happened upon this secret deal when their attorney filed a routine access-to-information request. The Cree had hoped to use this information to estimate Quebec's energy needs. But when the Cree attorney showed up at an access hearing, one he expected to be simply pro forma, Hydro-Quebec arrived with a cadre of its own lawyers. The Cree attorney said, "We said, if they're reacting so strongly, it's because there's something very, very fishy about it."[19] When the less-than-public dealing came to light through a leak, even the Parti Québécois, staunch supporters of Quebec's energy independence, demanded that the injunction against public broadcast be lifted.

Despite the Cree's opposition and the growing public controversy, the province and the company plowed on. Hydro-Quebec and the Province refused to participate in a federal environmental review. Claiming provincial autonomy over environmental matters, Lise Bacon said: "We will not accept being subject to orders that come from a federal committee."[20] When a New York legislative committee met in early October of 1991 to review its $17 billion contract with Hydro-Quebec, the company refused even to attend the hearing. One company spokeswoman said: "New York is not the right place to decide the future of hydro projects in Quebec."[21] Another company spokesman said, "The contention that Canada can't conduct its own economic review is not only insulting, but it has no basis in fact."[22] An official from the Canadian Arctic Resources Council expressed quite different sentiments at the New York hearing: "It's somewhat embarrassing for Canadians to have to come to New York for a hearing on the James Bay project."[23]

Despite Hydro-Quebec's efforts to avoid a federal environmental review, a Canadian federal court judge ruled that, under the 1975 James Bay

Northern Quebec Agreement, the Great Whale project had to be submitted for federal review. Within a month, the province announced its own all-inclusive environmental impact assessment. The plan to separate the assessment of preliminary road construction from the dam construction was dropped. Despite this reconsideration, the project's supporters remained obstinate. When Lise Bacon was asked what would happen if the project did not pass the environmental review, she flatly stated, "We'll go nuclear, that's our answer."[24] When asked what had influenced their change of heart with regard to the environmental assessment, Bacon responded that " . . . it has nothing to do with pressure from the Cree, it has nothing to do with pressure from environmentalists, it has nothing to do with pressure from anyone."[25]

Talking With, Not At, the Other: The Mutual-Gains Approach

Mercredi, the Chief of the First Nations Assembly, once said, "The problem with this province is that there is no debate, there is no dialogue. I don't understand why people who are champions of their own rights, their language, their culture and their self-determination cannot come to the realization that we are comrades."[26] The debate surrounding James Bay II revolved around stark contrasts in both values and power: modern technology versus traditional technology; resource exploitation versus respect and care for nature; Western European-based culture versus indigenous culture; the strong versus the weak; and corporate interests versus individual interests. Ironically, both "sides" were seeking recognition of, and respect for, cultural autonomy and sovereignty. But in Hydro-Quebec's and Quebec's overwhelming need to hold the reins of power, in their intense effort to assert their own autonomy, they ended up ignoring and debasing the very principles they held dear when it came to dealing with the Cree.

Seek Common Principles—Despite Seemingly Stark Differences

Mercredi's insight provides an important lesson for companies and governments dealing with an angry public: Seek common principles—despite seemingly stark differences.

What if, instead of attempting to bulldoze forward, the province and its utility had taken the time to acknowledge the shared value of autonomy? What if Quebec and the utility had sought to underscore their respect for the Cree, just as they sought such recognition for themselves in federal constitutional negotiations? What if the province had said, "Yes, autonomy is of utmost importance to us, as it is to you. Therefore, might we sit down and discuss how best we can respect this common principle while serving our separate interests?"

Of course, we cannot know for sure what would have happened. We do know, though, that New York State voted to conduct its own environmental review of the project. We also know that the Cree were able to enlist the support of celebrities such as Jackson Browne, James Taylor, and Robert Kennedy, Jr., a well-connected environmental lawyer. We know that two New England colleges divested themselves of $8 million in Hydro-Quebec bonds, and that the *New York Times Magazine, National Geographic,* and the *New Scientist* wrote pieces skeptical of the proposed project. We know that the Cree felt compelled to seek redress in federal courts, international forums, and the media. Had Hydro-Quebec been able to emphasize the principle of autonomy, which linked them in spite of their differing interests, the company might have had a basis for initiating useful bilateral negotiations.

Why appeal to shared principles? We think that a reference to common values can alter adversarial relations by validating the core identity of others who value those same principles. As Northrup suggests, principles and identity are inextricably linked. If someone attacks our fundamental values, he attacks us. Once our identity is under attack, we have little choice but to defend ourselves: our survival depends on it. However, if someone recognizes a principle that is important to us, then we not only have something in common, but we feel less threatened, less that our survival is at stake. The more secure we are in our identity, the easier it is to focus on finding a resolution of our differences.

Appealing to shared principles can reframe a debate. Had Hydro-Quebec and the province suggested that hydro development in the North was inextricably bound up with the common quest of the two cultures for recognition and autonomy, the debate between them might have changed. In addition, a clear recognition of autonomy as a significant concern of both "sides" would have also more clearly brought to light another feature of the conflict: the countervailing notion of interdependence. Consumers in the northeastern United States were benefiting from electricity generated in Quebec; it was cheaper than many other sources and did not produce harmful emissions from the burning of fossil fuels (though hydropower production is not without environmental costs, as the James Bay I project painfully proved). In turn, the use of Hydro-Quebec electricity by U.S. consumers was affecting the lives of the Cree and their landscape. The light in a Manhattan apartment was connected, however indirectly, to the waters where Cree fisherman fished. If autonomy was a shared value, how might this common value be balanced with the fact that the actions of one political entity (be it a tribe, province, or nation) were having significant effects on many others?

Complexities such as these suggest that focusing on, and bringing to light, common principles will not, in itself, eliminate conflict. However, acknowledging shared values can be an important stepping-stone to more productive dialogue. Appealing to shared principles can help to begin the conversation. Without face-to-face dialogue conflict will almost certainly remain intractable.

> *Prescription 1: Search for shared or overarching principles on which to base a continuing dialogue.*

Consider That You Might Be Wrong

An important element in dealing with values disputes involves getting all sides to look inward. When values disputes arise, it is important to get each organization and individual to admit that they might be mistaken. Instead of defending ourselves when attacked, we must consider the fact that the other side had good reasons to attack. In Hydro-Quebec's eyes, for instance, the Cree's charges required countercharges. The Cree were not merely challenging a multibillion-dollar energy project, they were attacking the hopes and dreams of thousands of politicians, managers, and engineers. Even after Quebec's new leader put the Great Whale project "on ice" in 1994, Hydro-Quebec officials refused to admit that they had done anything wrong. Jacques Guevremont, the utility's representative in the United States, told the *Hartford Courant* defiantly: "If [this project were] to disappear, what are you left with? Some people want Hydro-Quebec to disappear. It's very nice to say, but who is going to feed you electricity [in the future when demand once again increases]?"[27]

Unfortunately, this refusal to reconsider, while understandable, causes problems. There are at least two reasons why it is important to take the time, when faced with a dispute over values, to reconsider the merits of the positions all sides have taken. First, even if we continue to believe our "cause" is right, our critics may be suggesting a resolution of differences that benefits us even more on a more practical level. Second, simply put, we may be wrong. Defending an unethical or incorrect position may hurt our ability to pursue our own interests over time.

Was Hydro-Quebec wrong? The Cree certainly thought so. The public outcry suggested so. The markets for electricity, at least for the while, indicated that they were. The final environmental impact reviews from both Canada's federal and provincial governments concluded that they were. On the other hand, time tends to render a clearer verdict. It may be that in ten or twenty years Canada and the United States will desperately need the power Quebec could have supplied. It is also possible that the environmental damage done by dam building would have been far less than the impact of equivalent nuclear-power-, oil-, gas-, or coal-fired plants. In any case, one thing is for certain: The utility was never able to admit that the Cree had any legitimate concerns. It took a customer, an outsider, and a foreigner—the president of the New York Power Authority—to suggest that the Cree had grounds to complain.

When David Freeman, the 68-year-old leader of the New York Power Authority, canceled a 20-year, $5-billion contract with Hydro-Quebec in 1994 (which was supposed to extend from 1999 to 2018), he cited financial and environmental reasons for doing so. Freeman did not hesitate to explain that the decision was based on flattened power demand. But he added, because he heard his customers' concerns, that the impacts on the environment and on the Cree were also of concern to the Power Authority. Furthermore, as he put it, "We've just about cleaned out nature's store down here in the United States, and it's precisely because we've done such a bad job with our own environment that we think we're in a position to warn you folks up in Canada about some of the mistakes we've made."[28] Freeman explained how the Tennessee Valley Authority had flooded the ancestral lands of the Cherokee, perhaps needlessly. This experience was enough, for him, to raise concern about the Cree. Freeman's statements, which, of course, earned the applause of environmentalists and the Cree, were certainly never spoken by Hydro-Quebec officials.

Shortly after Quebec Premier Jacques Parizeau came to power, he shelved the Great Whale project. "The grand dream is over," he told the press. "Former premier Robert Bourassa dreamed of exporting 12,000 megawatts. Well, we're only exporting 1,000. Contracts were canceled."[29] The new premier did not actually cancel the project because he agreed that the Cree "were right." Rather, it did not make business sense to continue. Had the utility been able to make this decision earlier *and* in a different way, they would have saved a substantial amount of money and won enormous good-will throughout the United States and Europe.

When parties focus primarily on their respective positions, such as "no build" or "build," great amounts of energy are spent shoring up these stands, whether or not they have substantive merit. In times of conflict, as in times of war, admitting weaknesses is tantamount to colluding with the enemy. Unfortunately, this leads disputing parties to discount new information that might improve their ability to satisfy their interests. While the Cree framed the public debate in terms of values, they also focused a great deal of their effort to analyzing why, in quite practical terms, the Great Whale project was economically unfeasible. When they came to the United States, they enlisted experts who agreed that the power produced by the massive project would not be needed, at least for the immediate future. The demand for electric power was leveling off. The cancellation of two contracts by the New York Power Authority, one in 1992 for $13 billion and one in 1994 for $5 billion, proved this. American utilities were finding that it was more cost-effective, in many instances, to "produce" power and reduce the environmental impacts of electricity production through greater conservation efforts—the installation of more efficient lighting, air conditioners, electric motors, and other equipment—and new pricing strategies. Quebec might have maintained its autonomy *and* addressed some of the Cree's concerns by seeking to develop energy conservation programs of its own, perhaps even with the support of the Cree.

Some energy experts in Quebec thought that the debate, however belated and painful, did bring Hydro-Quebec's energy planning into the 1990s. A spokeswoman for a Quebec energy-research group said, "The Cree brought the notion of replacing new projects with energy conservation. . . . The Cree have helped Quebec avoid making a serious mistake. They helped Quebec make the transition to a more modern way of doing things."[30] If Hydro-Quebec had been open to considering the evidence the Cree had submitted, without worrying about defending the position it had taken, it might have saved both its reputation and its money.

> *Prescription 2: Keep an open mind, be open to reason, and consider carefully that you might be wrong.*

Consider Substantial Community Improvement Through a Fair Process, Not Compensation Only for the Few

In the past, promoters of large-scale development, such as Hydro-Quebec, have made an unfortunate mistake. They have believed (or hoped), encouraged by numerous experts, that they could mitigate or compensate any negative impacts their projects might have. For instance, in 1975, the Cree and Inuit of James Bay settled for $231 million in return for granting Hydro-Quebec the right to develop extensive portions of their land. As James Bay II moved forward, the province and its utility assumed that they would negotiate further compensation.[31]

But in the spring of 1989, the Cree set a different course. While some Cree businessmen argued on behalf of the project, making note of the economic gains it would bring, delegates from Whapmagoostui—Great Whale—argued that they did not want the same problems that plagued the southern villages as a result of James Bay I. The elders decided to fight, not as a negotiating tactic to gain more money from the utility, but on principle. "Enough is enough; we want to preserve our way of life," they asserted. In March of 1989, when the Cree announced their decision, a reporter asked Chief Coon Come, "'How much money do you want? What's your bottom line?"[32] Coon Come later noted, ". . . [W]e weren't interested in making a deal. We were sincere. Our people knew all about the damage the first phase of the project had caused . . . and they didn't want to see it happen again."[33]

The utility was willing to pay handsomely. What was wrong with their strategy? According to economic theory, nothing. The winners in public decisions ought to be able to compensate the losers, to make them whole. If developments are truly valued by society, then there ought to be sufficient "gain" so that a tax on the gainers can be used to compensate the losers. This seemed to work in 1975. In that negotiation, the Cree received hundreds of millions of dollars. They also obtained a police force, a school board, and health and social services. Infant mortality rates went down and life expectancy increased. They negotiated a hunter-and-trapper-security program that guaranteed a minimum income of some $10,000 for those who spent at least 125 days each year in the bush. They gained exclusive jurisdiction over some of their lands, autonomy they had lost in 1912 when all Cree ancestral lands were turned over to Quebec without their consent. Ironically, the money the Cree gained in the 1975 deal enabled them to fight Great Whale. During the five-year battle from 1989 to 1994, the Cree spent more than

$8 million on the campaign, hiring energy experts to estimate long-term energy demand, soliciting the services of Hill and Knowlton, a large public-relations firm, and enlisting attorneys to handle various legal skirmishes.[34]

On the other hand, the Cree had already experienced, under James Bay I, major increases in mercury poisoning, alcoholism, domestic violence, and teenage suicide. Traditional burial, hunting, and fishing grounds had been submerged. Numerous fishing spots along the wild northern rapids, key not only to the subsistence economy but also to the mythology and folklore of the tribe, had been lost. In practice, it seems, the assumption of the "winners" being able to compensate the "losers" financially had not worked. Why? It is not possible to counterbalance with financial compensation the increased risk of mercury poisoning, alcoholism, family violence, and teenage suicide. As one reporter put it: "For the natives, it is equivalent to the citizens of French Canada being told by a group of outside agitators that while they'll be financially compensated, from now on they can no longer enjoy the benefits of Quebecois culture, including the food they eat and the way they spend their spare time."[35]

We all make implicit trade-offs. Some people trade the safety of a helmet for the thrill of riding a motorcycle with the wind in their hair. Some trade living closer to a nuclear-power plant for lower housing prices. Some trade a probable longer life span for the pleasure (or habit) of smoking. When made explicit, these trade-offs can be used to derive an estimate of how much the community seems to "value" a life. When asked to do so directly, however, some people react with aversion: "We won't sell out for a few lousy dollars! We won't put our children's lives on the line for $100,000!" Experts have mistakenly reduced "values," in the broad sense, into a common but mistaken dollar measure. Beyond this, such "willingness-to-pay surveys" sidestep the problem of actually working out agreement together in a community with diverse views. The average that a group of interviewees might be willing to pay does not reflect the highest (i.e., incalculable) amounts demanded by a few extremists.

The question of how much compensation should be paid was not the only one at stake. The process for answering the question was riddled with concerns about fairness and due process. Civil engineers had drawn up their plans in the 1960s. Electrical engineers had designed power grids. Geologists had pondered maps. But neither the Cree nor the Inuit were informed of the project prior to its public announcement. No environmental assessment was ever undertaken (nor was one required by law, at the time). While a deal was negotiated in 1975, this "agreement" was marred by the fact that the Cree believed they had no choice but to accept a settlement to minimize the impacts the impending James Bay I project was certain to bring. Although the Cree won a temporary court injunction against the project in 1973, the injunction was soon overturned and the province was able to move ahead with construction. A senior member of the Canadian House of Commons argued at the time, "It is not acceptable that we approve of a process which has had the effect of forcing upon native people in a distant part of this land agreements which in all reasonable likelihood they would not have accepted had they been able to negotiate free of the constraints that were placed upon them."[36]

Even if the original agreement had been negotiated willingly, a Canadian justice [judge], Réjean Paul, concluded in 1991 that both the federal and provincial governments had been delinquent in honoring the intent of the treaty. The justice's Cree-Naskapi Commission accused the government of making agreements, and then repeatedly reneging. The less-than-thorough environmental review also raised doubts about the fairness of the decision. All major projects north of the 49th parallel were exempted from otherwise required public hearings. One Cree spokesperson described the lack of due process as "environmental racism," charging, "You can do what you please to the environment in Quebec if the only direct victims are indigenous people."[37] In the environmental assessment process, even when review committees incorporated Cree members they were in the minority. Their advice was only considered advisory, with the final decision remaining in the hands of government officials. In short, the Cree were not offered a fair process for incorporating their concerns into the decisions.

If indigenous peoples, and other groups adversely affected by proposed development, are going to accept additional risks in their lives, it will not be only because compensation is paid. Unless decision makers respond to a community's sense of its *own* needs, unless host communities find themselves, when all is said and done, better off in their own eyes, and unless decision makers include, rather than exclude, citizens in decision making, the affected people will continue to resist.

To escape the difficulties posed when values conflict, the planners of the Great Whale project, and others like it, should have proceeded with four principles in mind:

1. Fairness in process and substance matters, especially when there have been past inequities.

2. Discussion around the design and implementation of controversial developments requires meaningful input from all stakeholders.
3. A community must be left substantially better off if it is expected to
"host" a development.
4. Decision-makers (including citizens, as stated in principle 2) should
have access to the best technical advice available, but technicians should
not make what are essentially political decisions.

We can imagine a different process from the one used by Hydro-Quebec
that incorporates these four principles. This process would seek to achieve
substantial improvements in the lives of an affected group rather than merely
to offer "suitable" compensation, and it would keep the stakeholders engaged
in, rather than alienated from, the process.

Step 1: Principled Leadership. At the outset, key leaders (both in the private
and public sectors) would make it clear that the proposed development
would follow the four principles we have enunciated. Some leaders prefer to
avoid such principled statements for fear of locking themselves into commitments they cannot meet. But by not promising from the start a fair, inclusive, and technically proficient process that leaves the host community better
off, leaders sow the seeds of distrust that will block their efforts. Certainly,
in the case of James Bay II, both provincial and utility leaders generated
enormous hostility. They discounted the concerns of the Cree. They excluded the Cree from decision making. They assumed that financial compensation was sufficient. They took their case to the courts only to have the
Cree take their case, in turn, to the public.

Step 2: Informal Assessment. In addition to complex technical analyses justifying the development, an informal assessment—or stakeholder analysis—
should be undertaken to ensure that the needs of the affected community
are clear. This assessment could be completed in two steps. First, the
development's promoter ought to hire a professional facilitator to interview
community leaders, citizens, and opinion makers to better understand their
concerns. If the community does not have, or cannot identify, significant
needs, there will be little chance of framing the proposed development in a
way that will seem useful in the eyes of the community.

Some might say that, in the James Bay case, the Cree had no needs
around which to frame the negotiation, regardless of how great the needs of

the electricity consumers might have been. Was not the Cree's stand based solely on principle? Did they not want more than anything else to be left alone? That was not quite the case. Following the construction of James Bay I, the Cree population more than doubled—from 5,000 in 1975 to 12,000 in 1995. By 2005, the population is expected to reach 20,000. Even the vast Cree territory is becoming insufficient to meet the needs of this burgeoning population. The indigenous way of life is painfully, but irreversibly, changing. Wood-frame housing and trucks are replacing huts and canoes. Fur, once a staple of trade between the Cree and the Hudson Bay Trading Company, now provides, by some accounts, less than 5 percent of Cree income. Hunting and fishing account (depending on the source) for only 20 percent of Cree income.

As it turns out, the Cree community had many needs. After the Great Whale project was postponed, the Cree sat down with the provincial government to discuss numerous concerns. Topics of discussion included Quebec's financial participation in Cree community programs such as water distribution and sewerage, care of the elderly and disabled, economic development, revenue sharing from mining and forestry, and the development and operation of a regional government. This short list suggests that mere dollars were not what was most important. Instead, the Cree appeared to be looking for a partnership. As Coon Come told the Montreal press: "We've got to find how we can coexist . . . and how we, as Northerners, can be co-partners, be full participants and have a say on what happens in our own backyard."[38]

Step 3: Stakeholder Involvement. Once leaders have enunciated basic principles to guide the interaction, and the promoter has conducted an informal assessment of community needs, stakeholders must organize themselves. A professional neutral should be tapped to convene a citizens' forum. The informal needs assessment should have already identified key constituency groups to include in the citizens' forum. In the case of the Cree, stakeholder groups might have included church groups, tribal councils, health providers, and even outside advocacy groups with whom the community felt comfortable. If representatives of stakeholder groups are not obvious, the neutral can caucus various advisors to help clusters of organizations select representatives. It is incumbent upon the neutral to help identify and bring on board representatives of the community at large, even when such representatives are not obvious. In a case involving significant cultural differences, such as James Bay, it would be important to involve a neutral with significant experience with, and understanding of, the Cree's and Quebec's various conflict-handling mechanisms and traditional means of resolving disputes.

Step 4: Joint Assessment. Once the stakeholder group is convened, citizens should be engaged in improving upon the informal needs assessment conducted by the neutral. Practical solutions ought to be developed, and their costs ought to be ascertained with the aid of citizens. When discussions require technical know-how, the citizens' group ought to be provided access to specialized help, either through panels of experts selected from the community or through outside experts selected by the citizens' forum who can advise them on a continuing basis. Citizens ought to have a say, not only as to which technical experts are used, but also as to how technical studies are framed, interpreted, and presented to the public. In our view, Quebec's environmental review would not have been sufficient. The Cree, understandably, appealed to the federal government in the hope that its assessment would be fairer.

Step 5: Citizen or Consumer Choice. The next step can be a difficult one for many promoters to accept. They do not want to leave their fate in the hands of a community, especially an angry one. However, as the Cree's successful campaign suggests, the fates of many (though not all) development projects are, one way or another, influenced by the community that must bear the impacts. Once a "package" has been developed by the stakeholders interested in participating, the whole community ought to have the final say in accepting or rejecting the deal. This means a vote, referendum, or similar means of approval.

Because we would want to avoid substantial minorities within a community having to bear the cost of a facility that they truly believe will not leave them better off, the voting rule ought to involve more than a simple majority. Before voting, however, the citizens' forum should be careful to inform the community about the voting rule, the arguments for and against the package, and the guarantees and contingencies that have been negotiated. The forum might produce a newsletter, and cable-access television can broadcast forum meetings. The press should be kept up to date, and citizen representatives should be asked to report to their constituencies on a regular basis.

Step 6: Ongoing Learning. Once a development has been approved, the citizens' forum should not disband. The ongoing process should be keyed to seeking information (including the opinions of all stakeholders), using that information to make decisions (jointly with stakeholders), and gathering feedback to ensure that plans are proceeding as imagined. For instance, if impacts or risks, such as mercury poisoning, are worse than expected, then citizens ought to be involved in formulating revised mitigation strategies. If the community has been involved all along it is more likely to participate in and accept such revisions. If a portion of the package proves unrealistic, then stakeholders ought to decide what should happen instead. In short, the process should allow for ongoing learning and revision.

Rethinking Winners and Losers. The best developments make everyone a winner: the community whose residents' lives are improved; the citizens of the larger state, province, or nation; the government which has helped develop the project; and the developer who stands to make a fair profit. An ideal development would avoid a siting process in which the "profit-hungry" promoter, the "incompetent" state, and the "trouble-making" community are vilified. Of course, the best of all possible worlds is not the world we know. Even when mutual-gains principles are used properly, there are apt to be losers. We suspect those losers might include: (1) people who cannot demonstrate that they are worse off, but object to the development on grounds of principle; (2) people who are slightly worse off despite sincere efforts to make them better off; and (3) people who are posturing for personal (or political) gain.

The fact that there may be losers raises some very difficult questions. How far should those in favor of a development go to please the minority? What size minority is acceptable? We think that all development ought to aspire to make everyone better off. Long before the majority begins deciding just how many losers (perceived or real) are acceptable, supporters should promise to strive to leave absolutely no one worse off and make most everyone in the community substantially better off.

Of course, this may not always be possible. It may be too difficult to garner support from those most affected, who, no matter how much their community benefits, may believe that they personally stand to lose. Some individuals and groups may still oppose a development for fear of setting an unwanted precedent (even though it is difficult to say how well and how long such principled stands will measure up against the real gains an ideal development would bring).

We think a simple majority, and even a super majority, is not enough to justify a highly controversial development. Bourassa's purported statement,

"Seven million Quebecers can't be wrong," suggests the wrong voting rule. What if there were only a few hundred Cree left unhappy? What then? We suggest that a line ought to be drawn liberally to ensure that almost all parties in a host community perceive themselves as better off. Furthermore, these hard decisions must be made with, not for, the citizens in each community.

In the end, some parties will be left unhappy; perhaps, still angry. This is unavoidable. However, such tough decisions about how much minority dissent is acceptable will be easier if leaders adhere to stated principles, worry about the perceived fairness of the process, encourage the community to organize and think creatively, and work to forge innovative partnerships.

> *Prescription 3: Seek to achieve real gains and substantial improvements, as seen through critics' eyes, rather than offering "appropriate" compensation to offset significant losses.*

Ignoring the Principles of the Mutual-Gains Approach Intensifies Cultural Conflict

At every turn, in an attempt to maintain their independence and autonomy, officials from both the province and Hydro-Quebec alienated the public. When honesty and disclosure might have alleviated concern, or put accurate information on the table, the company instead denounced the Cree concerns and adamantly refused to share information. The company appeared indifferent and stubborn. Their attempts to thwart public opposition only increased criticism of the company. As one letter writer to the *Montreal Gazette* indicated, "If Hydro-Quebec is so sure that the further development of the James Bay complex will have no alarming impact on the environment, would it not be more reassuring if it made its findings public?"[39] The *Montreal Gazette* editorialized: "The Bourassa government and Hydro-Quebec are reaping the bitter fruits of their own arrogant mishandling of the Great Whale power project."[40]

The case of Hydro-Quebec and the Cree parallels many other crises. While the development of Northern Quebec certainly brought into sharp contrast vastly different cultures and highlighted the centuries-old mistreatment of indigenous peoples in North America, Hydro-Quebec's public-relations approach suggests that stonewalling exacerbates controversy, regardless of the cultural context. Hydro-Quebec belittled and ignored its critics. Secret dealings eroded trust. Hydro-Quebec, fiercely asserting its autonomy, refused to listen. This inflexibility encouraged the Cree to seek alliances in the United States and Europe. In time, Hydro-Quebec found itself facing an international array of opponents ranging from the New York Power Authority to international tribunals. The Hydro-Quebec case underscores, we hope, the dangers of the conventional decide-announce-defend approach to public relations, particularly when charges of racism and cultural insensitivity can be raised.

> *Prescription 4: Stonewalling, belittling, and ignoring critics, especially when cultural differences are involved, create misunderstanding, polarize opinion, and increase criticism.*

Animal Rights

"A rat is a pig is a dog is a boy." *Ingrid Newkirk, People for the Ethical Treatment of Animals*

"Animism should be aligned with quackery, cults, and terrorism." *John Vane, British Nobel Prize winner*

"I believe more strongly than ever that animal research is a moral abomination that will come to be viewed as one of the foulest events in human history." *Steve Siegal, Trans-Species, Unlimited*

"[They] are nothing more than animal rights terrorists . . . [who] have tried to foster a siege mentality among our scientists and at our nation's laboratories." *Louis W. Sullivan, M.D., former U.S. Secretary of Health and Human Services*

These are some of the voices in the debate over animal rights and the use of animals in scientific research. On the side of "science," the critics of animal-rights activists cite the numerous cases where violent means have been used against upstanding scientists, destroying years of careful planning and experimentation. In April of 1987, animal rights terrorists set fire to the University of California at Davis' Veterinary Diagnostic Laboratory, causing $4.5 million in damages. In April of 1989, some 1,000 animals were released by activists from laboratories at the University of Arizona and words like "scum" and "Nazis" were painted on the walls. In February of 1992, terrorists set fire to a mink research lab, causing about $75,000 in damage and destroying 32 years of research. Researchers, such as world-renowned heart surgeon Dr. Michael DeBakey, exclaimed: "If these people succeed, they're going to destroy the research that will lead to cures of disease and treatment of health."[41]

On the side of "morality," the critics of scientific research involving animals cite numerous instances in which violence has been directed against helpless creatures. In 1976, activists used letter writing, picketing and even bomb threats to get the American Museum of Natural History in New York City to halt its studies of the neurological bases of sexual behavior because they involved injuring experimental animals—cats in this case—by removing part of their brains, severing nerves in their genitals, and destroying their sense of smell. In 1981, one activist, posing as a volunteer, exposed a laboratory that severed the nerves of the limbs of macaques and rhesus monkeys as part of a neurological research project. The activists found monkeys in filthy cages attacking their own numb limbs, no longer able to recognize their arms as their own. In 1985, activists released 650 animals from the University of California at Riverside, including a baby macaque monkey whose eyes had been stitched shut as part of a sight-deprivation research project.

Listening Whether You Agree or Not: The Mutual-Gains Approach

The animal-rights debate has been presented in rhetorical extremes, or as a "clash of absolutes," to borrow a phrase from Laurence Tribe.[42] Human life is set against animal life. The possibility of relieving human pain and suffering through scientific research is set against the reality of injuring and killing animals to achieve this end. Not surprisingly, such debates soon become personalized. They are transformed, as Northrup points out, from disagreements over principles and values to distortions and increasingly rigid "ideologies" about the perceived "enemy." A rhetorical chasm opens up between the contending camps. It is as if the parties were at war—neither side acknowledging the other, neither side granting the other any legitimacy.

Is there a way out? Can such a divide be bridged? Can the parties at least find a way to talk to each other across the gap?

Examine History to Better Understand Today

In a culture that values the fleeting present and is often ignorant of past events, it may appear as if one controversy arises after another—like the newest pop record, clothing fashion, or crazy fad—seemingly out of nowhere. However, debates over values often recur over extended periods. Furthermore, the content of each episode may be unique, but the underlying debate goes on. An understanding of, and appreciation for, the long history of such value disputes can provide clues to their resolution. Furthermore, by understanding the history of a dispute, we can better understand our critics, an important step toward productive dialogue.

Some of the critics of the modern-day animal-rights movement act as if the animal-rights movement arose out of nowhere, driven by a few fanatical crackpots. More cautious critics suggest that the activists are disassociated from the "realities" of life, that they are being unrealistic. One critic explained the rise of the animal rights movement partly in terms of increased urbanization. "Many American[s] no longer need to come in direct contact with farms or wildlife. To them, milk comes from a carton, not a cow."[43]

However, the concern for animals and the opposition to their use in experimentation appears to have a much longer history. The animal rights movement has arisen out of a long history of animal protection. Harriet Ritvo of the Massachusetts Institute of Technology (MIT) points out that lay criticism of animal experimentation accompanied the dawning of the scientific revolution in the seventeenth century. Critics skeptical of scientific experimentation have been around as long as science. By the early nineteenth century, concerns for animals began to be organized, and institutions were formed to further the interests of animals. In 1824, the Royal Society for the Prevention of Cruelty to Animals was founded. In the 1830s, Britain enacted legislation to protect animals in commercial use and to stop the sport of dog fighting. By mid-century, British concern was focused on animal use in scientific experimentation. In 1876, the British passed the Cruelty to Animals Act, which outlined regulatory procedures governing their scientific use.

In the United States, the history of animal protection followed Britain's lead. In 1866, a wealthy New Yorker started the American Society for the Prevention of Cruelty to Animals (ASPCA). In 1884, the Massachusetts legislature passed laws banning vivisection in primary and secondary schools. In 1892, the American Humane Association called for a prohibition on painful experiments on animals. While staunch antivivisectionists remained on the periphery of the humane movement through the first half of the twentieth century, humane groups began to splinter after World War II.

Some members of the American Society (ASPCA) broke away to form the Humane Society of the United States in 1954. A more radical group called Friends of Animals was organized in 1957, focusing its attention on animal dealers who collected stray dogs for research. The concern for commercial and domestic animals became increasingly linked with animal research. Imagine, the advocates said, if your beloved pet, lost on the street, were picked up by a disreputable animal dealer, sold to a laboratory, and then painfully experimented on before being thrown away. Not surprisingly, the Laboratory Animal Welfare Act was passed in 1966 to license dealers and set minimum standards for animal care.

While the best-known social movements of the 1960s focused on women's liberation and the rights of women and people of color, there was also growing opposition to hunting, trapping, the wearing of furs, and animal slaughter for food, as well as animal experimentation. Throughout the 1960s and 1970s, more and more organizations formed, some of them adamantly opposed to animal experimentation. Several were quite harsh in their assessment of the more conservative and wealthy humane societies, which accepted animal experimentation as necessary for improving human health. By 1990, the movement included 600 groups with ten to fifteen million members and assets valued at roughly $50 million.[44]

The history of the animal-rights movement suggests that the advancement of science and concern about the use of animals for experimentation has been inextricably linked for centuries. The animal-rights movement is not merely a faddish contemporary notion; rather, it is an outgrowth of public concern that has ebbed and flowed since the rise of the scientific revolution. History suggests that the animal-rights movement is far more complex than its most vocal critics would have the public believe. By understanding the history of this movement, we can better understand (though not necessarily create agreement between) both sides. Historical understanding can help managers accurately estimate the force of their critics' arguments. While animal rights might have seemed a fringe and unimportant movement in the 1970s, even a cursory review of the history books would have suggested its potential public appeal. Better understanding of the historical roots of anger and citizen protest can also keep officials and managers from jumping to short-sighted conclusions about their critics' beliefs and actions. Historical understanding can help those dealing with an angry public move beyond stereotyping, demonization, and ridicule that only increase polarization and conflict.

Prescription 5: Look to history to better understand the critics' arguments and beliefs.

Seek Reason Amid Emotion, Not Reason at the Expense of Emotion

Assaulted from all sides, many physicians have struck back with the claim that animal-rights advocates are irrational. The venerable British journal *Nature* included an article on animal rights under the headline "Can reason defeat unreason?" In the editorial, Barbara Culliton offered a stark contrast: "The animal rights people go for the heart, the biologists for the head." She concluded, "Meanwhile, the research community at large has yet to learn that some arguments cannot be won by dry, safe, reasoned discourse."[45] When the public gets angry, a typical and frequent charge is, "They're being overly emotional. They're ignoring the facts. They're whipping the crowd into a frenzy so nobody can think straight!" Is it true, at least in the case of the animal-rights movement?

Two philosophers have been credited with giving the "animal-rights" movement both impetus and form. In 1975 Peter Singer, an Australian philosopher, published *Animal Liberation*. He offered a utilitarian argument grounded in the work of the eighteenth-century philosopher Jeremy Bentham. Singer argued that the pleasure or pain of animals ought to be taken into account when considering an action. Because animals, like humans, are sensing (or sentient) beings, their suffering can no more be left out of a moral argument than can the suffering of children, women, or humans weaker in political, physical, or mental strength (i.e., minority populations, the physically handicapped, and the mentally handicapped). Singer went on to suggest that this ethical position did not mean all beings deserved equal *treatment*. Instead, he insisted on equal *consideration*. In short, he argued against "speciesism," but not for animal rights on par with human rights. Like utilitarians more generally, Singer argued that infliction of pain on animals might be justified if aggregate benefits outweighed individual pain. His point was, however, that the suffering of animals must enter into such a calculation.

In 1983 Tom Regan, an American professor of philosophy, published a work entitled *The Case of Animal Rights*. Regan's philosophical stance differed from Singer's in that he raised doubts about the relevance of large-scale cost-benefit calculations. While Singer argued against the inequality of speciesism, Regan argued against the inequality of unequal rights. He asserted that because animals, particularly mammals, have many complex attributes—they can remember, prefer one thing over another, and have intentions—they are "subjects," like humans, and not merely objects to be acted upon. Like humans, animals have a value of their own, distinct and separable from their value to humans beings. In other words, animals have inalienable moral rights. Unlike Singer, Regan argued that inflicting suffering on animals cannot be justified merely because the greater good might be served. Thus, he concluded, animal experimentation is morally unjustified. Animals' rights are violated when they are used as a means to an end for other beings. Tom Regan had reframed the animal protection debate in terms of rights.

Whether we agree with these philosophical arguments or not, one writer in the *Journal of the American Medical Association* concluded, "Despite their radical conclusions, both Singer and Regan are very much in the mainstream in their ethical methods. Consequently, the charge that they are motivated primarily by emotion is unconvincing to anyone who takes the time to read their work and is familiar with modern ethics."[46] A closer look at these two philosophers of and proponents for better treatment of animals suggests that, in contrast to the charge leveled by many scientists, their arguments for particular positions have been well thought out. Thus, accusations of emotionalism leveled against the animal-rights movement are not easy to sustain. Indeed, the charges of emotionalism might, in themselves, be criticized as nothing more than a strategy aimed at eliciting emotions.

In our experience, when the hearts and minds of the public are at stake all parties seek to influence opinion through emotion. Pictures of wide-eyed, caged monkeys with tubes sticking out of their chests are meant to elicit our sympathy. But comments such as, "If this movement is successful, untold millions will suffer the ravages of disease," are also aimed at playing on the emotions of the listener, chiefly the emotion of fear.[47] Dr. Frederick Goodwin, former administrator for the Alcohol, Drug Abuse, and Mental Health Administration, claimed, "To the extent that animal rights proponents succeed, they will irreparably damage medical practice."[48] The National Association for Biomedical Research requested that researchers submit to them family photos and letters from their children for a family album to be presented to then-President and Mrs. Bush. This had little to do with the merits of their argument.

In another instance, when the *Wall Street Journal* ran an article on the battle over the introduction of a curriculum concerning animal experimentation in public schools, the executive director of Americans for Medical Progress (AMP) responded, "These activists shrewdly manipulate audiences with non-threatening, seemingly logical arguments. Teachers, students and parents are sucked in by their honey-sweet lines and fail to recognize the swarming hive they are stepping into."[49] AMP's statement is hardly an appeal only to reason. Just like shocking pictures, sentimental appeals to families and apocalyptic statements are intended to provoke an emotional response, not a reasoned one.

We think that charges of emotionalism, in almost any public dispute, are disingenuous: human beings are motivated by a complex set of reasons, ideas, beliefs, *and* emotions. Moreover, charges of irrationality rarely help to resolve a conflict; on the contrary, they tend to exacerbate it. Hectoring the public with charges that it is being "unreasonable" or "emotional" undercuts the possibility of dialogue. "You are being emotional," the accusers charge, implying that their critics are "hysterical," "irrational," and ultimately "crazy," and therefore not to be taken seriously. But actions or words that trivialize people's concerns only encourage them to become even more "emotional," fueling their anger. The less the public thinks it is being taken seriously, the louder it becomes.

To make matters even worse, when one side frames the debate in terms of reason versus unreason, the "rational" accuser implies that no further discussion is possible—after all, how do you reason with someone who is unreasonable? Further public debate is rendered pointless. In her *Nature* editorial, Culliton made an odd statement: "The past decade is evidence enough that the animal-rights movement is not about reason. It is about eliminating the use of animals in research."[50] She does not make it clear why eliminating the use of animals is unreasonable. Obviously, she disagrees with the animal-rights activists, and by deeming their position "unreasonable" she leaves no room for debate.

We also think there is another danger in leveling the charge of emotionalism. Those who make such charges may seriously underestimate their adversaries' tactical capabilities. Take for instance the case of one of the first widely known "successes" of the animal-rights movement. Jasper and Nelkin, in their book *The Animal Rights Crusade*, trace the history of the modern-day movement from the strategic efforts of Henry Spira to bring the cause of animal rights to the public's attention in the 1970s. A veteran of civil-rights and labor battles, Spira and his colleagues sought, with consummate skill (and perhaps a measure of luck), a likely target to epitomize their growing concern for animal justice. Reviewing numerous scientific abstracts and grant proposals, they came upon two experiments on cats being undertaken at the American Museum of Natural History in New York by a team of psychologists. The experiments, aimed at learning more about the neurological bases of sexual behavior, involved removing parts of living cats' brains and destroying their sense of smell. For Spira, this was a perfect target for mobilizing public sentiment. First, the target was in the heart of New York. Second, the experiments were gruesome and seemingly unnecessary.

Spira enlisted the support of local animal-protection organizations. In a free weekly publication called *Our Town,* Spira denounced the experiments. In June of 1976, 400 letters arrived at the Museum; in July, 650 letters; and in August, 1,500. Protesters with placards such as "Curiosity kills cats" appeared in front of the museum. Congress got involved and asked the National Institutes of Health (NIH) to review its decision to fund such research. Congressman Ed Koch, future mayor of New York, jumped into the fray, arguing effectively: "'Now tell me, after you have taken a deranged male cat with brain lesions and you place it in a room and you find that it is going to mount a rabbit instead of a female cat, what have you got?"[51] Within a year and a half, the American Museum abandoned its cat laboratory. In 1980 the American Museum abolished its whole experimental program. The animal-rights movement had won its first major victory, using quite rational and effective organizing techniques.

It would be a frightening world if people used only reason or only emotion. In reality, it is far more likely that both "sides" will use both reason and emotion. After all, the public has both hearts and minds, and those who wish to advance their cause most always appeal to both. It is best to acknowledge strong emotion and, at the same time, appeal to reasoned arguments.

Prescription 6: Acknowledge strong emotions but appeal to reasoned arguments.

Recognize Diversity on the Other Side

The animal-rights debate certainly highlights the tendency to portray the other side as monolithic and extreme. Scientists tend to view animal-rights activists as a bunch of "hysterical people" putting "animals before people," or as a "handful of extremists" depriving "millions" of the "life-saving" benefits of research.[52] On the other side, animal-rights activists portray scientists as "women and men in white coats" who practice "institutionalized cruelty" arising from "hideous compartmentalized thinking."[53] While extreme characterizations are aimed at winning the upper hand in the public debate, neither is likely to be true (although at least one worst offender reinforcing the stereotype can almost always be found on each side).

Are all scientists unfeeling technocrats opposed to animal rights? Clearly, the answer is no. Numerous scientists are engaged in research that may well improve the lives of both people and animals. An often-cited case is the rabies vaccine: Louis Pasteur used rabbits to develop a vaccine that has since prevented suffering and death in large numbers of both animals and humans.

With regard to the scientific use of animals, scientists hold a range of views. One MIT researcher, in a debate over a city ordinance in Cambridge, Massachusetts, wrote a letter to the head of a group championing regulation of animal use in laboratories, stating that scientific research did have "'an aura of elitism and seclusion'" and that, "in a measured tone," the scientist concluded, "I feel sure that by compromise well-meaning people can resolve the problems which we both feel so strongly about."[54] When the *Journal of the American Medical Association* published a report stating that use of animals in medical education "was essential," several letters reproached the AMA for "taking an unbending, unreasonable, and clearly minority position that conflicts with the policies of the best medical schools." (Indeed, one-fourth of American medical schools do not use animals in education, according to the survey of the AAMC.)[55] Twenty thousand doctors signed a petition requesting that the U.S. Surgical Company stop using live dogs to demonstrate the use of its surgical staples.[56] It would seem that all scientists do not share the view promulgated by extremists among them.

All animal-rights activists are not unreasonable zealots. One group of researchers used a survey to interview animal rights advocates at a march in Washington.[57] They found several interesting results: 79 percent of the protesters had at least some college education, and the median income of the protesters was $33,000 (of course this figure may be skewed, because the protesters included only those who could afford to travel to Washington for the march); 44 percent of the protesters surveyed were nurses, doctors, lawyers, engineers, professors, and other professional workers; and most reported that their opinions were shaped by a variety of news sources, a highly unusual finding in surveys of the population as a whole. In short, while holding fast to certain beliefs, these protesters exhibited traits that suggest they were well educated, well read, and employed in respectable professional jobs.

Researchers have also found that within the general animal-rights movement there is a spectrum of views and motivations. While 56 percent of the Washington protesters either disapproved or strongly disapproved of scientific research that does *not* harm animals, 26 percent of the protesters approved or strongly approved of the same kind of research. About the same number, 26 percent, felt that science does more good than harm despite concerns over animal experimentation.[58] While some activists had been drawn to the movement primarily out of emotion, others had formed their decision to protest after carefully considering ethical arguments such as those made by Singer and Regan. While some activists disavowed owning pets on the grounds that it is immoral, others strongly defended their choice to give and gain solace from animals they kept as pets.

While the leaders of opposing positions in a values dispute may often portray the conflict in extremes, a closer look at the parties in the animal rights controversy suggests something different. A diversity of views and opinions is as likely in these conflicts as is a consistent, unified view held jointly by everyone on the "same side." While the debate may appear to involve a clash of opposites, more likely the debate is characterized by a range of views and opinions that are not necessarily diametrically opposed.

Advocates of polarization may continue to take extreme positions because it improves their standing among their constituents. From an organizational standpoint, extreme and controversial statements may generate useful press coverage, and perhaps new paying members. In the longer term, however, it is unclear that extreme positions help advance an organization's agenda.

By contrast, when diverse and complex views are given voice they can become the raw material for crafting agreements that meet everyone's needs. In the language of negotiation, diverse parties—with their complex range of shared and differing interests (in the midst of their conflicting values)—can be brought together. This is why bringing diverse opinions into the debate is important: Productive dialogue can only begin when all the voices are part of the conversation.

> *Prescription # 7: Allow for and seek out diverse and complex views on all "sides."*

Beware the Pitfalls of "Rights Talk"

In the American experience, when the minority seeks redress from the majority, or the majority seeks immunity from the minority (so it can do as it pleases), citizens demand their rights.

The courtroom is usually the forum in which countervailing claims collide. Americans turn to the courts for resolution. In the great courtroom dramas of the day, from the O. J. Simpson trial to the mundane entertainment of television's *The People's Court*, a black-robed judge, elevated above the rest, presides. Two sides face a judge or jury. Prosecutors and defenders assumes their assigned roles. Voices are raised, fingers point, fists slam, and attorneys rebut each other until their parts are finished. Then a final verdict is rendered. One side, exultant, rises from its chairs in victory. The other, having lost, slumps back dejected.

Unfortunately rights talk, with its absolutes, shuts out the subtlety and leaves only winners and losers. The concerns of the "losers" are then left unattended. Within the context of rights, sensible solutions to real problems are often overlooked. The courts, bound by the law, often impose remedies that are less than satisfactory, even to the winner. Appeals are filed, and then everyone waits to see whether the court's mandate is implemented.

In Mary Ann Glendon's book, *Rights Talk: The Impoverishment of Political Discourse*, she asks, "The independent individualist, helmetless and free on the open road, becomes the most dependent of individuals in the spinal-injury ward. In the face of such facts, why does our rhetoric of rights so often shut out relationship and responsibility, along with reality?"[59] In America, at least, there is an undue emphasis on individual rights *without* corresponding attention to the responsibilities that go with them, or the limitations that must necessarily constrain individuals so that the social fabric of the nation can remain intact. Thus, although many rights are granted, there is very little attention to the difficulties of arbitrating among them. As Glendon points out, "Our rights talk, in its absoluteness, promotes unrealistic expectations, heightens social conflict, and inhibits dialogue that might lead toward consensus, accommodation, or at least the discovery of common ground."[60]

In the case of the animal-rights controversy, framing the debate in terms of rights led to further polarization. As soon as someone claimed that animals had rights, it came as no surprise that someone else claimed that humans had the right to seek medical care based on animal experimentation. This led to the difficult problem of deciding how best to arbitrate between the two claims. Anthropologist John Cole describes University of Pennsylvania trauma experiments which involved inflicting head injuries on baboons.[61] Animal-rights activists captured videotapes of this research and made them widely available. Videotapes of adults and children who believe that they owed their lives to the surgical and recuperative techniques gleaned from these experiments were not widely distributed. "Rights" talk leads to stark and terrible choices. How should we choose between the certain death of baboon babies and the possibility that human children might benefit from the death of the baboons?

Many of us refuse to accept such choices, preferring to explore still other alternatives. How can we make cars safer so that children are not hurt? Is there another way to do the trauma research so that it is not necessary to harm the baboons? We might try to develop new ways to train trauma physicians to be more effective. Unfortunately, when the debate becomes framed in "rights," the search for creative alternatives is stymied. As Glendon points out, "rights talk" in America tends to override any discussion of responsibilities. She explains that American law, unlike European law, imposes no duty to come to the aid of another person in mortal danger [so long as it does not put the rescuer in mortal danger]. In America, apparently, we are free to do as we choose, which includes choosing not to save another life. The animal-rights dispute, when framed in terms of rights, suffers from the same myopia. For instance, the following brief interchange took place during a forum, sponsored by *Harper's Magazine*, at Cooper Union for the Advancement of Science and Art, in New York City.

> There is a wide range of creatures—some of them human—for whom our rights language is not the best way to deal with them. I want people to deal with them out of a sense of fairness or a sense of humanity or a sense of duty, but not out of a claim to rights.   —*Arthur Caplan, Director of Center for Biomedical Ethics, University of Minnesota*

> I don't like your supremacist view of a custodial responsibility that grants you the luxury to be magnanimous to those beneath you. The rights of animals are not peripheral interests. In this case, we are talking about blood, guts, pain, and death.   —*Ingrid Newkirk, National Director, People for the Ethical Treatment of Animals*

When a critic of animal "rights" suggests that the language of responsibility ought to be taken seriously, the animal-rights activist, sensing, we suspect, a veiled attempt to discount her claims, quickly accuses Caplan of being paternalistic and "speciesist." But, by refusing to partake in the discussion of responsibility, Newkirk may very well undermine her own argument. Jasper and Nelkin use the example of domestic animals, dependent on human care. "What, indeed, would dachshunds and dairy cows do if left to their own devices?"[62] Don't human beings have some responsibility to these creatures, which, over time, have become dependent upon them? And furthermore, it is quite clear that Newkirk has taken responsibility upon herself for the well-being of animals: after all, unlike a sentient human, animals cannot lay their claims before a court of law in which rights are adjudicated.

It may be that Newkirk and others avoided the language of responsibility, as does American law, because it made the discussion more complex. If rights are intricately bound up with responsibilities, how do we, within the context of the law, not only grant animals rights, but also require them to hold responsibilities? Do we, like some medieval court, put horses on trial for eating another farmer's grain? To return to the deer herd at the Quabbin Reservoir mentioned at the outset of this chapter, do we put the deer on trial and jail them for over-browsing their habitat and killing future oak trees? If animals have rights, but cannot make claims for themselves, who ought to represent them? Should animal-rights activists become their guardians? What responsibilities would flow from this guardianship?

It is one thing to say that we should not needlessly kill baboons; it is quite another to say we should kill no other beings of any kind. "Most Americans sympathize with some relaxing of the strict boundaries between humans and other species, especially in the case of dogs and cats, but they resist when activists deny any relevant distinctions between species. Bees, snakes, and banana slugs simply do not arouse much compassion."[63] In the words of Glendon, when "rights" talk is carried too far, we may "trivialize" the "essential core" of rights we hold dear.[64] This makes the debate over rights even more difficult.

Andrew Rowan of the Tufts Center for Animals and Public Policy notes that two "middle-of-the-road" groups, the Hastings Center and the Institute of Medical Ethics, have convened working groups which have concluded that animal research does raise significant moral issues which are not easily brushed aside.[65] In other words, the use of animals in experimentation poses challenging ethical and moral questions. Unfortunately, "rights talk" does not help those who disagree about animal rights to pursue a constructive ethical discussion about the issues because "it does not do justice to the richness and variety of American moral sentiments."[66] This is not to say that the pursuit of rights for the disadvantaged, marginalized, or mistreated is doomed. The civil rights movement in America sought, with much success, to force American institutions to provide equal protection under the law for all, regardless of race, creed, or color. Glendon's critique reminds us, though, of the obstacles that emerge when we engage in "rights talk" rather than consensus building.

Prescription 8: Beware the pitfalls of "rights talk."

Seek Forums for Dialogue

In the conclusion of their book on the animal-rights movement, Jasper and Nelkin call for dialogue and compromise "basic to a democratic conversation."[67] Laurence Tribe argues that in a debate even as polarized and strident as abortion, given that it occurs in our democracy, "voting and persuasion are all we have."[68] Tribe suggests that while nothing should stop a group from arguing that its view is indeed better, pragmatically or morally, at the same time there is no view free from politics; even the Constitution is subject to change given political debate. The case of *Roe* v. *Wade*, which declared a right to abortion as a private choice and has led to twenty-plus years of debate, protest, and at times violence, strongly suggests that even the Supreme Court cannot be the final arbiter of values. Properly structured public discussion and debate are desperately needed.

Glendon concludes: In a democracy, where court decisions are insufficient to settle matters, where science fails to answer all questions, where the exercise of raw power leads not to resolution but to further plays of power, deliberation, with all its travails and difficulties, is the means we have at our disposal to settle difficult questions.[69] She states, "Only time will tell whether the public square can be effectively regained for an ongoing broad-based conversation about the means and ends of government, about what kind of society we are, and about what kind of future we hope to create for our children and posterity."[70] If deliberation, debate, and dialogue are the basis of hope in situations where values collide, then how we operationalize the conversation is absolutely crucial. We need to bring all the stakeholders together, in a joint problem-solving mode that goes beyond polarized rhetoric and rights talk.

Consider this: A dialogue among diverse parties about animal protection took place in Baltimore, Maryland in late 1993. Animal rights activists, scientists, and regulatory officials met for the first World Congress on Alternatives to Animal Use in the Life Sciences sponsored by the Johns Hopkins University School of Hygiene and Public Health. The event was neither conclusive in its deliberations nor representative of all interests. Organized medicine did not attend. A vice president for the American Medical Association did not attend. Some animal rights activists protested outside the Congress, claiming that the event was merely a ruse to buy time and avoid resolving the problem. More than 700 people did attend, however, including numerous scientists and long-time animal-rights leaders such as Henry Spira.

People from different sides were talking at last. Practical solutions and possibilities for reducing the use of animals in research were discussed in detail. Participants heard plenary sessions on "The Concepts of Alternatives," "The Role of Animals and Alternatives in Education," and "Science, Ethics, and Animals."[71] Toxicologists freely disagreed with one another about the effectiveness of alternatives to animal experimentation. Animal-protection advocates acknowledged the split in their ranks, from "pragmatists" to "fundamentalists."[72] One industrial toxicologist concluded that while it was "really too early for entrenched positions to be changed in public," the meeting was an "outstanding success" in opening up dialogue among the various parties involved in the dispute.[73] Diverse parties concerned about the issue were meeting face to face in a forum to deliberate in a constructive fashion.

It is possible for the parties involved in a value dispute to discuss their differences and to consider potential solutions in a civil manner. There are various forms that such deliberation can take, from short facilitated debates to multiyear consensus-building processes. All bring disputants with vastly different world views and values closer together.

Facilitated Dialogue versus Adversarial Debate

Imagine for a moment what might happen if, instead of a judge in an imposing black robe presiding, a professional facilitator in a dull beige suit sat among the opposing parties. Rather than asking each side to present its views, and then encouraging them to rebut each other's statements, what if the neutral pursued an entirely different tack? What if the neutral said, "I'm not going to make any final judgments; that's not my job. I'm here to help you explore what might serve your collective interests." What if the neutral asked, "In addition to your differences, what common values do you share?" Just this format was attempted in a television series called "The Search for Common Ground." In one episode, the abortion debate was highlighted. On one side of the camera sat a leader from the National Right to Life Committee, on the other a spokesperson for the National Abortion Rights Action Committee. In between sat a professional mediator.

The mediator posed the first question to the right-to-life advocate: "State your basic position on abortion." But then, surprisingly, the mediator turned to the pro-choice advocate and asked: "When he is done, please sum up as best you can his stated position." While the audience expected first one, then the other, to present their views, they were surprised when the neutral pressed each side to be sure it had understood the other's interests and concerns. The mediator, turning to the camera, said, "This is not a debate. We will not exploit conflict to hold your interest."

Of course the two advocates heatedly disagreed. The pro-choice advocate stated, "You missed the moral decision-making I discussed. Fetal life does have value, but in hard situations there are sometimes higher values. There is the morality of bringing a child into the world, into abuse, into poverty." The pro-life advocate responded: "We do not believe in the big killing the small, the mighty killing the weak. We are all created equal."

At one point, debating whether family planning counselors ought to encourage a woman seeking an abortion to listen to the heartbeat of the fetus, the pro-life advocate turned to the brass pin on his lapel and said, "These little feet are the size of a fetus's feet at ten weeks. So if you show these to the woman, and she sees them, then . . . ." The pro-choice advocate interjected: "You insult women. I sat here and told you I had an abortion after three children, and you show me these small feet. You are insulting the intelligence and compassion of women."

Nevertheless, amid the strong emotions and intense debate, the mediator sought potential points of agreement. "Do both of you agree that unwanted pregnancies should be minimized?" Both responded yes, but disagreed on how best to achieve that goal. The mediator asked: "Can you agree that in order to serve the well-being of women, they need better alternatives, such as adoption?" Both parties agreed. "Can you imagine," the mediator asked, "some kind of joint action you could take to reduce infant mortality?" Again, both responded yes. With the assistance of a neutral interlocutor, even in a debate as heated and polarized as the one that surrounds the abortion issue, at least some areas of common ground were uncovered. While the forum hardly brought the two opposing side to an agreement about abortion, it did identify some shared interests. As the mediator summed it up, "The lesson here is that beneath the stridency and strong emotion, there can be some common areas of agreement."

Collaborative Workshops Rather than Mutual Media Attacks

The "by-catch" in the U.S. fisheries has become a hot-button issue for fishermen and conservationists. When fishermen incidentally bring up sea turtles or dolphins in their nets, maiming or killing them, many environmentalists become concerned and angry. For some animal protectionists, the by-catch of mammals such as porpoises is unacceptable. The first widely publicized by-catch controversy—the by-catch of dolphins by tuna fishermen in the Pacific—led to a flurry of media activity and a nationwide boycott of canned tuna. Tuna fishermen and environmentalists headed to Washington to lobby, organized protest marches, issued angry press releases, and filed endless court briefs. By April 1991, the United States had placed an embargo on the import of Mexican tuna. Congress also prohibited the import of tuna products from countries that purchased from banned countries. In August of 1991, a panel established by the General Agreement on Tariffs and Trade (GATT) ruled that environmental concerns could not a be factor in barring imports, and that the U.S. embargo was unwarranted and illegal. What began as a congressional attempt to protect marine mammals in 1972 culminated in an international trade war, and eventually an overturning of an American law that attempted to regulate tuna fishing.

Who had won? At least a million dolphins died between 1972 and 1992. The U.S. tuna fleet practically disbanded: it has shrunk to nearly a fifth its original size. America, at least for a while, lost its ability to enforce its own environmental priorities in international markets. In short, nobody won.

Fortunately, fishermen and environmentalists alike learned something from this conflict. By-catch remains a sensitive issue, especially the by-catch of harbor porpoises caught in gill nets off Maine and sea turtles caught by shrimp trawlers in the Gulf of Mexico. But those involved in this issue are finding common ground. In December of 1994, a day-long conference held in Seattle brought together fishermen, scientists, regulators, and environmentalists to discuss "Win-win By-catch Solutions." Representatives of the different interests met in small groups to learn about approaches to reduce by-catch around the country. Attendees were told about collaborative efforts between hunters and antihunting activists to protect a 6.5-million acre waterfowl habitat in Canada. American regulators called for, and promised to prioritize, cooperative research proposals on gear modifications. One leading environmentalist and frequent critic of fishermen both admitted to past mistakes and promised to "listen," "tell the truth," "look for what works and makes sense," and to "stick by" fishermen to implement practical solutions.[74] While the day-long workshop did not "solve" the problem, it helped to bring diverse, and often disputing, parties together to think about how to deal with their differences. One Alaskan skipper concluded, after the day's workshop, "'I went into this thinking we'll all sit around and talk, we won't get anything done, it's not going to go anywhere, and nobody's going to be there who can make any decisions. I was wrong on all counts."[75] The workshop was so successful that another one was held the following spring on the East Coast.

There are other fisheries successes. In both 1988 and 1993, a skilled facilitator helped various parties weave together amendments to the Marine Mammal Protection Act. A working group of fishermen, environmentalists, and regulators met, with the aid of a mediator, to promote research, production, and implementation of the use of a net-mounted "pinger" to warn harbor porpoises in Maine away from gill nets.

Joint Problem-Solving Rather than Closed Decision-Making

Although the planned hunt of deer in the Quabbin reservation sparked significant controversy, the agency was able to address the problem of forest regeneration. While a small group of animal-rights advocates remained upset and unhappy with the plans of the MDC, a carefully planned and thoughtfully executed public-involvement process organized by the agency was able to garner significant public support for their actions. Not all but many environmentalists, after participating in the public debate, concluded that the hunt was unfortunate but necessary. One Audubon member wrote in his local newsletter, "The Metropolitan District Commission (MDC) personnel have done an impressive job of studying and documenting the issue, exploring alternatives to herd reduction, and explaining the issues to interested environmental groups and citizens across the Commonwealth."[76] *The Boston Globe* concluded: "Given the desirability of protecting the reservation from excessive intrusion by the public, sharply controlled hunting appears to be the best available compromise."[77]

What did the agency do to help address the public's concerns? Prior to initiating public presentations, workshops, and forums, the MDC conducted two years of scientific study. These studies helped the MDC determine that the impacts of deer browsing would have to be minimized, but the agency left completely open how that objective might be reached. As one staff member stated, "We didn't have a preconceived solution. We did focus on the problem and outcomes, but not on the means to getting there."[78] The initial studies did not reassure many of the MDC's critics. As one frustrated MDC staff member pointed out, "Research isn't going to help much in the public setting. Unfortunately, you read 300 articles on an issue, and it is dismissed in one newspaper article." However, the research did lay the groundwork for a reasonable justification (if not a perfect one) for the agency's actions. Perhaps the most convincing piece of evidence were several small plots of land that MDC fenced off from deer. Within a few years, the amount and diversity of growth inside the fence vastly exceeded the growth outside. This was tangible evidence of the impacts of overbrowsing. In addition, the agency also conducted an inventory of small-tree growth on unhunted and hunted lands. The inventory indicated a deficit of more than 50 million small trees in the unhunted forest surrounding the reservoir.

While the agency already had a citizens' advisory committee, MDC personnel realized that this issue would generate a marked increase in public concern. The more typical fishing and recreation interests on the committee were not likely to reflect the interests that would come forward. Thus, the agency concluded that greater public involvement was needed.[79] During the summer of 1989 the agency held slide shows, offered tours of the forest, and distributed copies of its technical reports. Agency personnel conducted more than 25 meetings with environmentalists, sportsmen, animal-rights activists, and forestry and wildlife organizations. In the following year, the agency held two all-day public workshops attended by 35 to 40 people each. Representatives of diverse interests discussed whether or not there was a problem and considered various options for controlling the herd (e.g., herd reduction, relocation, fencing, and alternative forestry practices). After seeing the difficulty of moderating the workshop using its own staff, the MDC hired a professional mediator to conduct subsequent workshops. In addition, after incorporating the comments from the all-day workshops in a revised draft of its management plan, the MDC held three facilitated educational forums. Rather than putting only agency staff in front of the room, the MDC invited a panel of seven speakers representing animal protection, hunting, forestry, and wilderness preservation points of view. In the forums, which involved some 600 attendees, panel members discussed the revised draft plan, answered questions, and debated the pros and cons of the suggested options.

The educational forums succeeded on several levels. First, they set a good precedent, reaching out to diverse stakeholders and acknowledging diverse opinions. One MDC scientist said, "We reviewed a whole issue without first setting a plan that people could attack and resist. We started early from the ground level. Our informational meetings were unique, with a panel and audience that could openly express both pro and con views."[80] Second, by remaining focused on the issues of forest regeneration and deer-herd reduction, the MDC avoided clouding the debate with other public concerns. Third, the process moved beyond opposing pronouncements and mutual attacks to more (though not always) respectful dialogue. The mediator, provided by the Massachusetts Office of Dispute Resolution, helped the MDC design the process. The neutral aided the agency staff in facing the conflict with "reasonable decorum," letting various disputing voices be heard, and framing the conversation in terms of "give and take" rather than "tell and listen." The mediator also trained the agency staff in the basics of conflict resolution, so they knew why they were taking particular actions. As one agency staff member pointed out, natural-resource professionals typically get plenty of training in technical problem-solving but little or no training in dealing with the public. Finally, the agency's approach prompted the staff to undergo some soul-searching. Staff members had to incorporate diverse views into their planning, which encouraged them, along the way, to reflect upon what they thought was right and good. One staff member stated, "Conflict can be a good thing as long as it is approached in an open and respectful way. It helps to clarify goals, philosophical viewpoints, and forces an organization to define what it stands for. It helps confront assumptions and helps reach clarification, if not outright resolution."[81]

The public-involvement process was by no means perfect. The agency could have included the public even earlier in the process, asking for input on the design and execution of the background studies. The MDC could have established a small focus group to help design the larger public-participation process. The agency could also have enlisted members of the public to help draft the management plan, or at least a general framework for the plan. But the agency still viewed the drafting of plans as its prerogative. This may result in a lengthy redrafting process and generate opposing position papers from sophisticated interest groups. It also means that the agency will have to respond to heaps of form letters from opponents. As some federal agencies have found, initially involving interested parties in the drafting of regulations, policies, or plans is much more effective. Outcomes are perceived as less biased, open and frank discussion of technical uncertainties is encouraged, decisions tend to take better account of both technical and political realities, and, most importantly, the stakeholders are more likely to "buy in" to the result.

In the end, the revised management plan did not satisfy either the strongest advocates of animal rights or the interests of those who had other bones to pick with the MDC. Indeed, the controversy created a painful rift in the environmental community. The underlying question of the "nature of nature," as Jan Dizard, an observer of the events, wrote, remains unanswered.[82] The state agency, however, facing a controversial task embedded with fundamental disagreements over values, provided a meaningful forum for citizens to voice their concerns, consider various options, and influence the outcome. A large majority of opponents may not have liked the agency's final actions, but they did not oppose them. In the end, the agency even earned some good will. As one environmental advocate said of the process: "I felt the MDC process was remarkably open. I have never seen an agency do so much."[83]

> *Prescription 9: Seek forums for discussion in which facilitated dialogue rather than adversarial debate, an airing of differences rather than attacks, and joint problem solving rather than unilateral decision making, dominate.*

CHAPTER VII

The Media

Consider the stereotypical image of the generic PR "flack." He hobnobs with the media's stars, slipping them inside tips in return for favorable coverage. He leaks information at the right time to the right people. To the question of truth as advertised, he (or she) replies: "There are two, three and sometimes four sides to everything. What is truth?" When the press gets tough, he returns articles with the "biased" coverage marked in neon highlighter. When a questionable client arrives at the door, the flack does not ask if he should take them on; he asks how the prospective client's "image" might best be sanitized and upgraded for the masses.

The real world of public relations and the media is far more complex. Some public-relations practitioners do advocate heavy-handed tactics: woo the press, stonewall the press, play reporters off against one another, and rely on hype rather than substance. On the other hand, many theorists and practitioners promote aboveboard, straightforward behavior toward the press and the public. Many practitioners believe in what they do and attempt to do it well. Many scholars and practitioners emphasize exactly the things at which public relations representatives are considered notoriously deficient: honesty, relationship-building, integrity, maintaining open lines of communication. Nonetheless a mistaken set of ideas remains fixed in the minds of many. Especially when a crisis ensues, these ideas are played out with unintended and sometimes disastrous results. A sound track of set notions, held by many but questioned by few, drowns out better ideas.

The Conventional Wisdom of Media Relations

Corporations and political institutions often presume that the press can and should be controlled and manipulated. For them, communicating with the media involves disseminating information to their liking. Decision-makers do not consider two-way communication, where institutions not only influence but are also open to influence. Image creation is their number one priority. The public's real concerns are brushed aside in order to maintain a good image, regardless of the substance beneath the veneer. Media relations is stripped of any consensus-building role it might play, and is instead narrowly defined in terms of advocacy for the company's view. In the conventional wisdom, the process of media relations is based on maintaining control over outcomes; all power to define issues, set agendas, and handle questions or concerns must be in the hands of the organization. There is no thought of sharing power or meeting the other parties' needs, let alone the media's. While a company or agency worries about its "image," the media worry about getting beneath that image to the "real story." Unfortunately, problem solving—ensuring that the needs of all stakeholders are met—is an activity left undone. Too often media relations, in practice, assumes that no one has responsibility for ensuring that interests on all sides are met.

Consider Exxon's handling of the *Exxon Valdez* oil spill. One prominent practitioner of corporate public relations wrote,

> There was a window of opportunity with the news media. The reporting initially and for a period of time following the disaster was factual and pretty straightforward even though media representatives were undoubtedly as horrified as the rest of us at the scope of the disaster. But as Exxon stumbled, fumbled, stonewalled, denied, shifted the blame, ducked responsibility and tried to manage the messages, the news media had no choice but to turn against them as well.[1]

Why did Exxon fail to capitalize on this initial window of opportunity? Exxon executives, like many of us, locked into a timeworn set of ideas, fell back into the default position typically adopted in a time of crisis. By stonewalling, whitewashing the problem, and sending up smoke screens, Exxon hoped to save the day, but instead squandered the opportunity to interact with the media in an aboveboard, nonadversarial manner that would have preserved some semblance of a working relationship and the possibility of addressing concerns of the affected stakeholders. The problem is that there are some faulty assumptions which underlie much public relations theory and practice. These mistaken but widely shared beliefs get in the way of developing sound and principled strategies for working with the media.

The Media as Adversary

Unfortunately, the assumption of the media as adversary underlies a great deal of public-relations practice. Consider the advice given in a case study in the *Harvard Business Review.* A business comes under media fire for indirectly funding a pro-life organization, one of whose members is accused of bombing an abortion clinic. In his response, a senior editor at Los Angeles-based *Investor's Business Daily* advises that the company ". . . consider accusing both the local newspaper and television station of being anti-business. Nowadays, an 'I'm a victim' defense is a sound strategy that may turn a potentially damaging story into a positive event."[2] The senior editor also advises the company (1) not to issue a formal press release, on the grounds that responding to an accusation only gives it credibility; (2) to go on the offensive by charting all the other organizations which might have given money to such political groups; and (3) to downplay the size of the company's financial contribution to the group. It would seem the media is but a passive observer at best, and, at worst, an enemy to be ignored, neutralized, or attacked. Loftier ideals expressed in some of the textbooks, such as "The bedrock of the practitioner-journalist relationship must be one of mutual trust and mutual advantage"[3] are brushed aside.

Even experts wise to the dangers of fighting with the media promote strategies intended to sidestep the media's influence and diminish their power. Those playing the "media game" mistakenly still believe that there can only be winners and losers. "If you talk to the people who count, if you've had contact with those groups who are most directly affected, media coverage simply becomes less and less relevant. You have reduced the media's power, yet built your own credibility."[4] We are all for talking to the people who count—namely, the stakeholders most affected by and concerned with your actions. But we do not see the value in treating media relations like a power game. If you are out to reduce their power, then there's no reason why they should not be out to reduce yours. Will such a battle bring reason, argument, and truth to the forefront? Will such a battle serve the public's interests? Will it really serve yours?

The Media as a Tool

William Greider, in his book *Who Will Tell the People?* relates the Alar case as an example of environmental advocates outspinning the spin doctors. Fenton Communications orchestrated the highly effective campaign against Alar, a pesticide used on apples, for about one-sixth of what the supporters of Alar spent to save the pesticide. Fenton helped get a spot on *60 Minutes*. They called on Meryl Streep to hold a press conference with the national president of the PTA, stating that Alar could make children sick. Because the critics could not afford television advertising, Fenton released an anti-Alar video at a press conference in the hopes that the press would take it and use it. They did.

Although the *Washington Post* and the *Wall Street Journal* both countered the claims that "Alar gives your kids cancer," and apple growers, the chemical industry, and the EPA countered the claims with numerous statistics, the pesticide was voluntarily withdrawn from the market by Uniroyal. As Greider points out, "Fenton's adroit manipulation of the news media enraged the apple growers and the chemical industry as well as their conservative defenders in the press, but his strategy simply followed the basic principles of mass communications developed by business itself."[5] Unfortunately, what the Alar case suggests is that the media is frequently used as a channel for innuendo rather than information, as a place to convey image rather than substance. Conservatives and liberals, business and advocacy groups alike can be faulted for treating the media (and the media playing along, or at the least, being played) as nothing more than an instrument of propaganda. The danger, as Christopher Lasch points out, is that "when words are used merely as instruments of publicity or propaganda, they lose their power to persuade. Soon they cease to mean anything at all."[6]

The Media Can Be Controlled

While the most experienced PR experts urge enlightened standards, the fact remains that the prevailing paradigm of media relations is rooted in a desire to control outcomes. Many practitioners still fall into the trap of thinking that the media are somehow controllable—that somehow, if you do all the right things, the media will fall into place. Even experts with more enlightened views still tend to believe that the media can be managed as if they were unequal subordinates rather than equal peers more open to persuasion and argument than to manipulation.

Take, for example, the crisis management plan prepared for Clorox by a Pittsburgh advertising and public-relations firm. It was leaked to Greenpeace in 1991 before it was adopted by the company. The plan offered several "scripts"—possible strategies for handling different kinds of crises—including a proposed announcement that the company would seek an independent, third-party review of a hypothetical study commissioned by Greenpeace. Why? Because ". . . the independent report will gain little media attention if it supports the company's position; its primary value will be to cause reporters to question Greenpeace's integrity and scientific capabilities." And later, in response to an imagined columnist's attack on chlorine bleach, the draft plan suggested an "industry association advertising campaign—'Stop Environmental Terrorism'—calling on Greenpeace and the columnist to be more responsible and less irrational in their approach" and "conducting research to determine if and how a slander lawsuit against the columnist . . . could be effective."[7] Is it any wonder the media become skeptical and cautious, even defensive and confrontational, when such schemes come to light?

What may be worse than professional communications firms giving dubious advice is the fact that "spin doctoring" and other strategies for media manipulation have become the conventional wisdom among nonpractitioners. As we mentioned in Chapter V, *Family Circle* magazine published an article on communities at risk because of environmental contamination, giving as one example Jacksonville, Arkansas. The Jacksonville community, or parts of it, responded angrily, with resolutions of censure and other forms of attempted pressure. The outcome? The *Jacksonville News* reprinted the article alleging that health in the city was at risk from toxic waste, and *Family Circle* ran a follow-up story in a "Special Report" later the same year. Did the offended town succeed in controlling the press? No.

Sadly, but hardly surprisingly, after the local paper reprinted the article the Jacksonville Chamber of Commerce allegedly discussed a boycott "designed to bleed the newspaper to death," and a state representative attacked the paper in a letter, asking "why on earth" the paper would voluntarily republish the article. In this case, one of the paper's owners apologized to the Chamber of Commerce. The actions of the city leadership, however, only added fuel to the fire, giving the impression that the city had something to hide. For the city's political and business leadership, the issue was not that the article had created fears in the minds of some residents; leadership was more intent on silencing criticism than in calming fears. While the local press might have bowed to the threats of local community leaders, *Family Circle* certainly did not. In the end, attempting to control the media led to a set of unintended and unwanted consequences quite beyond the town promoters' control.

Media Policy by Default

The conventional wisdom of media relations has worked its way into the public and corporate psyche. Advertising types claim that an image can be projected onto a suggestible public via the press. Flash the public enough pictures of clear blue water, flying seabirds, and panoramic views, all with a company logo firmly attached, and the public will come your way. Management types assume it's nobody's business but their business, and by God, they'll find a way to fix the problem by themselves. Don't admit mistakes. Don't show your warts. Charge ahead full steam. And of course, there is the "hard-hitting attorney" approach: Insist on restrictive policies regarding access to documents and decision makers; deny any possibility of responsibility or liability; challenge and attack all claims made by your critics. The best defense, clearly, is a good offense.

The set of responses that emerges from this mishmash of views includes the "usual" tactics: Communicating to presumably gullible media; seeking reputable pundits and "experts" to back up corporate and agency interpretations; stonewalling access to information; erecting a smoke screen to distract the public while concealing the real story; and attacking the media.

Media relations policy is made in a vacuum with lawyers advising one thing, advertising consultants urging another, and the public-relations department pushing in still a third direction. This is how Exxon got into trouble. Its incoherent approach to the press—the result of legalistic, image-making, and public relations concerns dictating inconsistent action—conveyed a message to the media of irresponsibility, lack of cooperation, and defensiveness. Dow Corning, in the controversy over the health risks of breast implants, also failed to address the problem of coherence. Rather than hand responsibility to a single experienced spokesperson early on, Dow Corning used lower-level representatives and changed them frequently. It was only when the company's new CEO stepped forward that they began to get good press for their handling of communications. Unfortunately, having settled one problem, Dow Corning created another by reversing itself and refusing to turn over an internal study for public scrutiny.

James Gruning, a prominent scholar of public relations, has identified both symbolic and behavioral elements of a relationship between an organization and the public. In his analysis, the manipulation of symbolic elements, namely the "image" of an organization, has crowded out any interest in behavioral considerations. As examples of the latter, Gruning identifies a number of attributes of effective behavioral relationships: reciprocity, trust, credibility, mutual respect, openness, mutual satisfaction, and mutual understanding.[8] These are exactly the kinds of concerns so often left by the wayside when business and government try to deal with the public. These concerns are also left out in dealing with the media. Business and government representatives must tend to these behavioral considerations in establishing relationships with the media, just as they must address them when they interact with the public. Well thought-out rationales rather than reactive defenses need to be employed when engaging the media.

The Mutual-Gains Approach to Dealing with the Media

Take Into Account the Interests of the Media

Reporters have jobs to do, just like everyone else. They have deadlines to meet and editors to please. Publishers must keep circulation up and advertisers on board, and keep up with a rapidly changing and highly competitive market. In keeping with the mutual-gains approach, managers attempting to address public controversies must take into account the interests of the media. As James Gannon, the former executive editor of the *Des Moines Register and Tribune,* once said in regard to why some organizations fare better with the media than others, "I think the difference is that those people have a better understanding of what the press needs and wants, and they recognize that it is in their interest to work with journalists, even at the risk of an occasional bruise or bonehead play."[9]

What would it mean to keep the interests of the press in mind? The press's livelihood depends on information. If they are provided information, they have the raw material they need. Denying the media information gets in the way of them doing their job. Denying reporters information, furthermore, encourages them to uncover everything they can. There is no better story than a cover-up: it creates an opportunity for a reporter to become a hero. For example, when the Quebec Cree representative showed up to gather seemingly straightforward information on utility–smelter contracts, a cadre of lawyers appeared seeking to prevent the release of the contracts. Hydro-Quebec was hiding something! That was a good story worth pursuing. It was not good news for Hydro-Quebec. As Mark Jurkowitz, ombudsman for the *Boston Globe*, has written, "Reporters who write nice, moving features end up on the inside pages. Those who catch people with their hands in the cookie jar make Page 1."[10]

This brings us to our second point: the media want a good story, not just good information. Anyone who has a story to tell is more likely to be heard, although this does not mean it is appropriate to concoct a story! Rather, it is important to ask, "Why does this issue matter to the public and to the press?" For an industrial plant, the fact that particulate emissions have fallen by 30 percent might be something to share with state environmental regulators, but why should the media or the public care? They don't care if concentrations in parts per billion have declined. What they want to know is whether the company is working hard to protect public health. They care whether or not children or elderly parents are less likely to have respiratory problems because of the drop in particulate emissions. Although the media are not exactly customers, it makes sense to respond to them as if they were: give them what they need, in a form they can use, within the schedule they must meet.

Lastly, don't treat the media like enemies or you will create a self-fulfilling prophecy. The case of Jacksonville, Arkansas mentioned earlier indicates that doing battle with the media causes them to respond in kind. At Three Mile Island, Metropolitan Edison's plant manager, exasperated by a barrage of questions at a press conference, responded, "I don't know why we need to tell you each and every thing we do."[11] That antagonistic statement, while understandable given the intense pressure facing the manager, hurt the company badly. The reporters' worst suspicion—the company was withholding valuable information—was confirmed. The manager's angry words were printed everywhere. Both these examples suggest: Difficult as it may be, especially in times of crisis, do not add fuel to the fire. Work with, not against the media.

Tell the Media What You Know and Don't Know

This is a major theme of the mutual-gains approach: Be honest. Tell the media what you know and admit what you don't know. Bland reassurances or unsupported claims of certainty are far worse than a simple "I don't know."

As straightforward as this advice is, it is often met with "But, but, but . . . ." But, the truth is what you make it, so shape it to suit your needs. But people don't want to hear the truth, they want to hear what is exciting, provocative, or otherwise stirring; people don't want facts, they want feelings. But your story is only as good as your opponent's story, so put a good story out there, and may the best one win. But, if I tell them what I don't know, the situation will appear out of control.

We reply: "Spin-doctoring" offers limited long-term gains and imposes numerous short-term costs. We have cited numerous cases, from the *Exxon Valdez* to Three Mile Island to the breast-implant controversy, where overly optimistic claims, half-truths, or outright denials have led to anger, criticism, and ultimately a loss of credibility in the eyes of the public. The fact is, in today's world the media have come to believe that their job is to shoot down the claims of powerful interests and institutions, be they corporations or government. The ombudsman for the *Washington Post* put it particularly well. "Journalists know the company/institution/government has the expertise and money to spread its good-news message. Newspapers think it's their job to make sure people hear the other side."[12] The media are motivated to counterbalance overly rosy projections and reassuring promises.

How reassuring was it that the Disney corporation, in attempting to site its historical theme park near Washington, D.C., claimed that their development was only "good news for Prince William County"?[13] Disney asserted, in a letter to the *Washington Post*, that they would mitigate traffic increases, control development, manage growth, respect the environment, all while bringing a "win-win" project with 12,000 new jobs and $1.68 billion in additional tax revenue to the region. No wonder the press felt the need to throw a little cold water on the proposal. Instead of making only positive projections, Disney would have been better off providing a balanced assessment: Pointing out the concerns of their critics, suggesting how they intended to address them, and acknowledging that the involvement of those concerned might be necessary to help shape acceptable solutions.

The fact is, the press will uncover the negatives, whether information is provided willingly or not. It is next to impossible to control all the information available. Numerous government agencies, consumer groups, environmental advocacy groups, labor unions, and eyewitnesses are all possible sources of contradictory information. For instance, at Three Mile Island, after the first unannounced release of radioactive steam, the lieutenaut governor's staff asked the plant manager, "Why didn't you tell the press?" He said he had never been asked, or the question did not come up, or something like that. Immediately, caution in dealing with Metropolitan Edison increased.[14] Needless to say, the press found out about the release when government officials revealed it to the public. Furthermore, the government officials expressed "disappointment" that Metropolitan Edison had not been more forthcoming. Surprises make good press, but they are not good news for embattled institutions.

There is another important reason why spinning a story, rather than telling the truth, no longer works: The opposition may be better at it. Consider again Disney's attempt to site the historical amusement park they had dubbed "America." One could argue that Disney is (or, at least, was) the master of public relations and image creation. They were the squeaky-clean company that brought us Space Mountain, the Hall of Presidents, and EPCOT Center. As the Disney corporation went about siting their "America" theme park, they seemed to make all the right moves. The initial announcement of the park was followed by numerous political and press endorsements. Buses of eager local supporters flocked to Virginia's State House in Richmond to lobby for the development. Ultimately, Disney convinced state lawmakers and the governor to offer $163 million in subsidies. One local writer quipped, "It's remarkable that a corporation a continent away, unknown to the community, could present this colonial-style invasion as a fait accompli and have the project immediately endorsed by everyone who counts."[15]

But in the end Disney was outspun. Disney did not take into account a long list of wealthy residents who cherished the quietude of the surrounding countryside (where many of them just happened to own homes and farms). The opposition gathered experts ranging from the former chief of public relations for NASA's space program to one of Ronald Reagan's prime handlers. After sponsoring studies that indicated traffic impacts and infrastructure costs would be substantial, the critics quickly moved the campaign from the local to the national level. The National Trust for Historic Preservation took out an ad in the *Washington Post* asking Disney to reconsider. In the end, over 200 well-known and respected historians decried the loss of America's heritage and the vulgarization of America's history. Suddenly, Disney was being criticized by George Will and Mary Matalin, not exactly the anti-development, anticorporation types they expected. The opponents convinced Disney that their plan was, after all, not a good idea; they accomplished this while spending only one-tenth of what Disney spent promoting the theme park. Less than a year after its announcement, Disney withdrew its plan.

Both the Disney case and the Alar case mentioned earlier suggest that it is crucial to maintain trust. The mass media provide a setting in which well-trained spokespeople or famous celebrities can tell white lies (or perhaps worse, carry on without knowing the truth). The American public in the 1990s is not convinced of its institutions' good intentions; much of the public is instead frustrated and cynical. It is time to begin rebuilding trust by approaching the media with more openness and honesty. This will not be easy, and it will take courage. Leaders who move in this direction (as we discuss in Chapter VIII) will meet internal resistance. Some will be "burned" by either malicious or incompetent reporting. Some will find themselves misquoted and misunderstood. Yet the status quo is not sustainable and should not be acceptable to companies, government, or the public. In the words of the NRC's Denton, the spokesman who attracted a great deal of public attention during the Three Mile Island crisis, "I believe we frequently underestimate the public's ability to understand the situation, and have therefore inadvertently or purposely withheld information because of our perception of the danger of a crisis mentality when none was warranted. This is exactly the wrong approach to take with the public. If we want the public's trust, we must trust the public."[16]

Make Available People with Authority Who Can Share Their Views Openly

People want to know what is happening from those who are in the best position to answer questions. People want leaders, not spokespeople, to tell them the story. Over the years, the public has become wary of public-relations experts and communications vice presidents. Too often, these individuals have presented bad news in a sugarcoated form that has not, as it turns out, gone down well. At the same time, chief executives and top officials have remained mute or unduly restrained by numerous legal and public-relations advisors. As David Finn, a public-relations advisor, pointed out over 15 years ago, corporate leaders too often hide behind corporate anonymity. Even though they may have strong ethical beliefs and deeply held values, in their role as chief executive or senior-level manager they hide their motivations behind the bottom line. When senior executives do issue statements, their personal convictions are molded into smooth-talking, impersonal corporate-speak. David Finn concluded, "In a sad way, we public-relations advisors who try to help the companies we work for often do harm by preventing the true personalities of top management from being seen by the public."[17] In the midst of many controversies, the heads of embattled organizations have failed to seize the opportunities for leadership, and have been buried by a barrage of criticism.

In the *Exxon Valdez* spill, for example, Exxon was soundly criticized for waiting so long before it sent a senior executive to the disaster site. Almost four days after the spill, in an effort to bring the disaster under control, Exxon sent the president of Exxon USA, William D. Stevens, from Houston to Valdez. Lawrence Rawl, Exxon's CEO, did not visit the site in the first week, nor did he appear in public. In four major newspapers over a six-month period, Rawl was quoted (and presumably available) one-third less than Exxon Shipping's President Smith. In the absence of a leader at the helm, the White House was left to comment, "There is a sense that nobody is in charge there." Even Rawl admitted, in an interview with *Fortune*, that it would have been better if he had been more visible from the beginning of the crisis.[18]

In contrast, a highlight in Dow Corning's otherwise painful hammering in the press came when Dow Corning's new CEO, Keith R. McKennon, arrived at the February FDA panel. Prior to his appearance, the company was criticized for delegating public communication responsibilities, first to an operations vice president, and then to yet another vice president (of health care). One panel member deemed McKennon's approach a "new spirit of cooperativity, and, to borrow a term, 'Glasnost.'"[19] Prior to the panel, McKennon told the press, "For me and Dow Corning, the overriding responsibility is to the women who have mammary implants. . . . If it hasn't been clear until now, we are going to cooperate absolutely with the Food and Drug Administration, and that means we're going to quit complaining about who is on the advisory panel and all that."[20] McKennon's interactions with the press caused the *New York Times* to state that " . . . the company has taken a new attitude on scientific questions and public opinion."[21]

Of course, the CEO of a corporation may not always be the best choice to communicate with the public. Disney's Michael Eisner managed to irritate more than a few critics and supporters alike when he spoke during the debate over the proposed "America" theme park. Eisner told *CBS This*

Morning that Virginians would be lucky to have Orlando (home of Disney World) in their state. Supporters quickly tried to distance themselves from his paternalistic statements. They sought to mute images of Orlando's 30,000-acre sprawling park with its tawdry outlying motels, sideshows, and greasy spoons in the midst of the rolling hills of Virginia. When pressed regarding Disney's intention to commercialize American history, Eisner retorted: "The First Amendment gives you the right to be plastic."[22] Clearly, these comments did not inspire trust. Someone with slightly less authority but more tact might have been more effective. The problem is that many CEOs tend to lead lives far removed from the experiences of most people. Sheltered in glassed-in corner offices with a host of subordinates to meet their every request and need, top executives are often unused to criticism. One only has to think of the 1992 presidential campaign and George Bush's surprise at the bar-code reader in the grocery check-out line, to realize the damage an insulated executive can cause.

In nationally covered events, only a few key people represent the institutions involved. During the six months following the *Exxon Valdez* spill, in four major newspapers, only *three* Exxon officials were quoted more than ten times. During this same time period, *two* State of Alaska officials were quoted at least three times more than anybody else representing the state.[23] Key spokespeople are extremely important. A few people can powerfully influence how the public views entire institutions. Spokespeople can help establish trust and credibility or, unfortunately, they can as easily erode trust and mar reputations.

In the end, it is people who are knowledgeable, nondefensive, and have the authority to make commitments who can help the most. Spokespeople do matter. In the end, who says it, how it is said, and what's said, all make a difference. We do need to add one caveat: All of these attributes are of little value if the spokesperson is not mandated to follow an agency or corporate policy that says, "Tell the public what you do and what you don't know." Institutional limitations can easily undermine even the best spokesperson's abilities.

Work to Convince the Media They Have an Educative Role

In a poll conducted by the Times Mirror Center for the People and the Press, 60 percent of those interviewed said journalists get "in the way of society solving its problems."[24] William Raspberry, a syndicated columnist, says, "Our training, the news values we inculcate, the feedback we get from our editors, all encourage us to look for trouble, for failure, for scandal, above all for conflict."[25] One study of the news media and congressional policy-making pessimistically concluded, "The news media rarely alerted the public to a forthcoming vote on an issue at any stage of the congressional process. The news media rarely explained how a pending issue might affect the average citizen."[26] In an essay on the lost art of argument, Christopher Lasch suggested that the media's attempt to inform the public has led to the equivalent of news as junk mail; the media deliver an unending set of messages without context and without meaning to people's day-to-day lives.[27] He pointed out that as much as 40 percent of all news in newspapers comes essentially unaltered from releases churned out by public-relations experts in business, government, and even religious institutions.

We think the media can do more than fan the flames of conflict by highlighting the extreme views in each debate; they can do more than merely inform people about decisions after they have been made. The media can help to educate, as well as inform and entertain, their readers and listeners. They can not only reflect a broad spectrum of views, but also explain the content of a public debate. In short, the media can play a powerful role in promoting civic discourse.

Over the last several years, a concept known as public journalism or civic journalism has emerged. Rather than reporting the latest inflammatory campaign remark or covering political campaigns like horse races, those involved in civic journalism attempt to promote the common good. Lisa Austin, Research Director for the Project on Public Life and the Press, has recorded numerous instances of this new kind of journalism.[28] For instance, the Portland *Oregonian,* at the kickoff of the 1994 campaign, outlined ways voters might judge candidates. They printed pieces on the importance of experience, vision, planning, and negotiating skills. Readers were invited to write in about what they felt were important qualities in Oregon's leaders. The paper attempted to help people think about the campaign, not merely respond to it. The Akron, Ohio, *Beacon-Journal* went even further. After reading its five-part series on the stark social and economic disparities between blacks and whites, over 22,000 people returned a pledge coupon stating they would fight racism. The paper's publisher hired two facilitators to work with groups who wanted to actively address the problem. Within a year, over 10,000 people were involved in the effort. In these cases, the media were not only responding to the public's (and the media's) right to know, but the public's (and the media's) desire and obligation to take action.

The media can be a highly effective tool for educating the public, not only about conflict but about attempts to resolve it. The media can provide a forum for citizens, not merely experts and pundits, to carry on a public dialogue. The media can be a place to spotlight the deliberations of citizens working on difficult issues. For instance, when citizen forums and other consensus-building groups are meeting, the press can communicate the content of ongoing deliberations to a much wider public. The press should be invited to observe the proceedings. They should be kept informed and given all documents generated for the group as a whole. The press ought to be able to reflect the full spectrum of opinion, not just the polarized extremes. Furthermore, if the ongoing process is reported well, and explained in sufficient detail, the public will see their fellow citizens working hard to resolve differences. This will encourage others to participate. When only the extremes and the confrontations are presented, this discourages participation by those who are watching from the sidelines.

The press, at times, can even play a role in brokering consensus. In a multiparty dialogue over the ranking of environmental issues in Louisiana, the dialogue's steering committee decided to release an interim agreement to the media. Television cameras zoomed in on the document, including several blank lines where some parties had not yet added their signatures. (Underneath the blank lines was written "the discussions continue," to make clear that others still had opportunity to influence the negotiations.) This publicity helped generate further discussion which eventually led to a final signed agreement.

As the Akron story suggests, this kind of educative role means that more than just the reporters need to be involved. Citizens and decision-makers need to reach the publishers and owners of newspapers to urge them to take part in the process of consensus building. Papers often need to be asked for such support so that they can feel comfortable providing it. The media respond to feedback from people who are persuasive and persistent.

This does not mean going to the publisher to complain about reportorial coverage; nor does it mean that one party should unilaterally lobby the publisher to endorse "its side" of the story. Threatening to pull advertising when an unfavorable story appears sends exactly the wrong message. Parties in conflict should approach the media together and ask them to play an educative role in ongoing efforts aimed at building consensus. If one side feels the media have presented a biased or unfair picture of their views, they should ask for space or time to present a rebuttal. If the media agree that a mistake has been made, they can issue a correction, a clarification or even, if appropriate, an apology.

If one side or the other approaches the media, they are likely to provoke a skeptical response. However, if contending stakeholders approach the media together, they are more likely to be able to make the case for a civic-journalism perspective. In a consensus-building process, it is a good idea to have a media subcommittee. This group can prepare joint press releases. They can pursue collaborative strategies for engaging the media as a partner in the ongoing effort. The subcommittee can approach the media together, bringing legitimacy to the discussion of a wide range of views.

Use a Neutral to Speak in a Single Voice

Capable spokespeople are important, but institutions that engage in consensus-building efforts can do even better. A neutral can support the efforts of the media subcommittee discussed above. A neutral can bring credibility to a process that a spokesperson or hired media star cannot. Rather than communicate only the views and opinions of one side, a neutral in a consensus-building effort can speak for a diverse group of stakeholders working together to resolve their differences. This means that rather than negotiating through the press, the stakeholders have an advocate for the process they have jointly undertaken. Rather than offering only one view, a neutral can express the perspective of the entire group in a language that is intended to acknowledge not only differences but areas of agreement as well.[29]

The neutral can help to educate the press about the process of consensus building. Rather than focus on the issues under debate, the neutral can focus on the ways in which a broad array of representatives were brought to the table, the ground rules that have been developed to ensure a collaborative, fair, and effective process, and the subtleties of joint fact-finding, option generation, and negotiation. This kind of information can help lend credibility to the substantive decisions that are eventually made. As mentioned above, the neutral may play an important role in meeting with a publisher or a radio or TV station owner to explain the process and bring to their attention ways in which they can actively support the efforts of the group as a whole. The media are less likely to be skeptical of, and thus more likely to listen to, someone accountable to a broad array of interests rather than someone in one "camp" or another.

One particular advantage of utilizing a neutral as a spokesperson is that such individuals must be accountable to the entire group. The neutral has a vested interest in being judicious in the comments he or she makes. If the neutral misspeaks or conveys information in a way that is problematic to anyone in the group, those with concerns can bring them to the attention of the entire forum. Since the neutral is beholden to everyone involved, he or she must make adjustments (or be replaced), whereas a spokesperson for one side is only beholden to that side, and thus cannot be held accountable by all the stakeholders.

In a Consensus-Building Process, Establish Ground Rules to Guide Media Interactions

A consensus-building group should establish ground rules governing the interactions that each stakeholder has with the media. In addition to opening the group's work to media scrutiny, the stakeholders should come to some agreement about how each participant will interact with journalists outside of group meetings. Simple ground rules can help establish an atmosphere of openness and mutual accountability. They can help prevent a forum from becoming merely a circus of accusations, proclamations, and grandstanding. In no way should these ground rules restrict people's access to the media. They should only guide participants about how to say what they want without undermining the dialogue. For instance, two common ground rules used in many consensus-building efforts are:

- Participants agree that they are free to make statements to the press regarding their own concerns or reactions to meetings, but that they should refrain from attributing statements or views to other participants.
- If stories appear in which a participant's remarks are misrepresented or misinterpreted, that individual should inform the group as soon as possible.

Sometimes, a third ground rule is added:

- Participants will not make derogatory or personally demeaning statements about others involved in the process.

These ground rules serve several purposes. First, they provide a way for participants to set behavioral expectations. This initiates and supports the process of building agreements (in that if they cannot agree on how to conduct themselves, they are highly unlikely to agree on matters of substance). Second, such common ground rules provide guidance for groups that are not used to interacting with the media. In turn, these agreed-upon rules of behavior can help to forestall behavior that reflects the heat of the moment but that is likely to be regretted later. In short, ground rules help set mutual standards of performance. Third, ground rules provide a basis for accountability to the group. If participants do not like what someone else has said about them, they have an agreed-upon protocol for addressing their concerns. At the point when a problem arises, it is usually impossible to talk about how the disagreement should be handled. Often, a media protocol frees the participants to speak more frankly.

Parties may continue to speak to the press, making statements, taking positions, and asserting arguments in order to get their fellow disputants to move in one direction or another. These actions are part of any negotiation, but they are usually more effectively handled face to face, in open forums, rather than through the media. Nevertheless, some participants will find the opportunity too tempting. At the very least, ground rules of the sort described above will force them to speak only for themselves, avoiding the blow-ups that usually result when views are attributed to others.

It may be tempting to adopt ground rules that keep a citizens' forum out of the spotlight. After all, negotiations are hard work. Sometimes difficult issues need to be brought to the table and discussed. Painful as they may be at the time, such interactions may be necessary to move the group toward agreement. In the glare of the spotlight, however, people may be reluctant to engage in the kind of forthright dialogue necessary to achieve such movement. They may be too inhibited. The media do not make a forgiving forum nor a place to try out new and difficult ideas.

In some cases, groups may decide that subcommittee meetings or private caucuses should be off limits to the media. While this may generate an atmosphere more conducive to negotiation, it may also infuriate the media, who then feel shut out. In a statewide transportation planning effort in Maine, for instance, the *Kennebec Journal* opposed smaller caucuses of stakeholders outside of the full advisory board meetings. One reporter said that outside of the public eye, citizens would never know "what was given up," what "compromises were made," and where "the real movement was."[30] The paper charged that the proceedings were "going on in secret." While each stakeholder group must decide how it can best participate in a problem-solving dialogue, we think it is very important to be aware of the costs of leaving the media out.

Of course, consensus-building processes can face precisely the opposite problem. Once the fury has died down and the parties have decided to move on to the hard work of detailed negotiation, the media often disappear. The reality is that much negotiation, like most of the workings of democracy, is boring. Reviewing four pages of ground rules, fleshing out the details of a technical data-gathering plan, or haggling over the wording of a mission statement, are simply not media moments. The kinds of discussions essential to resolving conflict rarely make the evening news. The media tends to be outcome-oriented rather than process-oriented; that is, the media want the final story—who won and who lost—and how everyone feels about it. They have neither the time nor the resources to analyze what was or was not accomplished, still less how it was accomplished.

To some degree, this is a reality that we may have to accept. There are, however, at least a few alternatives. First, the press can generate goodwill by regularly attending consensus-building meetings. By doing so, reporters can build trust, show a commitment to learning more about the issues and the process, and at the same time, gain greater access to all the parties for comment and analysis. Second, the facilitators can meet with station owners and newspaper publishers to discuss the importance of continued coverage of the process, not just occasional participation when conflict flares. Third, a consensus-building group can keep the public informed through additional communication channels.

Use Additional Means of Communication

In today's complex world, citizens have numerous means to gather information, including local newspapers, national newspapers, magazines, radio, newsletters, network television, cable access channels, and the Internet. In order to broaden the base of information still further, consensus-building processes can stimulate the creation of new ad hoc means of disseminating information.

The venues are numerous. In most consensus-building processes, the facilitators take exacting notes in order to prepare meeting summaries or "key points of agreement and disagreement." Unlike traditional minutes, these summaries attempt to capture the flow of conversation as substantive issues are discussed. In this way the process of decision making, not just the results, is added to the group's memory. In addition, in order to encourage debate rather than personal criticisms, such summaries do not attribute statements to individuals. These summaries are typically mailed directly to participants, the press, local libraries, and interested citizens who ask to be on the mailing list.

In a dispute over the siting of a hospital in Connecticut, the biweekly meetings of the sixty-plus citizens' group were broadcast live on a local public-access cable station. The meetings were videotaped in their totality, and broadcast at regularly scheduled dates and times four times a week for more than a year. This way, participants had an exact record of what went on, and nonattendees had an opportunity to see for themselves what had transpired at meetings. The cable broadcasts gave citizens an opportunity to compare their interpretation of events with the perspective offered by the more traditional media. In a consensus-building process intended to help a community organize a new city charter in Chelsea, Massachusetts, the cable connection went one step further: residents were able to call in to voice their opinions about ongoing discussions. This Chelsea project also offered a hot line to allow citizens to get up-to-date information about upcoming meetings, to obtain drafts of the proposed charter, and to voice their opinions.

Some citizens' groups hold large public forums or publish their own newsletters. For instance, the Portland, Oregon district of the Corps of Engineers convened an Environmental Advisory Board to allow broader input into district policy-making. Board members, once convened, identified a list of concerns such as wetland conservation, the use of general wetlands permits, and cooperation between the Corps and local governments. At the end of this phase, the Board held facilitated public meetings to inform the broader public of the selected issues they hoped to work on and to obtain additional feedback within the region. Environmental interests, in particular, wanted to "check in" with their constituents before proceeding further. The Board kept the public informed through a newsletter cleverly called *Cattales.* If groups do not want to publish their own newsletters, information about their efforts can be published in existing newsletters, trade journals, or other specialized publications.

Consensus-building groups can also use the traditional media in untraditional ways. Upon completion of a long process of building consensus, forums can work with local media outlets to develop special inserts about their work. These can lay out issues, findings, conclusions, recommendations, as well as unresolved questions in a way that a standard newspaper article cannot. For instance the *Boston Globe,* along with Harvard University and the Massachusetts Institute of Technology, sponsored a three-day conference stretched out over two months on transportation planning in metro Boston called "Shaping the Accessible Region." One reporter covered the full conference. A "jury" was selected to hear arguments. Experts in transportation, planning, and politics contributed to the conversation, the public was invited to observe, moderators guided the discussions, and all sessions were broadcast on the New England Cable News Channel. The jury, after assimilating all the different views, issued nine recommendations that were covered in a special 16-page newspaper insert, complete with photographs, charts, and color graphics. The conference jury called on the governor to convene a supplementary participatory process to pursue the issues addressed by the conference in more detail. The press (in this case, the publisher of the *Boston Globe*) played a significant role in triggering an important conversation about the future of the city.

Finally, in the world of cyberspace, whole new avenues for alternative communication are possible. Electronic bulletin boards and e-mail provide a way to reach thousands of people directly. In complex disputes with numerous stakeholders stretched across thousands of miles, the Internet offers the means both to convey information and to hold a conversation. For instance, Eurasian environmental groups working on biodiversity, monitoring major development, and reducing pollution on four continents are connected through the Sacred Earth Network's telecommunications project. Since 1989, 150 environmental groups across fifteen republics in the former Soviet Union have been plugged into e-mail. The project has provided new computers and hookups, as well as practical training on use and upkeep. On the network, numerous groups share ideas and experiences. They keep Western groups informed and up to date about ongoing activities, and they communicate among themselves within Eurasia to float new ideas, organize, and take action. E-mail is a powerful way to share existing information *and* develop new ideas and alliances.

Set an Example for the Media to Follow

If it is any consolation, the media has an angry public on its hands, too. In a 1995 poll taken by the American Bar Association, 41 percent of those polled had lost respect for defense lawyers after watching the endless trial of O. J. Simpson. But attorneys can take solace: 56 percent of those polled said they had lost respect for the news media.[31] The media are viewed by the public as part of the problem—polarizing the debate, turning complex arguments into overly simplified sound bites, and transforming the search for justice into a spectacle. Interestingly, while journalists often appeal to the public's right to know, the news media have displayed those same qualities they criticize in others when the spotlight has been turned back on them. All too often, the news media hide behind their First Amendment rights, refusing to accept responsibility for their mistakes and failing to acknowledge the concerns of their readers and viewers. For instance, when CBS News was under fire for faking footage from the Afghanistan war in 1989, the station's president instructed his staffers in the classic stonewall: Don't talk to the press, or else. On a personal level, one media critic and journalist put it this way: "Reporters don't seem to understand when you're calling on a story— they expect to be treated with kid gloves."[32]

In short, when it comes to dealing with an angry public, the press isn't necessarily better at it than anyone else. As a newsletter devoted to promoting media fairness through public accountability stated, "Members of the public have been ignored, shouted at, hung up on, told that as laymen they wouldn't understand . . . "[33] Research on libel suits suggests that many people sue not so much because a media report harmed them as because when they attempted to discuss their concerns with the media outlet, they were treated poorly. To make matters worse, the media seem hypocritical when they refuse to open themselves up to the same scrutiny they expect to apply to others. Here is an opportunity for other institutions and organizations to set an example. Employ the mutual-gains approach: Be honest, tell the truth, acknowledge people's concerns, accept responsibility, offer contingent agreements, build long-term relationships—and provide an example to the news media. They might learn something.

In some instances, the media have learned something. Some outlets have made progress in finding ways to hear the public's concerns. For years, *60 Minutes* has set aside part of its broadcast to read letters, many of them critical, from its viewers. ABC has televised "town meetings" on media issues. In Minnesota, the Minnesota Newspaper Association helped establish the independent nonprofit Minnesota News Council in 1970. Through the council, citizens have an opportunity to respond to, and be heard by, the media when they feel they have been treated unfairly. The Council is a "halfway" point between internal complaint mechanisms like letters to the editor and full-scale, expensive, and time-consuming libel suits.

The Minnesota Council is made up of 20 or so members, equally divided between media and nonmedia representatives, and chaired by a member of the state's Supreme Court. The council typically receives about eighty complaints a year. Complainants are first urged to negotiate directly with the media outlets in question. If the complainant is not satisfied with the outcome, they return to the council. Typically, the council convenes for a full public meeting when it has five to ten complaints to consider. The plaintiff waives the right to sue, but both parties agree to engage in good-faith efforts to resolve their differences. The council has no authority to sanction alleged offenders; instead, the hearing is held in full public view, and the results are widely publicized.

Gary Gilson, the council's executive director, cites a case that reached the council several years ago as an example of the real value of opening up the press to public feedback. The *Minneapolis Star-Tribune* ran a story about a 15-year old African-American girl, single and pregnant. She volunteered for the feature. One photo showed the girl lifting her blouse to display her rounded, pregnant belly. Some in the African-American community responded angrily, accusing the paper of perpetuating the problem of racism and blaming teenage pregnancy on black Americans. The council heard the case and ruled overwhelmingly in favor of not the complainants but the paper, even citing its work as an example of outstanding journalism.

Something interesting happened next. The paper's editor-in-chief was not satisfied with the outcome. Having heard the concerns expressed during the process, he realized that he had a problem on his hands: his paper was doing a poor job of covering communities of color. The editor-in-chief formed a task force of editors and reporters. Over several months, the task force worked to prepare news stories on communities of color. At the same time, the project team members kept diaries of their experience. At the end of the project the paper printed the stories, as well as excerpts from the staff's diaries. In those excerpts, one African-America journalist admitted that at lunch time when her white colleagues came to invite her to lunch, she hid in the corner. She knew they invited her out of a sense of obligation, perhaps midwestern "niceness," which nonetheless masked a general discomfort with her presence. One 35-year-old white editor admitted he had never had a conversation with a black person. The diaries revealed not a monolithic institution called the press but a place where diverse people with different views, fears, and opinions work. The public was given an honest look from the inside. "This was really a healthy exercise," says Gilson. "This public and media dialogue which was so important would have never happened without the council hearing the case in the first place"[34] While the media, like many businesses and government agencies, have a long way to go, forums like the News Council offer concrete hope for both protection of free speech and accountability to the public.

Summary

Sadly, in most public controversies, the news media become the medium for negotiation. The disputing parties churn out press release after press release, take out advertisements in newspapers and magazines, and distribute hastily made videos in the hope that, in the rush to deadlines, stations will broadcast them as "the news." Unfortunately, the media do not make the best forum for resolving public debates. Much like a children's game where a message is passed from person to person around a circle until the original statement is woefully altered, meanings become hopelessly distorted when shuttled back and forth via the media. There is no immediate opportunity for clarification or correction. Questions and responses are so limited and delayed as to make a meaningful conversation impossible. The subtleties of body language and facial expressions are lost. Freed from the respectfulness that face-to-face contact tends to elicit, parties let loose their most angry, contentious, and insulting statements. To make matters worse, the media are not neutral. Journalists have points of view. Editors and publishers hold ideologies and political views that must be taken into account. Media competitors' offerings must be met with equally compelling stories.

We think that there is another way to engage the news media. The media's concerns, interests, and needs, just like any other party in a negotiation, must be taken into account. The media should be a place where people can tell the truth, rather than make the "spin of the day." The media can play a role in educating, not merely enflaming, the public. The media can report on negotiations without having to be the only forum for negotiation. The media can add value by not only reporting, but also helping to resolve, difficult and complex conflicts. All of this will require, though, that the media and those who seek to manipulate them, adopt a new attitude toward media relations.

CHAPTER VIII

Principled Leadership

On an August day in 1979, William J. LeMessurier, the lead structural engineer for the new Citicorp Tower in New York City, came to the company's executive vice president, John S. Reed, and said, "I have a real problem for you, Sir."[1] What was the problem? LeMessurier had discovered that the bracing system in the new office tower was unusually sensitive to winds, known as quartering winds, blowing at 45-degree angles against the building. The building had already been built and the drawings, calculations, and estimations put away. But a phone call from a student asking about the building prompted LeMessurier to carry out some additional calculations. To his surprise, he found that the structure he had designed was in trouble.

As LeMessurier worked through his calculations, he became more worried. In addition to the innovative design's sensitivity to quartering winds, a change to the building's wind braces made during construction had caused them to be weaker than needed. The wind brace joints, to save money, had been bolted rather than welded. Given the leverage of high wind forces, the internal joints could experience a force four times that experienced by the walls of the building in a diagonal wind. This force was not taken into account when the bolts, rather than the welding, were put in place. To make matters worse, as LeMessurier investigated the problem, tests in a wind tunnel suggested that uneven winds in a severe storm might make the building vibrate. This would cause even more strain. After weeks of engineering calculations, wind-tunnel tests, and an analysis of New York City's weather patterns, LeMessurier drew an alarming conclusion: the Citicorp Building would experience catastrophic failure from a kind of storm that occurred, not once every hundred years, but once every sixteen years.

This story, recounted in the *New Yorker*, speaks to the question of leadership. William LeMessurier uncovered a flaw in the structure of a building for which he was the lead engineer. He labored hard to understand the extent of the problem. When he discovered for himself how great the risk was, he assumed responsibility. He could have remained silent, hoping for the best. Buckling under the pressure, he could have committed suicide, letting the world go on, and perhaps the building go down. The pressure he felt must have been enormous: The collapse of a $175-million symbol of Citicorp's financial eminence; the collapse of a real high-rise building killing thousands of unsuspecting victims; impending professional humiliation.

However, he decided to tell the truth—to admit his (and others') mistakes and to work hard to fix them, at the expense of his professional reputation, career, and livelihood. After assuring himself that his calculations and predictions were accurate, LeMessurier first contacted the lead architect's attorney, because he was unable to reach the architect, Hugh Stubbins. The next day, LeMessurier faced an office full of attorneys. They in turn contacted another structural engineer to review his predictions. After further deliberations, LeMessurier reached Stubbins, and together they approached Vice President John S. Reed. Moving to the top of the chain of command, Reed and LeMessurier approached the chairman of Citicorp, Walter Wriston. Wriston grabbed a yellow pad and began taking notes. Problem-solving had begun. Together, they devised a plan to shore up the building's flawed joints and to help stabilize the building while the repair work was done. By October, the "mistake" was fixed.

LeMessurier had displayed an essential element of leadership: honesty. LeMessurier had stood before a host of potential critics and openly admitted he had helped create a serious problem. As Arthur Nusbaum, a project manager for the building's original contractor, said of LeMessurier: "'It started with a guy who stood up and said, 'I got a problem, I made the problem, let's fix the problem.'"[2]

Doing the Right Thing

In one respect, this book is about public relations: How to interact with the public in a way that will minimize harm to and maximize gain for agencies and organizations, be they federal departments or Fortune 500 companies. In another respect, this book is about honesty, accountability, reputation, and integrity—ephemeral qualities that are hard to pin down. It is about the qualities we value above and beyond their ability to generate profits or votes: Decency, respect, and compassion. Thus, we did not feel we could end this book without a discussion of leadership, the kind necessary to put into practice the six deceptively simple principles that make up the mutual-gains approach to dealing with an angry public.

Because events that inspire anger can escalate so rapidly, it is important that leaders operate from a basic set of principles that offer guidance in turbulent moments. In the heat of a crisis, leadership—in the sense of making the right moves—must be exercised. Few people are prepared for the blitzkrieg of public attention that follows when a public controversy erupts. Even the most sophisticated managers can be thrown off guard. Disney's Michael Eisner told the *Washington Post*, "I'm shocked because I thought we were doing good," Eisner said in an interview with *Washington Post* editors and reporters. "I expected to be taken around on people's shoulders . . . ."[3] In public-relations crises, there simply is not enough time to work out a script. Events spin out of control, unsuspecting interests become players, and the media pile on. Furthermore, because controversies typically require quick thinking and rapid response, what occurs to those in the public eye to say comes as often from the gut as from the head. Thus implementing the mutual-gains approach requires more than a method or a formula. It requires more than a few simple rules and a day or two of study. Implementing the mutual-gains approach requires effective leadership.

Remember the hard-working, able plant manager we described in the hypothetical situation on pages 5–6 of this book? In real life, two weeks before a public hearing on Bill Colvin's plant's permit application, sulfur dioxide escaped from the plant. A truck had mistakenly pulled away while still hooked to a chemical feed line. The evening winds blew the sulfur dioxide across the channel to a neighboring shipyard where 27 plant workers were overcome with respiratory problems, including nausea and vomiting.

At the public hearing (which had already been scheduled prior to the accidental release), angry citizens demanded to know why the plant management had failed to show concern for the community. The recent accident, the injured workers, and the potential for future accidents were foremost in people's minds. Citizens asked why the company rarely held open meetings with residents, and why it failed to give widespread notice of meetings before they were held. Despite a litany of concerns, the hearing examiner realized that according to the letter of the law the permit should be granted. She offered Bill Colvin, the plant manager, two choices: Continue with the proceedings (which would almost certainly end with the permit being granted) or suspend the formal proceedings and initiate a discussion with the community in an attempt to address residents' broader concerns.

The neighborhood surrounding the plant posed all sorts of risks on top of those specifically related to his plant: freeways bordered the area on one side, railroad tracks carrying hazardous chemicals bordered another, and a refinery straddled a third. Most of the residents were not particularly well off, and very few worked at the plant. People might eventually grow tired of the issue and go on about their day-to-day lives. Colvin could have shut the door, hoping that the anger would die down. But he did not. Colvin turned to the examiner and said, "Let's take time out to talk."[4] In a pivotal moment, he displayed leadership.

What exactly do we mean by effective leadership? Warren Bennis, an astute student of leadership, said, "[I]t is not enough for a leader to do things right; he [or she] must do the right thing."[5] That is what both LeMessurier and the plant manager did: At a crucial moment, their instincts compelled them to do the right thing. It is at these key moments that the mutual-gains approach offers a framework for action. These basic principles provide direction for leaders whose instincts propel them to "do the right thing." Bill Colvin knew, without ever being formally trained in our approach, to acknowledge the concerns of others, to accept responsibility, to admit mistakes, to share power, to act in a trustworthy fashion at all times, and to focus on building long-term relationships. While numerous discussions, negotiations, and actions occurred, all were informed by this guiding set of principles.

Integrity, Honesty, and Trust

In recent surveys exploring the attributes of superior leaders, honesty has been identified more often than any other.[6] Honesty is key in the mutual-gains approach, a quality too often missing in the practice of public relations. Bennis uses the metaphor of a tripod to described how leaders generate and sustain trust, one of his key leadership ingredients. Bennis explains. "One leg of the tripod is ambition; another leg is competence; and the third leg is integrity, moral fabric. . . . I've seen too many leaders who have that formidable combination of competence and ambition absent integrity and they succeed only in the short term, if that."[7] The inspired leader seeks to build and repair her organization's relationship with the public and the public's trust in her organization. The mutual-gains leader acts in a trustworthy fashion at all times.

Unfortunately, in the dog-eat-dog world of public relations, honesty is too often ignored or even ridiculed. Winning is the name of the game. Swaying the public one way or another is the mission. "They won't act that way, so why should we?" people ask. Honesty is seen as the policy of fools and dupes. We, the authors, think that integrity and honesty are not liabilities. But we also think that leaders should not march blindly into the burning fires of vilification and blame. That is martyrdom, not leadership. Taking responsibility does not mean accepting blame willy-nilly. Listening to others' concerns does not necessarily mean agreeing with those who are concerned. Making contingent commitments does not mean promising whatever others demand.

Take the able plant manager. He was not simply caving in to "radical hysteria" or "unreasonable community pressure." Like any good businessman, he had a job to do: He had a plant to run, products to produce, shipments to make, customers to satisfy, bosses to please, and employees to pay. However, he saw that it was in his interest to engage in a dialogue with neighbors surrounding the plant. He could have sent the company's community relations designee or called in someone from corporate headquarters. He could have ignored the complaints. But he didn't. Colvin took responsibility for responding to people's concerns above and beyond the requirements of the law.

This did not mean the plant manager was giving up his negotiating power or offering self-sacrificing concessions. As it turned out, when he sat down to negotiate with community activists and an outside advocacy group, he worked hard to protect his company's interests. He did agree to support a Citizen's Advisory Group (CAG) and allow the community to have ongoing input into the plant's management. He agreed to adopt emergency notification procedures, including a plant siren and a localized radio-broadcast system, but he did not agree to limitations on the plant's production or production mix, even after the accidental spill. He agreed to help underwrite a citizens' health survey, but he wanted to review the scope of the study, and did not want to be bound by its results, since he had no control over its final design and implementation. He did not agree, nor hint, that possible health problems in the community had been caused by his operations when so many other risk factors were present. While the community wanted the company to closely monitor truckers hauling the company's chemicals through its streets, he could not agree to track haulers once they were outside the gates of the plant. Such oversight could have been prohibitively costly.

Toward the end of the negotiation, when activists seemed more intent on grandstanding than negotiating, on disagreeing rather than agreeing, Colvin asked his attorney to reschedule the full public hearing before the hearing examiner. The hearing examiner, in turn, sent out a letter stating that only the narrow issues concerning the permit (and not the community's many larger concerns) would be open for discussion. But rather than waiting patiently for the hearing that would grant his plant its permit, the manager called in his fellow negotiators to try one more time to work out an agreement. He pointed out that everyone had more to gain by settling than by walking away. Within days, the parties signed an agreement. What had begun as an angry confrontation and a potential public-relations liability for the company became a real success for both the community and the company (not to mention the others helped indirectly by the precedent-setting nature of the agreement that was finally negotiated). One city councilwoman said: "The company's willingness to take on community advisors inspired a vote of confidence from the community."[8] A community activist concluded, "The negotiations were successful. We now get along much better. They've shown they are willing to work in good faith with the community."[9]

While paying close attention to his interests, the plant manager was able to act in a trustworthy fashion, displaying integrity as well as competence. One community activist put it this way: "He responded to basic common-sense arguments. He made decisions independent of company pressures and the advice of attorneys. [He] just seemed to say, I am a plant manager and I want peace with this community."[10] Another community negotiator had this to say: "[He] talked to you up-front" and "[He] had a slow and easy way of talking. He comes through as a man telling the truth and being sincere."[11]

How to Inspire Trust

Political scientist Robert Axelrod had a simple question: When should a person cooperate and when should a person be selfish at the expense of the other?[12] To help answer this question he invited experts in game theory to submit computer programs for a tournament. Computer programs would "compete" against each other in repeated rounds of a scorable game called

"The Prisoner's Dilemma." After each round of play, programs would be awarded three points if they had been designed to cooperate on that round, one point if they had been programmed to defect (i.e., not cooperate), and five points if one defected while the other tried to cooperate. Fourteen programs were submitted; the simplest program, one written by Professor Anatol Rapoport of the University of Toronto, won.

The winning program employed a strategy best characterized as "tit-for-tat." That is, the program always began by cooperating (in the hope of encouraging a long-term cooperative relationship that would be worth 3 points to each side on every round), but thereafter, mimicked whatever the other side had done on the previous move. For example, if the other program had defected on the first round (thus gaining five points), tit-for-tat would defect on the next round. To test tit-for-tat's resilience, Axelrod organized a second full round of the game. Alexrod published the results of the first tournament and invited all comers to enter a second tournament. This time he received 62 entries, some quite complex. Surprisingly, tit-for-tat won again! From this winning entry, Axelrod (and others, like Douglas Hofstadter) have teased out these several simple prescriptions that seem to work well to encourage and sustain cooperative relationships.

- *Be cooperative:* Start out by being cooperative. Don't try to establish a tough reputation at the outset.
- *Be provokable:* If attacked, especially after an initial display of cooperation, let it be known that you will retaliate in kind. This should not be a bluff. Make it clear that you would prefer to cooperate, but you will not continue to cooperate if attacks continue.
- *Be forgiving:* If attacked, do not assume you will always be under attack. Consider that a mistake has been made. Don't remain provoked if it is possible to reestablish trust (although this may be difficult and require numerous small confidence-building steps).
- *Be clear:* Most of all, be explicit with regard to your intentions at each step along the way. Otherwise, your motives or interests may be misconstrued. This is why face-to-face dialogue is so important.

Of course, everyday interactions are not as simple as a computer game where the payoffs are clear and understood by all sides. Nonetheless, we think managers, executives, and officials who conduct themselves in this way are more likely to achieve success in public relations than are those who adopt a contentious or manipulative strategy at the outset (or, perhaps worse, have no strategy at all). The tit-for-tat strategy inspires trust and allows, over time, for cooperation with others. As Axelrod concludes:

> Once the word gets out that reciprocity works, it becomes the thing you do. If you expect others to reciprocate your defections as well as your cooperations, you will be wise to avoid starting any trouble. Moreover, you will be wise to defect after someone else defects, showing that you will not be exploited. Thus you too will be wise to use a strategy based upon reciprocity. So will everyone else.[13]

Sharing, Listening, and Learning

In the spring of 1995, two federal laboratories had reached a stalemate. Their federal department had launched a realignment spurred by the need for downsizing. As part of this initiative, the department had slated one lab for closing. But, when the other lab's congressional supporters got wind of the planned closure, they got on the horn with the right people. Within days, the other facility was slated for closing. Then that laboratory's congressman made his phone calls, and suddenly the tables were turned once again. Finally the department, frustrated with the political ping-pong game, told the two, "You figure out a merger plan together (or else)."

Under a very tight deadline and with the specter of institutional death looming, the upper-level managers formed a consolidation team and began to meet. Meetings were quite contentious and the interactions were riddled with disagreement and distrust. The two laboratories saw themselves as almost total opposites. "We represent fundamentally different cultures," the manager from the first lab said. "You're academic and research driven. We're market and customer driven. We've worked hard to become product focused and do not want to go back to your old ways of doing business."

Several managers from the second lab replied, "We've been competing for years. You've always relied on your political connections to undermine our funding. You promote your mission at the expense of your people." To make matters worse, Congress was threatening budget cuts and the department faced a 15 percent reduction in its total number of employees. While the managers involved in the face-to-face negotiations continued to wrestle with the merger idea, they told their colleagues away from the table that it just wouldn't work. Several described the potential merger as "a shotgun wedding of two people who hate each other."

Finally, out of frustration and fear, the two laboratories asked for the help of a neutral. After several days of intensive interviewing of mid- and top-level managers, 25 to 30 employees from each facility were brought together the following week to brainstorm the potential joint gains as well as the pitfalls of merging. At this two-day session, something very interesting happened.

During a late morning session with the whole group, the facilitator asked, "Why merge?" To start the conversation off, Bruce Burns (a pseudonym), a top-level manager, remarked to the group, "You know, we're only merging because we have to. That's the bottom line. We're being made to do this. Otherwise, we'd all go home." In response, a retiring top-level manager stood up and adamantly disagreed. "I think there are good reasons for this merger beyond the directive from headquarters. I think there are real benefits we can achieve through a merger." Other staff, mostly lower ranking than Bruce, also remarked on the potential for increased efficiency, increased political clout, and improved productivity through the sharing of ideas, research staff, and accumulated knowledge if the two laboratories merged. In effect, lower-level employees were telling their top-level managers to stop fighting, and instead to get on with the task of joining forces! Reluctantly, even somewhat unwittingly, Bruce had opened himself up to the sometimes painful but absolutely necessary activities of leadership: sharing, listening, and learning. By opening the discussion up to the 60 employees, rather than just the few on the consolidation team, by openly sharing his opinion and listening to disagreement, by being able to learn from others, Bruce had exercised leadership. From that point on, Bruce increasingly became an advocate for the consolidation.

The leadership required by the mutual-gains approach is not simply about knowing precisely what to do. Yes, technical skills, expertise, and knowledge are extremely important. As the Three Mile Island and James Bay cases suggest, however, the world's best engineers can be rendered helpless in the face of an angry public. The mutual-gains approach requires a three-step process of sharing information, listening to others, and learning from new information.

Leaders adopting the mutual-gains approach have to be willing to share what they know with others. After years of fighting to find the right answers in order to get ahead, after years of being rewarded for following the rules, managers who have risen to the top aren't always good at taking risks.

Top-level managers and officials aren't always skilled in sharing all that they know with others, in listening—especially to people "below" them on an organizational chart—and in changing their minds in the face of new information or better ideas. Since knowledge is power, sharing such power seems threatening and frightening. But the ability to share what we know with others so that they can make better informed judgments is essential to the mutual-gains approach. Roger Schwarz, writing on facilitative leadership, argues: "Facilitative leaders understand that valid information helps form the foundation of effective relationships. Working consistently with this value means that facilitative leaders share all relevant information with group members."[14]

The ability to listen to others is also essential. When high-ranking spokespeople or executives are being assaulted by those who are fearful, anxious, and angry, they must put aside their own feelings of defensiveness so they can listen carefully to what people have to say. This makes dealing with angry publics difficult. Good leaders, effective in times of crisis, must be as keyed into their audience's interests as their own. As so many of the cases in this book suggest, top-ranking officials are often more likely to be thinking about what their shareholders will think, what their attorneys have told them not to say, and how their words might be distorted by the media. Yet they will not be able to acknowledge the concerns of others if they cannot hear them. Listening must be active. This means reiterating what has been heard to be sure that the message has been received. Then it requires asking follow-up questions to probe underlying assumptions and concerns. For a principled leader, asking good questions is as important as providing the "right" answers.

Lastly, the mutual-gains leader must be able to learn. Sharing and listening are not enough. Knowing the answers and making decisions are not enough. Executives and officials must be able to learn. Muddling through difficult problems together with concerned stakeholders in the face of uncertainty is important. Multiple stakeholders can bring information to the table that the leader cannot otherwise know. Individuals, even those who are traditionally seen as critics or enemies, may have terrific ideas. Disagreement (not fighting) and deliberation can lead to clarity. Through discussion, a new and better understanding of the problem may arise. A leader must be able to learn through discussion and informed and respectful debate. The bottom line is: Reasoned argument matters.

What Leaders Value

Leaders who are able to institute the mutual-gains approach to dealing with an angry public are likely to value

- honesty and openness
- inclusion rather than exclusion
- decision making informed by, not driven blindly by, technical knowledge and expertise
- fairness as well as efficiency
- integrity as much as success;
- truth as well as efficacy
- both emotion and reason;
- creativity and chaos
- compassion as well as competence.

In addition, leaders most able to put the mutual-gains approach into action view problems from many angles. They acknowledge complexity rather than rushing to categorize situations in simplistic terms. These leaders are self-aware, able to see how others can contribute to both problems and solutions. These leaders know how to avoid demonizing adversaries or resorting to polarizing behavior out of frustration or fear. They are brave enough to admit mistakes and wise enough to listen to others who have constructive advice and new ideas. They are confident that joint problem-solving, teamwork, and collaboration—rather than coercion, raw competition, and victory—will serve them well. Their actions reflect a vision, both practical and idealistic, of how the world might and can be.

Leadership and Institutions

Thus far, we have focused on leadership as an individual quality: The sum of the traits and beliefs that are important to harnessing the mutual-gains approach. But leadership does not take place in a vacuum. It assumes meaning in the context of institutions, whether they are small businesses with a few employees or multibillion-dollar corporations with tens of thousands of employees. To utilize the mutual-gains approach, proponents will not only have to be good practitioners in a public setting, they will have to be effective advocates within their own agencies or organizations. Unless an entire organization is committed to the mutual-gains approach, an individual leader is likely to be ineffective.

Total Quality Management (TQM), reinventing government, market-driven government, and customer-focused strategies dominate organizational redesign today. Work and workers are organized increasingly in a lateral rather than a hierarchical fashion. That is, organizations are flatter, with fewer layers of management. Ground-level employees are being empowered to act without first having to check each decision "up the line." Managers are learning that "taking charge" means giving employees the support they need to become independent decision-makers.

Government services are being privatized or reinvented. With downsizing in government, public institutions find that they have to do more with less. With the growing belief that government is not the end-all when it comes to solving our most pressing social and environmental problems, both non-governmental organizations and businesses have had to become more adept at helping themselves. The mutual-gains approach to public relations is entirely consistent with these trends. Nonetheless, institutions can be remarkably resistant to change. The conventional wisdom—shared assumptions or expectations about the way things are supposed to be done—can be very slow to change. Implementing the mutual-gains approach will require, in many organizations, a fundamental alteration in basic rules of thumb. Such changes will have to be nurtured by inspired and inspiring leadership.

The fact of the matter is: The mutual-gains approach is not merely cosmetic. Neither a single leader nor a whole organization can readily change its posture toward the press, its attitude toward using outside facilitators, its reliance on official spokespersons, or its view toward engaging an angry public in a face-to-face dialogue. We wish that such adjustments required nothing more than a new press policy or an internal directive requiring all employees to change the way they act. Given the disputes in which we have been involved as neutrals and the many others we have studied, it is clear that this is not the case.

There are success stories of institutional change. The Corps of Engineers, for instance, has undergone fundamental shifts in the last twenty years. The Corps has taken great strides in adopting collaborative problem-solving methods consistent with the mutual-gains approach. Contractors and Corps engineers "partner" with one another to speed up construction schedules and improve safety as well as overall project quality. Corps planners work with hundreds, even thousands of citizens to engage diverse stakeholders in planning for future projects. Some Corps districts have invited environmental groups, town government officials, and businesses to help formulate district-level policies. At the national level, the Corps is partnering with trade organizations and other branches of the military to improve overall relations and increase fairness and consistency across cities and regions. However, after 25 years of experimentation, collaborative approaches are still resisted in some districts. Regardless of the stated policy, some districts merely go through the motions, simply to keep headquarters happy. District-level employees are still uncomfortable sharing information about the inner workings of the agency with the public or truly involving the public in decision making.[15]

What does it get to take an organization to change the way it deals with the public? What does it take to encourage an organization to begin using the principles of the mutual-gains approach? The following story, told by Peter T. Johnson, former administrator of the Bonneville Power Administration (BPA), is instructive.[16]

When Johnson came to the BPA in 1981, all seemed well. The BPA had been successful since 1937 in transmitting and marketing electric power. Johnson figured his new employer simply needed to continue as it had, perhaps with a few minor adjustments. He was wrong. Everywhere the BPA was immersed in controversy. Plans to extend transmission lines met with strong protest. Agreements with nuclear power plants turned out to be costly mistakes, leaving the BPA with a huge debt and an organizational black eye. Congress was working to diminish the BPA's authority nationally, while new organizations such as the Northwest Power Planning Council were challenging the BPA's authority regionally.

What had happened? Why was a successful and competent agency suddenly caught in a crossfire? BPA was caught in the beginnings of a fundamental paradigm shift that continues to create enormous difficulties for government institutions to this day. Agencies that were once the repository of specialized knowledge, manned by educated professionals, and charged with making decisions on behalf of the public at large, are being downsized, privatized or even eliminated. Government officials like Gifford Pinchot and Michael Straus, who built their federal natural resource agencies (the U.S. Forest Service and the Bureau of Reclamation, respectively) into enormous professionalized bureaucracies controlling immense quantities of land and water, are no longer asked to make decisions for the rest of us. The idea of progress through government intervention that once reigned has been replaced by a sense that government bureaucracies stifle creativity and work only to perpetuate themselves, not the public good.

The view of government agencies as independent, objective bureaucracies that would make decisions in the public interest was essential to the progressive reformer's philosophy. Michael Barzelay, a public-policy professor, argues that this conception of a professional government arose during the nineteenth century, as the United States changed from a primarily rural, agrarian, decentralized society to a primarily urban, industrial, and centralized society. In the best thinking of the time, the professional bureaucracy would end, once and for all, the corrupt politics of mid-nineteenth-century America. Decisions would be made "rationally" by trained experts rather than politically by the loyal operatives of party bosses. According to Barzelay, "Bureaucratically-minded reformers . . . placed a high value on the impersonal exercise of public authority. To this end, they argued that actions intended to control others should be based on the application of rules and that no action should be taken without authorization. When officials' actions could not be fully determined by applying rules, professional or technical expertise was to be relied on to make official action impersonal."[17]

This paradigm served the country well from the Depression through World War II, but the 1960s saw growing disillusionment with government, triggered by the Vietnam War and Watergate. The public came to distrust government agencies. The public wanted to know what the bureaucrats and elected officials were doing. It seemed that the government, once the watchdog of big business, needed a watchdog of its own. The task of government reform was begun yet again. "Sunshine laws" were added. Decision-makers and the various parties they were supposed to be regulating were allowed only limited communications. Citizens now had clear standing in the courts with the addition of "citizen suit" provisions in environmental legislation. Nongovernmental organizations emerged to monitor agency decision-making. Courts and agencies began to maintain voluminous and detailed records of all rule-making activities. But even these reforms were not enough. Procedural reforms led to problems that, in turn, had to be rectified. Elaborate procedural requirements took more time and cost more money. The "hard look" of more intensive court review delayed action. Greater access to information opened up technical debates to greater numbers of experts who often disagreed, creating more, not less, confusion. In addition, lobbying increased as the opened doors of government encouraged more groups to establish a Washington presence. While these reforms were aimed at creating accountability, it is questionable whether they increased it significantly, if at all.[18]

In the face of these vast societal changes, what did Peter Johnson and Bonneville Power do? Johnson decided the public ought to be invited to play a greater role in decision-making. That meant his organization would have to acknowledge the concerns of outsiders and share power in order to regain trust. Johnson says of his initial foray, "[at first] . . . all the apprehensions I had accumulated during my twenty years in the private sector began to surface"[19] His attorneys fueled his fears. How could the BPA release its important documents, open its policies to public scrutiny, and forfeit control? Surely all this would provide even more ammunition for the Authority's worst critics, the lawyers argued. Egged on by staff experienced in electoral politics who believed principles much like the mutual-gains approach were possible and practical, Johnson forged ahead. He was quick to realize that if the shift were to be effective, he would personally have to take it very seriously. "Any new approach would fail if we thought of it as something we did when we had political problems. We had to make a rock-solid, ethical commitment to be open and honest, whether or not it was to our presumed, near-term advantage."[20] Johnson freed his public-involvement staff to make decisions. The public-involvement staff was incorporated into Johnson's office. Funds were expended to compensate local communities and to help fund state oversight of the BPA's activities.

Within a few years, the BPA asked for an independent analysis of its new approach. The result? The Authority, to its surprise, was still viewed as "arrogant, insensitive, and uncaring."[21] While some parts of the BPA really took citizen concerns to heart, other parts marched ahead without consulting anyone. Stakeholders saw inconsistency and were not reluctant to point to it. The status report was sure to become a public-relations nightmare if it was released. Despite many internal recommendations to "deep six" the analysis, Johnson, with the encouragement of his staff, did the opposite— the Authority released the evaluation report to the media in full, along with a letter outlining the steps that the BPA intended to take to change further.

Now the real work began. The BPA had to truly change its collective attitude and develop new skills in working with the public. Performance requirements were added to all management job descriptions. Public-involvement planning requirements were put in place. Training programs were established for employees—from top to bottom. Old bureaucratic reporting forms were modified; BPA staff prepared more readable and shorter documents for public distribution. Citizens were given "issue alerts" to inform them of upcoming decisions and how they could participate. Perhaps most importantly, in the spirit of mutual gains, Johnson devoted two years to collaboratively developing with his staff a policy on public involvement. In addition, Johnson sat down, face-to-face, with his strongest critics—the environmental "crazies."

Over time, the work of Johnson and his staff paid off. After extensive public involvement, the Authority decided to put two nuclear plants "on ice." Nonetheless, BPA still found itself caught between investor-owned (IOU) and publicly-owned (POU) utilities. Given the decision, IOUs were stuck with nongenerating plants whose capital costs they could not incorporate into their rate base. Because of different regulations governing POUs, the POUs had already incorporated their share of the capital costs into their rates. IOUs had to suffer their mistake alone while POUs were allowed to charge it back to their customers. Needless to say, this created conflict. Furthermore, because Johnson was formerly in the private sector, the POUs expected, despite the BPA's statutory obligation to first take account of the interests of POUs, that he would support the IOUs. Johnson, instructed by the Secretary of Energy to ease the tension, had to find a way to avoid litigation and please the IOUs, the POUs, as well as numerous governors, senators, public-interest groups, and rate payers. Johnson, in keeping with the mutual-gains approach, decided to hold open public meetings. One IOU executive called Johnson when he announced this process and asked whether Johnson had ". . . gone mad to try to settle a giant and bitter lawsuit in a glass house?"[22] After more than a year and numerous setbacks and difficulties, an agreement was reached. Most stakeholders were satisfied. BPA (not to mention the IOUs and POUs) avoided litigation. IOUs were relieved of some of their financial burden through power trades and benchmarking to average prices at operating nuclear plants elsewhere in the country. A bitter suit had been resolved in a glass house open to public scrutiny.

Looking back over his tenure at the BPA, Johnson concluded: "Having seen BPA's many victories, I am more convinced than ever that public involvement is a tool that today's managers in both public and private institutions must understand. . . . While others are mired in disputes and litigation, astute practitioners of public involvement will have hammered out an agreement and gotten on with the project. In short, they will have made better decisions and found a new source of competitive advantage."[23]

Concluding Remarks

The need for the mutual-gains approach is now greater than ever. As government grows smaller, it must do a better job with less. Angry publics, conflict, and litigation will only drain limited funds that ought to be used instead to accomplish the tasks government has been empowered to do. Government must rebuild trust with the American people if it is to be entrusted to achieve its goals in an efficient and effective manner. Business, in many cases, no longer has government as a partner, for better or worse. The public will expect more and more accountability directly from private enterprise. The temptation, with fewer regulations and less money to enforce them, may be to ignore the public's concerns. The free market may seem like a license to do precisely as business pleases. This would be a terrible mistake. Freedom, as Mary Ann Glendon, a Harvard Law School professor, reminds us, can only work when responsibilities as well as rights are given their due. Over time, deception, dishonesty, and concealment will lead to more, not less, anger—anger America's business cannot afford in today's competitive international marketplace.

We cannot imagine how a corporate executive or public official could hold sway at home with his or her own employees if he or she employed strategies used all too often in the outside world. While TQM has effected significant change in the way businesses relate to employees and customers, TQM principles have not yet reached broadly into the realm of public relations. But it is time they did. The ways in which leaders deal with angry publics ought to parallel the best ways they deal with others inside their own organizations. In short, leaders must (1) realize that they are engaged in a search for mutually satisfactory outcomes; (2) negotiate as if long-term relationships mattered; (3) work to build trust regardless of what the other "side" does (because their credibility depends on it); and (4) build an organizational commitment that matches their individual commitment to honesty.

The six principles of the mutual-gains approach are simple. Using them in today's complex world is not. Putting these principles into action will require visionary, courageous, and collaborative leadership. As Johnson's and Bonneville Power Authority's story suggests, the road is difficult. Unfortunately, there are no shortcuts.

Notes

Chapter I. Introduction

1. Milo Geyelin, "Suits by firms exceed those by individuals," *Wall Street Journal*, December 1993, sec. B, p. 1.
2. Ibid.
3. Lorri Grube, "Litigation: Cost of litigation to US businesses," *Chief Executive* 19 (January 1995), p. 56.
4. Ibid.
5. Adrian Ladbury, "U.K. rethinks safety regulations," *Business Insurance* 28 (2 May 1994).
6. Ibid.
7. "Antipolitics '94: The anger ever deeper," *New York Times Magazine* (16 October 1994) p. 37.
8. Ibid.
9. Chris Reidy, "Term-limits supporters turn to ballot," *Boston Globe* (30 October 1994), p. 38.
10. U.S. auto insurance companies have lobbied for years to require auto manufacturers to install seatbelts, air bags, side impact protection, and other safety measures. While increasing the cost of automobiles, these would certainly lower the cost of auto insurance. In another example overseas, both U.K. employers and safety inspectors raised concern about the deregulation of workplace health and safety regulations. The chairman of a large association of insurers said: "'Risk managers in industry and commerce like myself are hoping that the sweeping away of hundreds of apparently superfluous regulations in our areas of responsibility will not result in an increase in the frequency and severity of loss events, particularly large-scale disasters. The prospect of saving hundreds of millions of pounds looks attractive. One slip like Piper Alpha, though, can cost a billion pounds." (Adrian Ladbury, "U.K. rethinks safety regulations," *Business Insurance*, 2 May 1994.)
11. "Public interest pretenders," *Consumer Reports* 59 (1994): 316–320.
12. Trip Gabriel, "Public relations has potent image at journalism schools," *New York Times*, 17 March 1994, sec. B, p. 1.

13. Allen H. Center and Patrick Jackson, *Public Relations Practice,* 4th ed. (Englewood Cliffs, NJ: Prentice Hall, 1990).
14. Scott M. Cutlip, Allen H. Center, and Glen M. Broom, *Effective Public Relations,* 6th ed. (Englewood Cliffs, NJ: Prentice Hall, 1985).
15. Kenneth N. Gilpin, "Man in the news: An embattled chairman," *New York Times,* 8 December 1984, sec. A, p. 7.
16. Thomas J. Lueck, "Crisis management at Carbide," *New York Times,* 14 December 1984, sec. D, p. 1.
17. Jesus Sanchez, "Alaska launches ad drive as spill hurts tourism," *Los Angeles Times,* 29 March 1989, sec. 4, p. 1 and "Alaska fighting effect of spill," *Newsday,* Nassau and Suffolk edition, 8 May 1989, p. 8.
18. Philip J. Hilts, "Grim findings on tobacco and a decade of frustration," *New York Times,* 18 June 1994, sec. A, p. 1.
19. ———,"Cigarette manufacturers debated the risks they denied," *New York Times,* 16 June 1994, sec. A, p. 1.
20. Richard Mauer, "Alaska aid assails oil industry for 'inadequate' response to spill," *New York Times,* 26 March 1989, sec. A, p. 1.
21. Timothy Egan, "Exxon concedes it cannot contain most of oil spill," *New York Times,* 30 March 1989, sec. A, p. 1.
22. "Crisis management plan: Wash, rinse, spin," *Harper's Magazine,* 284 (1991): 21–28.

Chapter II. Why Is the Public Angry?

1. "Baboon liver implant angers animal activists," *Chicago Tribune,* 1 July 1992, p. 11.
2. George Bush and Michael Dukakis, "Transcript of the Second Bush-Dukakis Debate," *New York Times,* 14 October 1988, sec. A, p. 14.
3. Broadcast of *Inside Washington* [Federal News Service] 15–16 October 1988.
4. Dale W. Griffin and Lee Ross, "Subjective construal, social inference, and human misunderstanding," *Advances in Experimental Social Psychology* 23 (1991), pp. 319–359.
5. Estimates of deaths vary widely. The *Boston Globe* reported the 7,000 figure on the tenth anniversary of the disaster (Dilip Ganguly, "Anger in India 10 years after Bhopal leak," *Boston Globe,* 4 December 1994). *The Ecologist,* on the other hand, cites estimates of eyewitnesses and local voluntary agencies at as many as 15,000 (Richard Morehouse, "Unfinished business: Bhopal ten years after," *The Ecologist,* 24/5).
6. Sanjoy Hazarika, "India police seize factory records of Union Carbide," *New York Times,* 7 December 1984, sec. A, p. 1.
7. Stephanie Abarbanel, "Toxic nightmare on Main Street," *Family Circle* (14 August 1990), pp. 77–128.
8. John F. Ahearne, "Telling the public about risks," *Bulletin of the Atomic Scientists* 46/7 (1990): 37(3).
9. Stephanie Abarbanel, "Toxic nightmare on Main Street," *Family Circle* (14 August 1990), pp. 77–128.
10. Susan Reed and Janice Carswell, "Animal passion," *People* (18 January 1993), p. 36.
11. Ibid, p. 39.
12. Neal D. Barnard, "The AMA and the physicians committee for responsible medicine," Letter to editor and reply, *Journal of the American Medical Association* 268/6 (1992): 788(2).

13. Janice Perrone, "Scientists tell of harassment by activists," *American Medical News* 35 (23–30 March 1992), p. 3.
14. Ibid.
15. Sam Howe Verhovek, "Power struggle," *New York Times Magazine* (12 January 1992): 16.
16. Peter Newman, "The beaching of a great whale," *Mclean's* 104/37 (1991): 38(1).
17. Dan Burke, "Power plays in Quebec," *Mclean's* 103/48 (1990): 23(2).
18. Benoit Aubin, "Vicious propaganda," *Montreal Gazette,* 13 September 1991.
19. David Kuechle, "Negotiating with an angry public: advice to corporate leaders," *Negotiation Journal* 1/4 (1985), pp. 326–327.
20. Roger Fisher, William Ury, and Bruce Patton, *Getting to Yes: Negotiating Agreement Without Giving In,* 2nd ed. (New York: Penguin Books, 1991).
21. Tim Smart, "Breast implants: What did the industry know, and when?" *Business Week* (10 June 1991): 94.
22. Thomas M. Burton, "Dow Corning refuses to give the FDA independent report on breast implants," *Wall Street Journal,* 15 January 1993, sec. B, p. 7.

Chapter III. The Mutual-Gains Approach

1. Max H. Bazerman and Margaret A. Neale, *Negotiating Rationally* (New York: The Free Press, 1992), p. 55.

Chapter IV. Accidents Will Happen

1. The Kemeny Commission was chaired by John G. Kemeny, a mathematician and president of Dartmouth College. Other members included the then Governor of Arizona, Bruce Babbitt, Patrick Haggerty, President, CEO, and Chairman of the Board of Texas Instruments, and eight other sociologists, engineers, attorneys, and citizens.
2. President's Commission on the Accident at TMI, chaired by John G. Kemeny, *The need for change: The legacy of TMI* (Washington, DC: U.S. Government Printing Office, 1979), p. 34. Social and psychological effects such as increased distrust of authority and chronic stress were marked. For more, see Maureen C. Hatch et al., "Cancer rates after the Three Mile Island nuclear accident and proximity of residence to the plant," *The American Journal of Public Health* 81/6 (1990): 719–724.
3. President's Commission on the Accident at TMI, chaired by John G. Kemeny, *The Need for Change: The Legacy of TMI* (Washington, DC: U.S. Government Printing Office, 1979), p. 122.
4. U.S. House of Representatives, Committee on Interior and Insular Affairs, Majority Staff, *Reporting of Information Concerning the Accident at Three Mile Island* (Washington, DC: U.S. Government Printing Office, 1981), p. 106.
5. President's Commission on the Accident at TMI, chaired by John G. Kemeny, *The Need for Change: The Legacy of TMI* (Washington, DC: U.S. Government Printing Office, 1979), p. 123.
6. President's Commission on the Accident at TMI, chaired by John G. Kemeny, *Task Force Report: Public's Right to Information* (Washington, DC: U.S. Government Printing Office, 1979), p. 85.

7. President's Commission on the Accident at TMI chaired by John G. Kemeny, *The Need for Change: The Legacy of TMI* (Washington, DC: U.S. Government Printing Office, 1979), p. 126.

8. Mitchell Rogovin et al., "Three Mile Island: A report to the commissioners and to the public," Pt. 3 in vol. 2 of *Nuclear Regulatory Commission Special Inquiry Group: Response to the Accident.* (Washington, DC: U.S. Nuclear Regulatory Commission, 1979), p. 1060.

9. President's Commission on the Accident at TMI, chaired by John G. Kemeny, *Task Force Report: Public's Right to Information* (Washington, DC: U.S. Government Printing Office, 1979), p. 98.

10. U.S. Senate, Committee on Environment and Public Works, Subcommittee on Nuclear Regulation, *Nuclear Accident and Recovery at Three Mile Island,* (Washington, DC: U.S. Government Printing Office, 1980), p. 144.

11. U.S. House of Representatives, Committee on Interior and Insular Affairs, Majority Staff, *Reporting of Information Concerning the Accident at Three Mile Island* (Washington, DC: U.S. Government Printing Office, 1981), p. 144.

12. Ibid., p. 115.

13. Ibid.

14. Ibid., p. 120.

15. Ibid., p. 133.

16. Mitchell Rogovin et al., "Three Mile Island: A report to the commissioners and to the public," Pt. 3 in Vol. 2 of *Nuclear Regulatory Commission Special Inquiry Group: Response to the Accident.* (Washington, DC: U.S. Nuclear Regulatory Commission, 1979), p. 1071.

17. President's Commission on the Accident at TMI, chaired by John G. Kemeny, *The Need for Change: The Legacy of TMI.* (Washington, DC: U.S. Government Printing Office, 1979), p. 131.

18. Donald Janson, "Radiation is released in accident at nuclear plant in Pennsylvania," *New York Times,* 29 March 1979, Sec. A, p. 1.

19. Ibid., sec. D, p. 22.

20. Ibid.

21. Richard D. Lyons, "Federal experts suggest filters caused accident: Utility differs," *New York Times,* 29 March 1979, sec. D, p. 22.

22. ———, "Atomic plant is still emitting radioactivity." *New York Times,* 30 March 1979, sec. A, p. 20.

23. Ben A. Franklin, "Nuclear foes see grave risk in Pennsylvania mishap, but utility aides are unalarmed," *New York Times,* 30 March 1979, sec. A, p. 19.

24. Ibid.

25. President's Commission on the Accident at TMI, chaired by John G. Kemeny, *The Need for Change: The legacy of TMI.* (Washington, DC: U.S. Government Printing Office, 1979), p. 135.

26. "Credibility meltdown, The," *New York Times.* 30 March 1979, sec. A, p. 30.

27. Richard D. Lyons, "Atomic plant is still emitting radioactivity," *New York Times,* 30 March 1979, sec. A, p. 20.

28. Ben A. Franklin, "Conflicting reports add to tension," *New York Times,* 31 March 1979, sec. A p. 1.

29. Ibid.

30. Ibid.

31. Ibid.

32. Richard D. Lyons, "Children evacuated: But Governor says later further pullouts are not thought likely," *New York Times*, 31 March 1979, sec. A p. 1.

33. Ibid.

34. David Burnham, "Congress is briefed: Carter aide at scene says danger to the public is believed remote," *New York Times*, 31 March 1979, sec. A p. 8.

35. Richard D. Lyons, "Children evacuated: But Governor says later further pullouts are not thought likely," *New York Times*, 31 March 1979, sec. A p. 8.

36. President's Commission on the Accident at TMI, chaired by John G. Kemeny, *Task Force Report: Public's Right to Information* (Washington, DC: U.S. Government Printing Office, 1979), p. 163.

37. David Burnham, "Congress is briefed: Carter aide at scene says danger to the public is believed remote," *New York Times*, 31 March 1979, sec. A p. 1.

38. B. Drummond Ayres, Jr., "Regulator of a nation's reactors: Harold Ray Denton," *New York Times*, 2 April 1979, sec. A, p. 15.

39. Richard D. Lyons, "Officials say nuclear power plant is cooler but still in crisis; trapped-gas danger persists; bubble size reduced: Wider evacuation possible, agency chief says—Carter to visit site," *New York Times*, 1 April 1979, sec A. p. 1.

40. "Problem seen easing," *New York Times*, 2 April 1979, sec. A, p. 1.

41. Harold Denton, Keynote speech to the Nuclear Energy Agency Workshop on Public Information During Nuclear Emergencies, 17–19 February, at Paris, France, 1988. In *Nuclear energy: Communicating with the Public* (Paris: Organization of Economic Cooperation and Development, 1991), p. 48.

42. Ibid.

43. Mitchell Rogovin et al., "Three Mile Island: A report to the commissioners and to the public," Part 3 in vol. 2 of *Nuclear Regulatory Commission Special Inquiry Group: Response to the Accident* (Washington, DC: U.S. Nuclear Regulatory Commission, 1979), p. 1069.

44. President's Commission on the Accident at TMI, chaired by John G. Kemeny, *Task Force Report: Public's Right to Information* (Washington, DC: U.S. Government Printing Office, 1979), p. 68.

45. Ibid., p. 69.

46. U.S. House Committee on Interior and Insular Affairs, Majority Staff, *Reporting of Information Concerning the Accident at Three Mile Island* (Washington, DC: U.S. Government Printing Office, 1981), p. 113.

47. Ben A. Franklin, "Conflicting reports add to tension," *New York Times*, 31 March 1979, sec A p. 1.

48. B. Drummond Ayres, Jr., "Regulator of a nation's reactors: Harold Ray Denton," *New York Times*, 2 April 1979, sec. A, p. 15.

49. President's Commission on the Accident at TMI, chaired by John G. Kemeny, *Task Force Report: Public's Right to Information* (Washington, DC: U.S. Government Printing Office, 1979), p. 61.

50. B. Drummond Ayres, Jr., "Regulator of a nation's reactors: Harold Ray Denton," *New York Times*, 2 April 1979, sec. A, p. 15.

51. B. Drummond Ayres, Jr., "Governor in an uncommon crisis: Richard Louis Thornburgh," *New York Times*, 4 April 1979, sec. A, p. 16.

52. President's Commission on the Accident at TMI, chaired by John G. Kemeny, *Task Force Report: Public's Right to Information* (Washington, DC: U.S. Government Printing Office, 1979), p. 54.

53. Ibid., p. 52.

54. Ibid., p. 53.

55. Consensus Building Institute (CBI), *Partnering, consensus building, and alternative dispute resolution: Current uses and opportunities in the U.S. Army Corps of Engineers,* (Fort Belvoir, VA: Office of Counsel and the Institute for Water Resources, U.S. Army Corps of Engineers, 1995).

56. David Vogel and Timothy Kessler, "Regulatory compliance," Paper presented at SSRC Conference on International Law and Global Environmental Change, Geneva, Switzerland, June 1993, p. 32.

57. Joseph DiMento, "They treated me like a criminal: Sanctions, enforcement characteristics, and compliance," In *Environmental Law and American Business: Dilemmas of Compliance,* (New York: Plenum Press, 1986), p. 170.

58. Art Davidson, *In the Wake of the* Exxon Valdez: *The Devastating Impact of the Alaska Oil Spill* (San Francisco: Sierra Club Books, 1990), 19.

59. Ibid., p. 104.

60. "In ten years you'll see nothing," *Fortune* 19 (8 May 1989): 50–51.

61. Keith Schneider, "Exxon is ordered to pay $5 billion for Alaska spill," *The New York Times,* 17 September 1994: sec. A, p. 1. Of course, Exxon quickly appealed the verdict, calling it "totally unwarranted and unfair," "Exxon to fight damage award in Valdez lawsuit," *National Petroleum News* (November 1994, vol. 86, no. 12), p. 8.

62. Art Davidson, *In the wake of the* Exxon Valdez: *The devastating impact of the Alaska oil spill,* (San Francisco: Sierra Club Books, 1990), pp. 223–224.

63. Ibid., p. 222.

64. Endispute, Inc, *Resolving Disputes Associated with the* Valdez *Accident,* (Boston: Endispute, Inc., 1989), p. 2.

65. Ibid., pp. 9–11.

66. Art Davidson, *In the Wake of the* Exxon Valdez: *The Devastating Impact of the Alaska Oil Spill* (San Francisco: Sierra Club Books, 1990), p. 115.

67. U.S. House of Representatives, Committee on Interior and Insular Affairs, Subcommittee on Water, Power, and Offshore Energy Resources, *Investigation of the* Exxon Valdez *Oil Spill: Oversight Hearings before the Subcommittee on Water, Power, and Offshore Energy Resources of the Committee on Interior and Insular Affairs,* 2 vols. 101st Congress, 1st sess, 5 May 1989 (Cordova, AK) and 7–8 May 1989 (Valdez, AK), (Washington, DC: U.S. Government Printing Office, 1989), p. 281.

68. John Keeble, *Out of the Channel: The* Exxon Valdez *Oil Spill in Prince William Sound,* (New York: HarperCollins, 1991), p. 75.

69. Ibid., p. 174.

70. Ibid., p. 176.

71. Ibid., p. 160.

72. U.S. House of Representatives, Committee on Interior and Insular Affairs, Subcommittee on Water, Power, and Offshore Energy Resources, *Investigation of the* Exxon Valdez *Oil Spill: Oversight Hearings before the Subcommittee on Water, Power, and Offshore Energy Resources of the Committee on Interior and Insular Affairs,* 2 vols. 101st Congress, 1st sess, 5 May 1989 (Cordova, AK) and 7–8 May 1989 (Valdez, AK) (Washington, DC: U.S. Government Printing Office, 1989), p. 11.

73. DeBenedictis, "Exxon fights oil-spill suits: Close to 150 cases are consolidated in two Anchorage actions," *American Bar Association Journal* 77 (Nov 1989): 18, cited in John Gallagher, "In the wake of the *Exxon Valdez:* Murky legal waters of liability and compensation," *New England Law Review* 25 (Winter 1990), p. 582.

74. For more information on the legal framework, see John Gallagher, "In the wake of the *Exxon Valdez*: Murky legal waters of liability and compensation," *New England Law Review* 25 (Winter 1990), pp. 571–616.

75. U.S House of Representatives, Committee on Interior and Insular Affairs, Subcommittee on Water, Power, and Offshore Energy Resources, *Investigation of the* Exxon Valdez *Oil Spill: Oversight Hearings before the Subcommittee on Water, Power, and Offshore Energy Resources of the Committee on Interior and Insular Affairs*, 2 vols. 101st Congress, 1st sess, 5 May 1989 (Cordova, AK) and 7–8 May 1989 (Valdez, AK) (Washington, DC: U.S. Government Printing Office, 1989), p. 37.

76. Ibid., p. 10.

77. Ibid., p. 10.

78. Ibid., p. 9.

79. Ibid., p. 12.

80. Ibid., p. 13.

81. John Keeble, *Out of the Channel: The* Exxon Valdez *Oil Spill in Prince William Sound* (New York: HarperCollins, 1991), p. 237.

82. Ibid., p. 237.

83. Ibid., p. 161.

84. U.S. House of Representatives, Committee on Interior and Insular Affairs, Subcommittee on Water, Power, and Offshore Energy Resources, *Investigation of the* Exxon Valdez *Oil Spill: Oversight Hearings before the Subcommittee on Water, Power, and Offshore Energy Resources of the Committee on Interior and Insular Affairs*, 2 vols. 101st Congress, 1st sess, 5 May 1989 (Cordova, AK) and 7–8 May 1989 (Valdez, AK), (Washington, DC: U.S. Government Printing Office, 1989), p. 12.

85. Art Davidson, *In the Wake of the* Exxon Valdez: *The Devastating Impact of the Alaska Oil Spill* (San Francisco: Sierra Club Books, 1990), pp. 115–116.

86. Ibid., p. 115.

87. Ibid., p. 229.

88. Ibid., pp. 146–147.

89. Ibid., p. 208.

90. George Laycock. "The disaster that won't go away." *Audubon* (September 1990), p. 108.

91. "Exxon says cleanup authorization was late," *New York Times*, 31 March 1989, sec. A, p. 12.

92. "In ten years you'll see nothing," *Fortune* 19 (8 May 1989), pp. 50–51.

93. "Exxon says cleanup authorization was late," *New York Times*, 31 March 1989, sec. A, p. 12.

94. Ibid.

95. John Holusha, "Exxon's public-relations problem," *New York Times*, 2 April 1989, sec D., p. 1.

96. "In ten years you'll see nothing," *Fortune* 19 (8 May 1989), pp. 50–51.

97. Michael Straube, "Is full compensation possible for the damages resulting from the *Exxon Valdez* oil spill?" *Environmental Law Reporter* 19 (August 1989): 10349.

98. Don Clark, "Big Pentium gamble puts Intel in the chips," *Phoenix Gazette*, 13 June 1995, sec. B, p. 3.

99. Chris Reidy, "Waiting on pines and needles," *Boston Globe*, 22 December 1994, p. 41.

100. See *Breaking the Impasse* and the newsletter *Consensus* for numerous examples of multiparty disputes resolved through stakeholder groups.

Chapter V. Risky Business

1. Bernard D. Reams, Ed., *Food and Drug Administration General and Plastic Surgery Devices Panel. Transcript of the panel meeting on February 18, 19, 20, 1992 on the topic of silicone gel-filled breast implants* (Buffalo, NY: William S. Hein and Co., Inc., 1992), 1:45.

2. Ibid., 1:73.

3. Ibid.

4. John Czrey, "So many chemicals, so few answers," *Business Week*, 13 March 1995, p. 98.

5. Walter Rosenbaum, "More choice: Risk assessment," In *Environmental Politics and Policy*, 2d ed. (Washington: Congressional Quarterly Press, 1991), p. 153.

6. The Conservation Foundation, *Risk Assessment and Risk Control*, (Washington, DC: The Conservation Foundation, 1985), p. 31.

7. Walter Rosenbaum, "More choice: Risk assessment," In *Environmental Politics and Policy*, 2nd ed. (Washington, DC: Congressional Quarterly Press, 1991), p. 149.

8. Environmental Resources Limited (ERL), *Guidance on managing risk and uncertainties in environmental decisions*, (Prepared for DGMH: Ministerie van Volkshuisvesting, Ruimtelijke Ordening en Milieubeheer, The Hague, The Netherlands, 1987), p. C8.

9. Walter Rosenbaum, "More choice: Risk assessment," In *Environmental Politics and Policy*, 2nd ed. (Washington, DC: Congressional Quarterly Press, 1991), p. 150.

10. Ibid., 152.

11. Ibid., 153.

12. Connie Ozawa, *Recasting Science: Consensual Procedures in Public Policy Making*, (San Francisco: Westview Press, 1991), p. 52.

13. Paul Slovic, B. Fischhoff, and S. Lichtenstein, "Rating the risks: The structure of expert and lay perceptions," in *Environmental Impact Assessment, Technology Assessment and Risk Analysis*, edited by V.T. Covello et al. (New York: Springer-Verlag, 1985).

14. It is important to note, that while suggestive, the comparison between the Roper polls and the EPA's own risk assessment were not highly rigorous. EPA had listed 31 problem areas, whereas only 20 of those areas could be found in the polling data. Furthermore, it's not at all certain that the categories presented to the public, such as "genetic engineering" or "non-nuclear radiation" were as rigorously defined as and clearly associated with the categories constructed by the EPA.

15. Environmental Resources Limited (ERL), *Guidance on Managing Risk and Uncertainties in Environmental Decisions*, (Prepared for DGMH: Ministerie van Volkshuisvesting, Ruimtelijke Ordening en Milieubeheer, The Hague, The Netherlands, 1987), p. C11.

16. Ortwin Renn, William J. Burns, Jeanne X. Kasperson, Roger E. Kasperson, and Paul Slovic, "The social amplification of risk: Theoretical foundations and empirical applications," *Journal of Social Issues* 48/4 (1992): 154.

17. William Leiss and Christina Chociolko, *Risk and Responsibility*, (Buffalo, NY: McGill-Queen's University Press, 1994), p. 52.

18. In a sense, this is nothing more than the free rider problem often discussed in relation to public goods and market failures, or the utilitarian view that humans seek to experience pleasure and avoid pain.

19. John F. Ahearne, "Telling the public about risks," *Bulletin of the Atomic Scientists* 46/7 (1990): 37.

20. Richard Wilson and Edmund A.C. Crouch, "Risk assessment and comparison: An introduction," *Science* 236 (17 April 1987): 267–270.

21. For a controversy that centered around uncertainty, it's ironic that even the number of devices implanted could not be estimated with any accuracy. Manufacturers and surgeons estimated the 2 million number, but this number was based on devices, including saline implants, sold, not implanted. A survey of households by the National Center for Health Statistics estimated that only 1 million women had received the implants (*New York Times*, 29 January 1992). One employee of Dow Corning told reporters: "Until there's an implant registry established, we'll probably never know how many . . . . We know of no methodology to determine the number of women with silicone breast implants" (Ibid.).

22. Jean Seligman et al., "Another tempest in a C cup." *Newsweek*, 23 March 1992, p. 67, and Tim Smart, "Breast implants: What did the industry know and when?" *Business Week*, 10 June 1991, p. 94.

23. Philip J. Hilts, "FDA seeks halt in breast implants made of silicone," *New York Times*, 7 January 1992, sec. A, p. 1.

24. Ibid.

25. Bernard D. Reams, Ed., *Food and Drug Administration General and Plastic Surgery Devices Panel. Transcript of the panel meeting on February 18, 19, 20, 1992 on the topic of silicone gel-filled breast implants* (Buffalo, NY: William S. Hein and Co., Inc., 1992), 2:466.

26. Philip J. Hilts, "Experts suggest U.S. sharply limit breast implants," *New York Times*, 21 February 1992, sec. A, p. 1.

27. "FDA does and doesn't," *Wall Street Journal*, 24 February 1992, sec. A, p. 14.

28. Philip J. Hilts, "As it quits implant business, maker says product is safe," *New York Times*, 20 March 1992, sec. A, p. 12.

29. Sherine E. Gabriel et al., "Risk of connective-tissue diseases and other disorders after breast implantation," *New England Journal of Medicine*, 16 June 1994, p. 1697.

30. "Do breast implants cause systemic disease? Science in the courtroom," *New England Journal of Medicine*, 16 June 1994, p. 1749.

31. "The $4.3 billion mistake," Editorial, *Wall Street Journal*, 17 June 1994, sec. A, p. 14.

32. "Breast implant update," *New York Times*, 18 June 1994, pp. 1, 20. This was a bit of revisionist history on the *Times'* part. The paper never flatly stated that the implants were unsafe. However, the *Times'* strong support of Kessler's actions along with the detailed reporting on the charges of numerous product liability suits certainly suggested that the paper thought the implants were anything but safe.

33. Philip J. Hilts, "Experts suggest U.S. sharply limit breast implants," *New York Times*, 21 February 1992, sec. A, p. 1.

34. Bernard D. Reams, Ed., *Food and Drug Administration General and Plastic Surgery Devices Panel. Transcript of the panel meeting on February 18, 19, 20, 1992 on the topic of silicone gel-filled breast implants* (Buffalo, NY: William S. Hein and Co., Inc., 1992), 1:46.

35. Bernard D. Reams, Ed., *Food and Drug Administration General and Plastic Surgery Devices Panel. Transcript of the panel meeting on November 12, 13, 14 1991 on the topic of silicone gel-filled breast implants* (Buffalo, NY: William S. Hein and Co., Inc., 1991), 2:48.

36. Bernard D. Reams, Ed., *Food and Drug Administration General and Plastic Surgery Devices Panel. Transcript of the panel meeting on February 18, 19, 20, 1992 on the topic of silicone gel-filled breast implants* (Buffalo, NY: William S. Hein and Co., Inc., 1992), 1:73.

37. Ibid., 1:101–102.

38. Ibid., 1:98, 105.

39. Ibid., 1:137–139.

40. Ibid., 1:181.

41. Ibid., 1:107–110, 169.

42. Ibid., 1:175–176.

43. Philip J. Hilts, "FDA seeks halt in breast implants made of silicone," *New York Times*, 7 January 1992, sec. A, p. 1. Kessler was purported to say that despite all the panels, hearings, and discussions, we knew more about the life of an automobile tire than about that of a breast implant. Jack Fisher, "The silicone controversy—when will science prevail?" *New England Journal of Medicine*, 18 June 1992, p. 1698.

44. Bernard D. Reams, Ed., *Food and Drug Administration General and Plastic Surgery Devices Panel. Transcript of the panel meeting on November 12, 13, 14 1991 on the topic of silicone gel-filled breast implants*, (Buffalo, NY: William S. Hein and Co., Inc., 1991), 2:93.

45. Ibid., 2:100.

46. Ibid., 2:101.

47. Bernard D. Reams, Ed., *Food and Drug Administration General and Plastic Surgery Devices Panel. Transcript of the panel meeting on February 18, 19, 20, 1992 on the topic of silicone gel-filled breast implants* (Buffalo, NY: William S. Hein and Co., Inc., 1992), 2:185.

48. Ibid.

49. Bernard D. Reams, Ed., *Food and Drug Administration General and Plastic Surgery Devices Panel. Transcript of the panel meeting on November 12, 13, 14 1991 on the topic of silicone gel-filled breast implants* (Buffalo, NY: William S. Hein and Co., Inc., 1991), 2:18.

50. Ibid., 2:27.

51. Ibid., 2:41.

52. Ibid., 2:53.

53. U.S. House of Representatives, Committee on Government Operations, Human Resources and Intergovernmental Relations Subcommittee, *The FDA's regulation of silicone breast implants: A staff report prepared by the Human Resources and Intergovernmental Relations Subcommittee*, December 1992, (Washington, DC: U.S. Government Printing Office, 1993), p. 36.

54. Ibid., pp. 36–37.

55. Bernard D. Reams, Ed., *Food and Drug Administration General and Plastic Surgery Devices Panel. Transcript of the panel meeting on February 18, 19, 20, 1992 on the topic of silicone gel-filled breast implants* (Buffalo, NY: William S. Hein and Co., Inc., 1992), 3:231.

56. Philip J. Hilts, "Top manufacturer of breast implants replaces its chief," *New York Times*, 11 February 1992, sec A, p. 1.

57. Bernard D. Reams, Ed., *Food and Drug Administration General and Plastic Surgery Devices Panel. Transcript of the panel meeting on February 18, 19, 20, 1992 on the topic of silicone gel-filled breast implants* (Buffalo, NY: William S. Hein and Co., Inc., 1992), 2:15.

58. Ibid., 2:19.

59. Peter M. Sandman, "Mass media and environmental risk: Seven principles," *Risk: Health, Safety, and Environment* (Summer 1994), p. 260.

60. Thomas M. Burton and Scott McMurray, "Dow Corning still keeps implant data from public despite vow of openness," *Wall Street Journal*, 18 February 1992, sec. B, p. 3.

61. Thomas M. Burton, "Dow Corning refuses to give the FDA independent report on breast implants," *Wall Street Journal*, 15 January 1993, sec. B, p. 7.

62. Ibid.

63. Bernard D. Reams, ed., *Food and Drug Administration General and Plastic Surgery Devices Panel. Transcript of the panel meeting on February 18, 19, 20, 1992 on the topic of silicone gel-filled breast implants* (Buffalo, NY: William S. Hein and Co., Inc., 1992), 3:219.

64. Marsha F. Goldsmith, "Image of perfection once the goal—Now some women just seek damages," *Journal of the American Medical Association* 267/18 (1991), p. 2440.

65. Bernard D. Reams, Ed., *Food and Drug Administration General and Plastic Surgery Devices Panel. Transcript of the panel meeting on February 18, 19, 20, 1992 on the topic of silicone gel-filled breast implants* (Buffalo, NY: William S. Hein and Co., Inc., 1992), 2:145–146.

66. U.S. House of Representatives, Committee on Government Operations, Human Resources and Intergovernmental Relations Subcommittee, *The FDA's regulation of silicone breast implants: A staff report prepared by the Human Resources and Intergovernmental Relations Subcommittee*, December 1992, (Washington, DC: U.S. Government Printing Office, 1993), p. 11.

67. Ibid., p. 10.

68. Bernard D. Reams, Ed., *Food and Drug Administration General and Plastic Surgery Devices Panel. Transcript of the panel meeting on February 18, 19, 20, 1992 on the topic of silicone gel-filled breast implants* (Buffalo, NY: William S. Hein and Co., Inc., 1992), 1:47.

69. U.S. House of Representatives, Committee on Government Operations, Human Resources and Intergovernmental Relations Subcommittee, *The FDA's regulation of silicone breast implants: A staff report prepared by the Human Resources and Intergovernmental Relations Subcommittee*, December 1992, (Washington, DC: U.S. Government Printing Office, 1993), p. 18.

70. Bernard D. Reams, Ed., *Food and Drug Administration General and Plastic Surgery Devices Panel. Transcript of the panel meeting on February 18, 19, 20, 1992 on the topic of silicone gel-filled breast implants* (Buffalo, NY: William S. Hein and Co., Inc., 1992), 1:52.

71. U.S. House of Representatives, Committee on Government Operations, Human Resources and Intergovernmental Relations Subcommittee, *The FDA's regulation of silicone breast implants: A staff report prepared by the Human Resources and Intergovernmental Relations Subcommittee*, December 1992, (Washington, DC: U.S. Government Printing Office, 1993), p. 35.

72. Ibid., p. 13.
73. Tim Smart, "Breast implants: What did the industry know when?" *Business Week*, 10 June 1991, p. 95.
74. Ibid., p. 98.
75. Ibid.
76. Bernard D. Reams, Ed., *Food and Drug Administration General and Plastic Surgery Devices Panel. Transcript of the panel meeting on February 18, 19, 20, 1992 on the topic of silicone gel-filled breast implants* (Buffalo, NY: William S. Hein and Co., Inc., 1992), 2:433–434.
77. William Leiss and Christina Chociolko, *Risk and Responsibility*. (Buffalo, NY: McGill-Queen's University Press, 1994), 270.
78. Bernard D. Reams, Ed., *Food and Drug Administration General and Plastic Surgery Devices Panel. Transcript of the panel meeting on November 12, 13, 14 1991 on the topic of breast implants* (Buffalo, NY: William S. Hein and Co., Inc., 1991), 2:27.
79. Philip J. Hilts, "Maker of silicone breast implants says data show them to be safe," *New York Times*, 14 January 1992, sec. A, p. 1.
80. Bernard D. Reams, Ed., *Food and Drug Administration General and Plastic Surgery Devices Panel. Transcript of the panel meeting on November 12, 13, 14 1991 on the topic of breast implants* (Buffalo, NY: William S. Hein and Co., Inc., 1991), 1:310.
81. Ibid., 3:194.
82. "Science abdicates," *Wall Street Journal*, 9 January 1992, sec. A, p. 12.
83. We also find it a tad ironic that the usually well-reasoned voice of the *New England Journal of Medicine*, certainly one of the strongest voices calling for a return to science, was perhaps too quick to cite a very questionable poll, sponsored by the American Society of Plastic and Reconstructive Surgeons, which found that 90 percent of women with breast implants were satisfied with their implants.
84. Bernard D. Reams, Ed., *Food and Drug Administration General and Plastic Surgery Devices Panel. Transcript of the panel meeting on February 18, 19, 20, 1992 on the topic of silicone gel-filled breast implants* (Buffalo, NY: William S. Hein and Co., Inc., 1992), 1:188.
85. Ibid., 1:216.
86. Breast implant update," Editorial, *New York Times*, 18 June 1994, pp. 1, 20.
87. Bernard D. Reams, Ed., *Food and Drug Administration General and Plastic Surgery Devices Panel. Transcript of the panel meeting on February 18, 19, 20, 1992 on the topic of silicone gel-filled breast implants* (Buffalo, NY: William S. Hein and Co., Inc., 1992), 3:245.
88. William Leiss and Christina Chociolko, *Risk and Responsibility*. (Buffalo, NY: McGill-Queen's University Press, 1994), p. 263.
89. Bernard D. Reams, Ed., *Food and Drug Administration General and Plastic Surgery Devices Panel. Transcript of the panel meeting on February 18, 19, 20, 1992 on the topic of silicone gel-filled breast implants* (Buffalo, NY: William S. Hein and Co., Inc., 1992), 2:210–211.
90. Ibid., 2:194.
91. Ibid., 2:449–451.
92. U.S. House of Representatives, Committee on Government Operations, Human Resources and Intergovernmental Relations Subcommittee, *The FDA's regulation of silicone breast implants: A staff report prepared by the Human Resources and Intergovernmental Relations Subcommittee*, December 1992, (Washington, DC: U.S. Government Tourist Office, 1993), p. 63.

93. Ibid., p. 127.
94. Bernard D. Reams, Ed., *Food and Drug Administration General and Plastic Surgery Devices Panel. Transcript of the panel meeting on February 18, 19, 20, 1992 on the topic of silicone gel-filled breast implants* (Buffalo, NY: William S. Hein and Co., Inc., 1992), 2:437.
95. Ibid., 2:204.
96. The former director and president of the board of Y-Me, New England, had her stand-in testify (she left the hearings before she could speak, for personal reasons) that she had resigned from the board for fear her negative position on the implants would result in funding problems for her organizations. She had had her own silicone implants removed and found they were leaking silicone. This survivor's stand-in expressed grave fear that the widely scattered members of the breast-cancer support network had been co-opted by the industry. This survivor believed reconstruction was in women's best interest, but not necessarily reconstruction with silicone breast implants.
97. Connie Ozawa, *Recasting Science: Consensual Procedures in Public Policy Making* (San Francisco: Westview Press, 1991).
98. Administrative Conference of the United States (ACUS), chaired by Thomasina V. Rogers, *Toward Improved Agency Dispute Resolution: Implementing the ADR Act,* (Washington, DC: U.S. Government Printing Office, 1995).
99. "EPA doesn't want to 'be jerked around' by city," *New Bedford Standard Times,* September 1993.
100. "Pollution remedy is hotly debated," *New York Times,* 10 October 1993.
101. "EPA makes two good moves toward repairing its image," *New Bedford Standard Times,* 21 November 1993.
102. "Mediation among PCB interest groups begins," *New Bedford Standard Times,* 8 December 1993.
103. Ibid.
104. Medical journals noted, at most, only a few hundred reported cases, while plaintiff's attorneys argued that there were tens of thousands of such cases.
105. Mark A. Peterson, "Giving away money: Comparative comments on claims resolution facilities," *Law and Contemporary Problems* 53/4 (1990), pp. 113–114.
106. See Deborah H. Hensler, "Assessing claims resolution facilities: What we need to know," *Law and Contemporary Problems* 53/4 (1990), pp. 176–181.
107. Lawrence Fitzpatrick, "The center for claims resolution," *Law and Contemporary Problems* 53/4 (1990), p. 13.
108. Patrick Field, Howard Raiffa, and Lawrence Susskind, "Risk and justice: Rethinking the concept of compensation," *Annals of the American Academy of Political and Social Science,* 1996 forthcoming.

Chapter VI. When Values Collide

1. According to one agency official, this defiant act lost some of its punch when the protesters found they had chained themselves, not to the Commissioner's radiator, but to a radiator in an adjacent empty office.
2. Holly Angelo. "Vigil mourns Quabbin deer hunt," *Springfield Union-News,* 23 December 1991.
3. Bruce Gadaip. "Stunted deer show wisdom of hunt," *Worcester Telegram,* 2 January 1991.

4. William L. Ury, Jeanne M. Brett, and Stephan B. Goldberg, *Getting Disputes Resolved* (Cambridge, MA: Project on Negotiation Books, 1993.)

5. Christopher Moore, *The Mediation Process* (San Francisco: Jossey Bass, 1986).

6. Terrell A. Northrup, "The dynamic of identity in personal and social conflict," In *Intractable Conflicts and their Transformations*, ed. by Louis Kriesbergy, Terrell A. Northrup, and Stuart J. Thornson (Syracuse, NY: Syracuse University Press, 1989).

7. Stephen Homes. "The Secret History of Self-Interest," In *Beyond Self-Interest*, ed. by Jane J. Mansbridge (Chicago: University of Chicago Press, 1990).

8. Anthony Oberschall, *Social Movements: Ideologies, Interests, and Identities* (New Brunswick, NJ: Transaction Publishers, 1993).

9. Vamik D. Volkan, *The Need to Have Enemies and Allies: From Clinical Practice to International Relationships* (Northvale, NJ: Jason Aronson, Inc., 1988).

10. Ibid.

11. Peter C. Newman, "The beaching of a great whale," *Maclean's*, 16 September 1991, p. 38.

12. Andre Picard, "James Bay II," *Amicus Journal*, Fall 1990: 13.

13. Ibid., p. 14.

14. Sam Howe Verhovek, "Power struggle," *New York Times Magazine*, 12 January 1992, p. 26.

15. Ibid., p. 26.

16. Philip Authier, "Staying popular with voters is tough Bourassa says after poll shows drop," *Montreal Gazette*, 25 October 1991, sec. A, p. 5.

17. Peter C. Newman, "The beaching of a great whale," *Maclean's*, 16 September 1991, p. 38.

18. Tu Thanh Ha, "Liberal, PQ stung by ad 'insulting to Quebecers,'" *Montreal Gazette*, 23 October 1991, sec. A, p. 1.

19. Graeme Hamilton, "Power to the people," *Montreal Gazette*, 26 November 1994, sec. B, p. 1.

20. Barry Came, "Power plays in Quebec," *Maclean's*, 22 July 1991, p. 12.

21. Jacquie McNish, "New York could pull plug on deal with Hydro-Quebec," [Toronto] *Globe and Mail*, 1 October 1991, sec. B, p. 1.

22. Ibid.

23. Sarah Scott, "Hydro will have to make a deal," *Montreal Gazette*, 1 October 1991, sec. A, p. 1.

24. Philip Authier and Graeme Hamilton, "We'll accept one impact study of Great Whale, Minister says," *Montreal Gazette*, 3 October 1991, sec. A, p. 7.

25. Ibid.

26. Tu Thanh Ha, "Liberal, PQ stung by ad 'insulting to Quebecers,'" *Montreal Gazette*, 23 October 1991, sec. A, p. 1.

27. Susan Kinsman, "Quebec ruling could affect future power supply," *Hartford Courant*, 5 December 1994, sec. A, p. 3.

28. Barry Came, "Cowboy capitalist," *Maclean's*, 2 May 1994, p. 14.

29. Philip Authier, "Our power-exporting dream is over," *Montreal Gazette*, 2 December 1994, sec. A, p. 6.

30. Graeme Hamilton, "Power to the people," *Montreal Gazette*, 26 November 1994, sec. B, p. 1.

31. The Inuit, rather than fight the utility, decided to negotiate because they felt they could not defeat it. In April of 1994, six months before the project was put "on ice," the Inuit settled with Hydro-Quebec for $556 million over fifty years.

32. Jack Aubry, "The beach of a whale," *Ottawa Citizen*, 26 November 1994, sec. B, p. 3.
33. Ibid.
34. Of course, Hydro-Quebec spent its own funds on such matters. In 1992, Hydro-Quebec paid Burson-Marsteller, yet another large public-relations firm, $2.3 million for its services in Europe, Canada, and the United States. In 1994, the company spent almost $200,000 lobbying its cause in Rhode Island alone. The utility spent some $250 million on its impact study, not to mention unknown funds on attorneys to defend their cause in court.
35. Peter C. Newman, "The beaching of a great whale," *Maclean's*, 16 September 1991, p. 38.
36. United Nations, Transnational Investments and Operations on the Lands of Indigenous Peoples, Commission on Human Rights, Sub-Commission on Prevention and Discrimination and Protection of Minorities, *Report of the United Nations Transnational Corporations and Management Division pursuant to Sub-Commission Resolution 1990/26*, 44th sess. (1992), p. 14.
37. Andre Picard, "James Bay II," *Amicus Journal* (Fall 1990): 16.
38. Philip Authier, "Quebec Cree resume talks with PQ" *Montreal Gazette*, 24 May 1995, sec. A, p. 1.
39. G. L. Roy, Letter to the Editor: "More to a river than hydro development," *Montreal Gazette*, 17 September 1991, sec. B, p. 2.
40. "Chickens come home to roost." Editorial. *Montreal Gazette*, 12 October 1991.
41. Susan Reed and Janice Carswell, "Animal passion," *People*, 18 January 1993, p. 37.
42. Laurence H. Tribe, *Abortion: The Clash of Absolutes* (New York: W. W. Norton and Company, 1992).
43. Daniel T. Oliver, "Our needs outweigh animal rights. . ." Scripps-Howard News Service, November 1993.
44. Wesley V. Jamison and William M. Lunch, "Rights of animals, perceptions of science, and political activism: Profile of American animal rights activists," *Science, Technology, and Human Values* 17/4 (1992): 443.
45. Barbara Culliton, "Can reason defeat unreason?" *Nature* 351 (13 June 1991): 517.
46. Richard P. Vance, "An introduction to the philosophical presuppositions of the animal liberation/rights movement," *Journal of the American Medical Association* 268/13 (7 October 1992): 1716.
47. Janice Perrone, "Scientists tell of harassment by activists," *American Medical News*, 23–30 March 1992, p. 3.
48. Frederick K. Goodwin, Letter to the Editor: "From the Alcohol, Drug Abuse, and Mental Health Administration," *Journal of the American Medical Association* 263/7 (1990): 936.
49. Susan E. Paris, Letter to the Editor: "A rat is not a pig is not a boy," *Wall Street Journal*, 7 October 1992, sec A, p. 17. Interestingly, the AMP was launched to defend animal experimentation by the United States Surgical Corporation, a major manufacturer of medical supplies and a focus of animal rights activists protests because of their use of dogs to train doctors in using surgical staplers.
50. Barbara Culliton, "Can reason defeat unreason?" *Nature* 351 (13 June 1991): 517.
51. James M. Jasper and Dorothy Nelkin, *The Animal Rights Crusade: The Growth of Moral Protest* (New York: The Free Press, 1992).
52. Lynda Birke and Mike Michael. "Views from behind the barricade," *New Scientist*, 4 April 1992, p. 29.
53. "Just like us?" *Harper's Magazine* 277, August 1988, p. 45.

54. Scott Sanders and James M. Jasper, "Civil politics in the animal rights conflict: God terms versus casuistry in Cambridge, Massachusetts," *Science, Technology, and Human Values* 19/2 (1994): 179.
55. W. David Zitzkat, Letter to the Editor: "Use of animals in medical education," *Journal of the American Medical Association* 266/24 (1991): 3432.
56. Neal D. Barnard, Letter to the Editor: "The AMA and the Physicians Committee for Responsible Medicine," *Journal of the American Medical Association* 268/6 (1992): 788.
57. Wesley V. Jamison and William M. Lunch, "Rights of animals, perceptions of science, and political activism: Profile of American animal rights activists," *Science, Technology, and Human Values* 17/4 (1992): 438–457.
58. Ibid.
59. Mary Ann Glendon, *Rights Talk: The Impoverishment of Political Discourse* (New York: The Free Press, 1991), p. 46.
60. Ibid., p. 14.
61. John C. Cole, "Animal rights and wrongs," *The Humanist* (July/August 1990): 13–14.
62. James M. Jasper and Dorothy Nelkin, *The Animal Rights Crusade: The Growth of Moral Protest.* (New York: The Free Press, 1992), p. 171.
63. Ibid.
64. Mary Ann Glendon, *Rights Talk: The Impoverishment of Political Discourse* (New York: The Free Press, 1991), p. 16.
65. Andrew N. Rowan, Letter to the Editor: "Is justification of animal research necessary?" *Journal of the American Medical Association* 269/9 (1993): 1114.
66. Mary Ann Glendon, *Rights Talk: The Impoverishment of Political Discourse* (New York: The Free Press, 1991), p. 172.
67. James M. Jasper and Dorothy Nelkin, *The Animal Rights Crusade: The Growth of Moral Protest* (New York: The Free Press, 1992), p. 176.
68. Laurence H. Tribe, *Abortion: The Clash of Absolutes* (New York: W. W. Norton and Company, 1992), p. 240.
69. Mary Ann Glendon, *Rights Talk: The Impoverishment of Political Discourse* (New York: The Free Press, 1991), p. 182.
70. Ibid.
71. Anne Wolven Garrett, "World Congress on Alternatives," *Drug and Cosmetic Industry* 153/6 (1993): 12.
72. Paul Cotton, "Animals and science benefit from replace, reduce, refine effort," *Journal of the American Medical Association* 270/24 (1993): 2907.
73. Susan Katz Miller, "Moderates bury the hatchets over animal tests. . . as activists end up in the laboratory," *New Scientists* 27 (November 1993): 6.
74. Brad Warren, "Heading off the by-catch boulder," *National Fisherman,* (February 1995): 20.
75. Ibid.
76. Massachusetts Audubon Society "Dialogue" page in MDC press files, n.d.
77. "Cutting the Quabbin deer herd," *Boston Globe,* 4 November 1989, p. 22.
78. Interview with the authors, December 1993.
79. The private Trustees of Reservations had previously held a controlled hunt on Massachusetts' North Shore. That hunt generated a great deal of unwanted and negative press.

80. Interview with the authors, December 1993.
81. Ibid.
82. Jan E. Dizard, *Going Wild: Hunting, Animal Rights, and the Contested Meaning of Nature* (Amherst: University of Massachusetts Press, 1994).
83. Interview with the authors, December 1993. Name withheld by request.

Chapter VII. The Media

1. James E. Lukaszewski, "Managing bad news in America: It's getting tougher and it's getting worse," *Vital Speeches of the Day* 56/18 (1990), p. 572.
2. Sandi Sonnenfeld, "Media policy—What media policy?" *Harvard Business Review,* July–August 1994, p. 20.
3. Scott M. Cutlip, Allen H. Center, and Glen M. Broom, *Effective Public Relations,* 6th ed. (Englewood Cliffs, NJ: Prentice-Hall, Inc., 1985), p. 425.
4. James E. Lukaszewski, *Influencing Public Attitudes* (Leesburg, VA: Issue Action Publications, Inc., 1992), p. 32.
5. William Greider, *Who Will Tell the People? The Betrayal of American Democracy* (New York: Touchstone Books, 1992), p. 322.
6. Christopher Lasch, "Journalism, publicity and the lost art of argument," *Media Studies Journal* (Spring 1995), p. 91.
7. "Crisis management plan: Wash, rinse, spin," *Harper's Magazine* 284/1695 (August 1991), pp. 24–25.
8. James E. Gruning, "Image and substance: From symbolic to behavioral relationships," *Public Relations Review* 19/2 (1993), p. 135.
9. James P. Gannon, "Business and the media," *Vital Speeches of the Day* 46/5 (15 December 1979): 133–136.
10. Mark Jurkowitz, "A kinder gentler press?" *Boston Globe*, 1 May 1995, p. 15.
11. Ben A. Franklin, "Conflicting reports add to tension," *New York Times,* 31 March 1979, p. 1.
12. Joann Byrd, "The wonderful/horrible world of Disney," *Washington Post,* 22 May 1994, sec. C, p. 6. Byrd noted that the *Washington Post's* reports of negative impacts and opposition outweighed its reports of the project's advantages and supporters about three to one.
13. Mark Pacala (Senior Vice President and General Manager, Disney Enterprises), "In defense of Disney's America," *Washington Post,* 28 January 1994, sec. A, p. 23.
14. U.S Senate, Committee on Environment and Public Works, Subcommittee on Nuclear Regulation, *Nuclear Accident and Recovery at Three Mile Island* (Washington, DC: U.S. Government Printing Office, 1980).
15. Richard Squires, "Disney's Trojan mouse," *Washington Post,* 23 January 1994, sec. C, p. 1.
16. Harold Denton, keynote speech delivered to the Nuclear Energy Agency Workshop on Public Information During Nuclear Emergencies, Paris, France, February 17–19, 1988, published in *Nuclear Energy: Communicating with the Public* (Paris: Organization of Economic Cooperation and Development, 1991).
17. David Finn, "Public invisibility of corporate leaders," *Harvard Business Review,* November-December 1980, pp. 102–110.
18. "In Ten Years, You'll See Nothing," *Fortune* (8 May 1989), pp. 50–51.

19. Bernard D. Reams, ed., *Food and Drug Administration General and Plastic Surgery Devices Panel, Transcript of the panel meeting on February 18, 19, 20, 1992 on the topic of silicone-gel-filled breast implants* (Buffalo, NY: William S. Hein and Co., Inc., 1992), 3:231.

20. Philip J. Hilts, "Top manufacturer of breast implant replaces its chief," *New York Times*, 11 February 1992, sec. A, p. 1.

21. Matthew L. Wald, "An ex-chemist's formula for Dow Corning," *New York Times*, 17 February 1992, sec. D, p. 1.

22. William F. Powers, "Eisner says Disney won't back down," *Washington Post*, 14 June 1994, sec. A, p. 1.

23. In 72 stories, Frank Iarossi was quoted 39 times, Don Cornett 22 times, and Lawrence Rawl 11 times. In 120 stories, Dennis Kelso was quoted 42 times and Steve Cowper was quoted 30 times. Interestingly, the President, George Bush, was quoted in stories about the spill only 11 times. See Conrad Smith, "News sources and power elites in news coverage of the *Exxon Valdez* oil spill," *Journalism Quarterly* Summer, 70/2 (Summer 1993).

24. Mark Jurkowitz, "A kinder gentler press?" *Boston Globe*, 1 May 1995, p. 15.

25. "The raspberry prescription," *Newsworthy* [Minnesota News Council newsletter], Fall 1994, p. 5.

26. Joseph D. Keefer, "The news media's failure to facilitate citizen participation in the Congressional policymaking process," *Journalism Quarterly* 70/2 (Summer 1993), p. 421.

27. Christopher Lasch, "Journalism, publicity and the lost art of argument," *Media Studies Journal* (Spring 1995), p. 91.

28. Lisa Austin, "'Public journalism' redefines the media's role," *Consensus*, 24 (October 1994), p. 2.

29. The last 20 years has seen the rise of the professional "neutral." Acting as a facilitator or mediator, these professionals assist disputing parties in convening the appropriate group, selecting representatives, setting agendas, conducting productive meetings, interacting with the media, and drafting final agreements. The quarterly newsletter *Consensus* carries a resource listing of professional neutrals. In addition, 18 states now have state-run conflict resolution programs that can assist parties in identifying appropriate neutrals.

30. Karen L. Khor, "The media: Friend or foe?" *Consensus* 24 (October 1994), pp. 4–5.

31. Mark Jurkowitz, "A kinder gentler press?" *Boston Globe*, 1 May 1995, p. 15.

32. Jane Hall, "Hazards of the trade," *Media Studies Journal* (Spring 1995), p. 36.

33. "News Council workshop will help media handle complaints effectively," *Newsworthy* [Minnesota News Council newsletter], Fall 1994, p. 7.

34. Gary Gilson, interview with the authors, 26 July 1995.

Chapter VIII. Principled Leadership

1. Joe Morgenstern, "The fifty-nine-story crisis," *The New Yorker*, 29 May 1995, pp. 45–53.

2. Ibid., p. 52.

3. William F. Powers, "Eisner says Disney won't back down," *Washington Post*, 14 June, sec. A, p. 1.

4. Patrick Field and Michael Wheeler, "Negotiating the right to know," Harvard Business School Case Study, N9-395-062, 1995.

5. Warren Bennis, *On Becoming a Leader* (Reading, MA: Addison-Wesley Publishing Co., 1989), p. 30.
6. James M. Kouzes and Jarry A. Posner, *The Leadership Challenge* (San Francisco: Jossey-Bass, 1987), p. 17.
7. Warren Bennis, *On Becoming a Leader.* (Reading, MA: Addison-Wesley Publishing Co., 1989), p. xiv.
8. Patrick Field and Michael Wheeler, "Negotiating the right to know," Harvard Business School Case Study N9-395-062, 1995, p. 14.
9. Ibid., p. 14.
10. Ibid., p. 12.
11. Ibid.
12. Robert Axelrod, *The Evolution of Cooperation* (New York: Basic Books, 1984).
13. Ibid., p. 189.
14. Roger Schwarz, *The Skilled Facilitator: Practical Wisdom for Developing Effective Groups* (San Francisco: Jossey-Bass, 1994), p. 251.
15. Consensus Building Institute (CBI), *Partnering, consensus building, and alternative dispute resolution: Current uses and opportunities in the U.S. Army Corps of Engineers,* (Fort Belvoir, VA: Office of Counsel and the Institute for Water Resources, U.S. Army Corps of Engineers, 1995).
16. Peter T. Johnson, "How I turned a critical public into useful consultants," *Harvard Business Review*, January-February 1993: 56–66.
17. Michael Barzelay, *Breaking through Bureaucracy.* Worth noting: Despite the notion of "public service," some of these great progressive bureaucrats of the first half of the twentieth century loved to serve the public, but disliked people. Frances Perkins, Secretary of Labor under F.D.R., was heard to say of Robert Moses, an early reformer of New York City and State government, and later the brilliant and powerful head of the Port Authority of New York and New Jersey, "He doesn't love the people . . . . He loves the public, but not as people."
18. See Lawrence Susskind and Jeffrey Cruikshank, *Breaking the Impasse: Consensual Approaches to Resolving Public Disputes* (New York: Basic Books, 1987).
19. Peter T. Johnson, "How I turned a critical public into useful consultants," *Harvard Business Review* (January-February 1993), p. 58.
20. Ibid., p. 58.
21. Ibid., p. 59.
22. Ibid., p. 65.
23. Ibid., p. 66.

Bibliography

Chapter I. Introduction

"Alaska fighting effect of spill." *Newsday*, 24 May 1989: 8.

"Antipolitics '94: The anger ever deeper." *New York Times Magazine*, 16 October 1994, 37.

Center, Allen H., and Patrick Jackson. *Public Relations Practice*, 4th ed. Englewood Cliffs, NJ: Prentice Hall, 1990.

"Crisis management plan: Wash, rinse, spin." *Harper's*, 284 (1991): 21–28.

Cutlip, Scott M., Allen H. Center, and Glen M. Broom. *Effective Public Relations*, 6th ed. Englewood Cliffs, NJ: Prentice Hall, 1985.

Egan, Timothy. "Exxon concedes it cannot contain most of oil spill." *New York Times*, 30 March 1989, sec. A, p. 1.

Gabriel, Trip. "Public relations has potent image at journalism schools." *New York Times*, 17 March 1994, sec. B, p. 1.

Geyelin, Milo. "Suits by firms exceed those by individuals." *Wall Street Journal*, December 1993, Sec. B, p. 1.

Gilpin, Kenneth N. "Man in the news: An embattled chairman." *New York Times*, 8 December 1984, sec. A, p. 7.

Grube, Lorri. "Litigation: Cost of litigation to US businesses." *Chief Executive* 19 (January 1995): 56.

Hilts, Philip J. "Cigarette manufacturers debated the risks they denied." *New York Times*, 16 June 1994, sec. A, p. 1.

———. "Grim findings on tobacco and a decade of frustration." *New York Times*, 18 June 1994, sec. A, p. 1.

Ladbury, Adrian. "U.K. rethinks safety regulations." *Business Insurance* 28 (2 May 1994).

Lueck, Thomas J. "Crisis management at Carbide." *New York Times*, 14 December 1984, sec. D, p. 1.

Mauer, Richard. "Alaska aid assails oil industry for 'inadequate' response to spill." *New York Times*, 26 March 1989, sec. A, p. 1.

"Public interest pretenders." *Consumer Reports* 59 (1994): 316–320.

Reidy, Chris. "Term-limits supporters turn to ballot." *Boston Globe,* 30 October 1994, p. 38.

Sanchez, Jesus. "Alaska launches ad drive as spill hurts tourism." *Los Angeles Times,* 29 March 1989, sec. 4, p. 1.

Chapter II. Why Is the Public Angry?

Abarbanel, Stephanie. "Toxic nightmare on Main Street." *Family Circle,* 14 August 1990, pp. 77–128.

Ahearne, John F. "Telling the public about risks." *Bulletin of the Atomic Scientists* 46/7 (1990): 37(3).

Aubin, Benoit. "Vicious propaganda." *Montreal Gazette,* 13 September 1991.

"Baboon liver implant angers animal activists." *Chicago Tribune,* 1 July 1992, p. 11.

Barnard, Neal D. "The AMA and the Physicians Committee for Responsible Medicine." Letter to editor and reply. *Journal of the American Medical Association* 268/6 (1992): 788(2).

Broadcast of *Inside Washington,* Federal News Service, 15–16 October 1988.

Burke, Dan. "Power plays in Quebec." *Maclean's* 103/48 (1990): 23(2).

Burton, Thomas M. "Dow Corning refuses to give the FDA independent report on breast implants." *Wall Street Journal,* 15 January 1993, sec. B, p. 7.

Bush, George, and Michael Dukakis. "Transcript of the second Bush-Dukakis debate." *New York Times,* 14 October 1988, sec. A, p. 14.

Fisher, Roger, William Ury, and Bruce Patton. *Getting to Yes: Negotiating Agreement Without Giving In,* 2nd ed. New York: Penguin Books, 1991.

Ganguly, Dilip. "Anger in India 10 years after Bhopal leak." *Boston Globe,* 4 December 1994, p. 7.

Griffin, Dale W., and Lee Ross. "Subjective construal, social inference, and human misunderstanding." *Advances in Experimental Social Psychology* 23 (1991): 319–359.

Hazarika, Sanjoy. "India police seize factory records of Union Carbide." *New York Times,* 7 December 1984, sec. A, p. 1.

Kuechle, David. "Negotiating with an angry public: Advice to corporate leaders." *Negotiation Journal* 1/4 (1985): 326–327.

Morehouse, Richard. "Unfinished business: Bhopal ten years after." *The Ecologist* 24/5 (1994).

Newman, Peter. "The beaching of a great whale." *Maclean's* 104/37 (1991): 38(1).

Perrone, Janice. "Scientists tell of harassment by activists." *American Medical News* 35 (23–30 March 1992).

Reed, Susan, and Janice Carswell. "Animal passion." *People,* 18 January 1993, pp. 35–39.

Smart, Tim. "Breast implants: What did the industry know, and when?" *Business Week* (10 June 1991): pp. 94–98.

Verhovek, Sam Howe. "Power struggle." *New York Times Magazine,* 12 January 1992, p. 16.

Chapter III. The Mutual-Gains Approach

Bazerman, Max H., and Margaret A. Neale. *Negotiating Rationally.* New York: The Free Press, 1992.

Chapter IV. Accidents Will Happen

Case: Three Mile Island

Ayres, B. Drummond, Jr. "Governor in an uncommon crisis: Richard Louis Thornburgh." *New York Times,* 4 April 1979, sec. A, p. 16.

———. "Regulator of a nation's reactors: Harold Ray Denton." *New York Times,* 2 April 1979, sec. A, p. 15.

Burnham, David. "Congress is briefed: Carter aide at scene says danger to the public is believed remote." *New York Times,* 31 March 1979, sec. A, p. 1.

Consensus Building Institute (CBI). *Partnering, consensus building, and alternative dispute resolution: Current uses and opportunities in the U.S. Army Corps of Engineers.* Fort Belvoir, VA: Office of Counsel and the Institute for Water Resources, U.S. Army Corps of Engineers, 1995.

"The credibility meltdown." *New York Times.* 30 March 1979, sec. A, p. 30.

Denton, Harold. Keynote speech delivered to the Nuclear Energy Agency Workshop on Public Information During Nuclear Emergencies, 17–19 February, 1988, Paris, France, published in *Nuclear Energy: Communicating With the Public.* Paris: Organization of Economic Cooperation and Development, 1991.

DiMento, Joseph. "They treated me like a criminal: Sanctions, enforcement characteristics, and compliance." In *Environmental Law and American Business: Dilemmas of Compliance.* New York: Plenum Press, 1989, pp. 77–102.

Franklin, Ben A. "Conflicting reports add to tension." *New York Times,* 31 March 1979, sec. A, p. 1.

———. "Nuclear foes see grave risk in Pennsylvania mishap, but utility aides are unalarmed." *New York Times,* 30 March 1979, sec. A, p. 19.

Hatch, Maureen C., et al. "Cancer rates after the Three Mile Island nuclear accident and proximity of residence to the plant." *American Journal of Public Health* 81 (1991): 719–724.

Janson, Donald. "Radiation is released in accident at nuclear plant in Pennsylvania." *New York Times,* 29 March 1979, sec. A, p. 1.

King, Wayne. "Concern rises in South Carolina, home of many nuclear reactors." *New York Times,* 1 April 1979, p. 30.

Lyons, Richard D. "Atomic plant is still emitting radioactivity." *New York Times,* 30 March 1979, sec. A, p. 1.

———. "Children evacuated: But Governor says later further pullouts are not thought likely." *New York Times,* 31 March 1979, sec. A, p. 1.

———. "Federal experts suggest filters caused accident: Utility differs." *New York Times,* 29 March 1979, sec. D, p. 22.

———. "Officials say nuclear power plant is cooler but still in crisis; trapped-gas danger persists; bubble size reduced. Wider evacuation possible, agency chief says—Carter to visit site." *New York Times,* 1 April 1979, sec. A, p. 1.

———. "Problem seen easing." *New York Times,* 2 April 1979, sec. A, p. 1.

Mohr, Charles. "Thornburgh weighs risks of radiation." *New York Times,* 3 April 1979, sec. A, p. 14.

Morone, Joseph G., and Edward J Woodhouse. *The Demise of Nuclear Energy?* New Haven: Yale University Press, 1989.

President's Commission on the Accident at TMI, chaired by John G. Kemeny. *The Need for Change: The Legacy of TMI.* Washington, DC: U.S. Government Printing Office, 1979.

———. Task force report: *Public's Right to Information.* Washington, DC: U.S. Government Printing Office, 1979.

Rogovin, Mitchell, et al. "Three Mile Island: A report to the Commissioners and to the public." Part 3 in Vol. 2 of *Nuclear Regulatory Commission Special Inquiry Group: Response to the Accident.* Washington, DC: U.S. Nuclear Regulatory Commission, 1979.

Sullivan, Walter. "Anatomy of atomic plant mishap." *New York Times,* 1 April 1979, p. 32.

U.S. Senate. Committee on Environment and Public Works. Subcommittee on Nuclear Regulation. *Nuclear Accident and Recovery at Three Mile Island.* Washington, DC: U.S. Government Printing Office, 1980.

U.S. House of Representatives. Committee on Interior and Insular Affairs, Majority Staff. *Reporting of Information Concerning the Accident at Three Mile Island.* Washington, DC: U.S. Government Printing Office, 1981.

Vogel, David, and Timothy Kessler. "Regulatory compliance." Paper presented at SSRC Conference on International Law and Global Environmental Change. Geneva, Switzerland, June 1993.

Willliamson, Oliver E. "Calculativeness, trust, and economic organization." *Journal of Law and Economics* 36 (1993): 453–486.

Case: Exxon Valdez

"Alaskan oil spill." *Management Review* (April 1990): 13–21.

Boston Globe. 13 February 1991–26 November 1992, passim.

Chafee, Bruce. "U.S. preparedness for clean-up of major oil spills." Unpublished paper written for *Policy and Management of Chemicals in the Environment.* Cambridge, MA: Massachusetts Institute of Technology Press, 1992.

Clark, Don. "Big Pentium gamble puts Intel in the chips." *Phoenix Gazette,* 13 June 1995, sec. B, p. 3.

Davidson, Art. *In the wake of the* Exxon Valdez: *The devastating impact of the Alaska oil spill.* San Francisco: Sierra Club Books, 1990.

Endispute, Inc. *Resolving Disputes Associated with the* Valdez *Accident.* Boston: Endispute, Inc., 1989.

"Evidence of *Valdez* damage released." *National Parks Magazine* 66 (July/August 1991): 13.

"Exxon says cleanup authorization was late." *New York Times,* 31 March 1989, sec. A, p. 12.

"Exxon to fight damage award in *Valdez* lawsuit." *National Petroleum News.* November 1994, vol. 86, no. 12: p. 8.

Gallagher, John. "In the wake of the *Exxon Valdez*: Murky legal waters of liability and compensation." *New England Law Review* 25 (Winter 1990): 571–616.

Graham, Frank Jr. "Talk of the trail." *Audubon* 91 (September 1989): 10.

Holusha, John. "Exxon's public-relations problem," *New York Times,* 2 April 1989, sec. D, p. 1.

Horton, Tom. "Paradise lost." *Rolling Stone,* 14 December 1989, pp. 150–246.

"In ten years you'll see nothing." *Fortune* 19 (8 May 1989): 50–54.

Keeble, John. *Out of the Channel: The* Exxon Valdez *Oil Spill in Prince William Sound.* New York: HarperCollins, 1991.

Laycock, George. "The disaster that won't go away." *Audubon* 92 (September 1990): 106–108.

Lemonick, Michael D. "Alaska's billion-dollar quandary." *Time* 140 (28 September 1992): 60–61.

Reidy, Chris. "Waiting on pines [*sic*] and needles." *Boston Globe*, 22 December 1994, p. 41.

Schneider, Keith. "Exxon is ordered to pay $5 billion for Alaska spill." *New York Times*, 17 September 1994, sec. A, p. 1.

"Special report." *The Amicus Journal* (Summer 1989): 12–20.

Straube, Michael. "Is full compensation possible for the damages resulting from the *Exxon Valdez* oil spill?" *Environmental Law Reporter* 19 (August 1989): 10338–10350.

U.S. House of Representatives. Committee on Interior and Insular Affairs. Subcommittee on Water, Power, and Offshore Energy Resources. *Investigation of the* Exxon Valdez *Oil Spill: Oversight Hearings before the Subcommittee on Water, Power, and Offshore Energy Resources of the Committee on Interior and Insular Affairs*, 2 vols. 101st Congress, 1st sess. 5 May 1989 (Cordova, AK) and 7–8 May 1989 (Valdez, AK). Washington, DC: U.S. Government Printing Office, 1989.

Chapter V. Risky Business

"The $4.3 billion mistake." Editorial. *Wall Street Journal*, 17 June 1994, sec. A, p. 14.

Ahearne, John F. "Telling the public about risks." *Bulletin of the Atomic Scientists* 46/7 (1990): 37–39.

American Conference of the United States (ACUS), chaired by Thomasina V. Rogers. *Toward Improved Agency Dispute Resolution: Implementing the ADR.* Washington, DC: U.S. Government Printing Office, 1995.

"Breast implant update." Editorial. *New York Times*, 18 June 1994, pp. 1, 20.

Burton, Thomas M. "Dow Corning refuses to give the FDA independent report on breast implants." *Wall Street Journal*, 15 January 1993, sec. B, p. 7.

———, and Scott McMurray. "Dow Corning still keeps implant data from public despite vow of openness." *Wall Street Journal*, 18 February 1992, sec. B, p. 3.

Carey, John. "So many chemicals, so few answers." *Business Week*, 13 March 1995, p. 98.

The Conservation Foundation. *Risk Assessment and Risk Control.* Washington, DC: The Conservation Foundation, 1985.

"Do breast implants cause systemic disease? Science in the courtroom." *New England Journal of Medicine*, 16 June 1994, p. 1749.

Environmental Resources Limited (ERL). *Guidance on Managing Risk and Uncertainties in Environmental Decisions.* Prepared for DGMH: Ministerie van Volkshuisvesting, Ruimtelijke Ordening en Milieubeheer. The Hague, 1987.

"EPA doesn't want to 'be jerked around' by city." *New Bedford Standard Times*, September 1993.

"EPA makes two good moves toward repairing its image." *New Bedford Standard Times*, 21 November 1993.

"FDA does and doesn't." *Wall Street Journal*, 24 February 1992, sec. A, p. 14.

Field, Patrick, Howard Raiffa, and Lawrence Susskind. "Risk and justice: Rethinking the concept of compensation." *Annals of the American Academy of Political and Social Science*, 1996 forthcoming.

Fisher, Jack. "The silicone controversy–When will science prevail? *New England Journal of Medicine*, 18 June 1992, p. 1698.

Fitzpatrick, Lawrence. "The Center for Claims Resolution." *Law and Contemporary Problems* 53/4 (1990): 13–26.

Gabriel, Sherine E., et al. "Risk of connective-tissue diseases and other disorders after breast implantation." *New England Journal of Medicine*, 16 June 1994, p. 1697.

Goldsmith, Marsha F. "Image of perfection once the goal—Now some women just seek damages." *Journal of the American Medical Association* 267/18 (1991): 2439–2442.

Gough, Michael. "Environmental exposures and cancer risks." *Resources* (Winter 1990): 9–12.

Hensler, Deborah H. "Assessing claims resolution facilities: What we need to know." *Law and Contemporary Problems* 53/4 (1990): 175–188.

Hilts, Philip J. "As it quits implant business, maker says product is safe." *New York Times*, 20 March 1992, sec. A, p. 12.

———. "Experts suggest U.S. sharply limit breast implants." *New York Times*, 21 February 1992, sec. A, p. 1.

———. "FDA seeks halt in breast implants made of silicone." *New York Times*, 7 January 1992, sec. A, p. 1.

———. "Maker of silicone breast implants says data show them to be safe." *New York Times*, 14 January 1992, sec. A, p. 1.

———. "Top manufacturer of breast implants replaces its chief." *New York Times*. 11 February 1992, sec. A, p. 1.

Johnson, Branden B., Peter M. Sandman, and Paul Miller. "Testing the role of technical information in public risk perception." *Risk: Issues in Health and Safety* 3 (1992): 341–364.

Leiss, William, and Christina Chociolko. *Risk and responsibility*. Buffalo, NY: McGill-Queen's University Press, 1994.

"Mediation among PCB interest groups begins." *New Bedford Standard Times*, 8 December 1993.

National Research Council (NRC). *Improving risk communication*. Washington: National Academy Press, 1989.

Ozawa, Connie. *Recasting Science: Consensual Procedures in Public Policy Making*. San Francisco: Westview Press, 1991.

Peterson, Mark A. "Giving away money: Comparative comments on claims resolution facilities." *Law and Contemporary Problems* 53/4 (1990): 113–136.

"Pollution remedy is hotly debated." *New York Times*, 10 January 1993.

Reams, Bernard D., ed. *Food and Drug Administration General and Plastic Surgery Devices Panel. Transcript of the panel meeting on November 12, 13, 14 1991 on the topic of breast implants. Transcript of the panel meeting on February 18, 19, 20, 1992 on the topic of silicone gel-filled breast implants*. Buffalo, NY: William S. Hein and Co., Inc., 1992.

Renn, Ortwin, William J. Burns, Jeanne X. Kasperson, Roger E. Kasperson, and Paul Slovic. "The social amplification of risk: Theoretical foundations and empirical applications." *Journal of Social Issues* 48/4 (1992): 137–160.

Rosenbaum, Walter. "More choice: Risk assessment." In *Environmental Politics and Policy,* 2d ed. Washington, DC: Congressional Quarterly Press, 1991.

Sandman, Peter M. "Mass media and environmental risk: Seven principles." *Risk: Health, Safety, and Environment* (Summer 1994): 251–260.

"Science abdicates." *Wall Street Journal.* 9 January 1992, sec. A, p. 12.

Seligman, Jan, et al. "Another Tempest in a C Cup." *Newsweek* (23 March 1992): 67.

Slovic, Paul. "Perception of risk." *Science* 236 (17 April 1987): 280–285.

———, B. Fischhoff, and S. Lichtenstein. "Rating the risks: The structure of expert and lay perceptions." In *Environmental impact assessment, Technology Assessment and Risk Analysis,* edited by V.T. Covello et al. New York: Springer-Verlag, 1985.

Smart, Tim. "Breast Implants: What Did the Industry Know and When?" *Business Week* (10 June 1991): 94–98.

U.S. Environmental Protection Agency, Office of Policy Analysis. *Unfinished Business. A Comparative Assessment of Environmental Problems.* Vol. 1, *Overview.* Washington, DC: U.S. Government Printing Office, 1987.

U.S. House of Representatives. Select Committee on Aging, Subcommittee on Housing and Consumer Interests. *Breast implants: Ramifications of the FDA ruling on consumers.* Hearing before the Subcommittee on Housing and Consumer Interests. 30 April 1992. Washington, DC: U.S. Government Printing Office, 1992.

U.S. House of Representatives. Committee on Government Operations. Human Resources and Intergovernmental Relations Subcommittee. *The FDA's regulation of silicone breast implants:* A staff report prepared by the Human Resources and Intergovernmental Relations Subcommittee. December 1992. Washington, DC: U.S. Government Printing Office, 1993.

Wilson, Richard, and Edmund A. C. Crouch. "Risk assessment and comparison: An introduction." *Science* 236 (17 April 1987): 267–270.

Chapter VI. When Values Collide

Angelo, Holly. "Vigil mourns Quabbin deer hunt." *Springfield Union-News,* 23 December 1991.

Aubry, Jack. "The beach of a whale." *Ottawa Citizen,* 26 November 1994, sec. B, p. 3.

Authier, Philip. "Staying popular with voters is tough Bourassa says after poll shows drop." *Montreal Gazette,* 25 October 1991, sec. A, p. 5.

———. "Our power-exporting dream is over." *Montreal Gazette,* 2 December 1994, sec. A, p. 6.

———. "Quebec Cree resume talks with PQ." *Montreal Gazette,* 24 May 1995, sec. A, p. 1.

———, and Graeme Hamilton. "We'll accept one impact study of Great Whale, Minister says." *Montreal Gazette,* 3 October 1991, sec. A, p. 7.

Barnard, Neal D. "Letter to the Editor: The AMA and the Physicians Committee for Responsible Medicine." *Journal of the American Medical Association* 268/6 (1992), p. 788.

Birke, Lynda, and Mike Michael. "Views from behind the barricade." *New Scientist,* 4 April 1992, p. 29.

Bourassa, Robert. *Power from the North.* Scarborough, Ont.: Prentice-Hall Canada, 1985.

Came, Barry. "Power plays in Quebec." *Maclean's,* 22 July 1991, p. 12.

———. "Cowboy capitalist." *Maclean's*, 2 May 1994, p. 14.

"Chickens come home to roost." Editorial. *Montreal Gazette*, 12 October 1991.

Cole, John R. "Animal rights and wrongs." *The Humanist*, July/August 1990: 12–42.

Cotton, Paul. "Animals and science benefit from replace, reduce, refine effort." *Journal of the American Medical Association* 270/24 (1993): 2967.

Culliton, Barbara. "Can reason defeat unreason?" *Nature* 351 (13 June 1991): 517.

"Cutting the Quabbin deer herd." *Boston Globe*, 4 November 1989, p. 22.

Dizard, Jan E. *Going Wild: Hunting, Animal Rights, and the Contested Meaning of Nature.* Amherst: University of Massachusetts Press, 1994.

Gadaip, Bruce. "Stunted deer show wisdom of hunt." *Worcester Telegram*, 2 January 1991.

Garrett, Anne Wolven. "World Congress on Alternatives." *Drug and Cosmetic Industry* 153/6 (1993), p. 12.

Glendon, Mary Ann. *Rights Talk: The Impoverishment of Political Discourse.* New York: The Free Press, 1991.

Goodwin, Frederick K. "Letter to the Editor: From the Alcohol, Drug Abuse, and Mental Health Administration." *Journal of the American Medical Association* 263/7 (1990): 936.

Hamilton, Graeme. "Power to the people." *Montreal Gazette*, 26 November 1994, sec. B, p. 1.

Herzog, Harold A. "The movement is my life: The psychology of animal rights activism." *Journal of Social Issues* 49/1 (1993): 103–119.

Holmes, Stephen. "The Secret History of Self-Interest." In Jane J. Mansbridge, Ed., *Beyond Self-Interest.* Chicago: University of Chicago Press, 1990.

Jamison, Wesley V., and William M. Lunch. "Rights of animals, perceptions of science, and political activism: Profile of American animal rights activists." *Science, Technology, and Human Values* 17/4 (1992): 438–457.

Jasper, James M., and Dorothy Nelkin. *The Animal Rights Crusade: The Growth of Moral Protest.* New York: The Free Press, 1992.

Johnson, William. "Damming Judgment." *Montreal Gazette*, 13 September 1991, sec. B, p. 3.

"Just like us?" *Harper's* 277 (August 1988), p. 45.

Kelman, Herbert C. "Applying a human needs perspective to the practice of conflict resolution." In John Burton, Ed., *Conflict: Human Needs Theory*, vol. 2. New York: Macmillan, 1990.

Kinsman, Susan. "Quebec ruling could affect future power supply." *Hartford Courant*, 5 December 1994, sec. A, p. 3.

Luanda, Brishkai, Catherine Morris, and Michelle LeBaron Duryea. *Conflict and Culture: Report of the Multiculturalism and Dispute Resolution Project.* Victoria, BC: University of Victoria Institute for Dispute Resolution, 1994.

McNish, Jacquie. "New York could pull plug on deal with Hydro-Quebec." *Globe and Mail*, 1 October 1991, sec. B, p. 1.

Michael, Mike, and Lynda Birke. "Accounting for identify and disreputable "'others'." *Science, Technology, and Human Values* 19/2 (1994): 189–204.

Miller, Susan Katz. "Moderates bury the hatchets over animal tests . . . as activists end up in the laboratory." *New Scientist* 27 November 1993: 6–7.

Moore, Christopher. *The Mediation Process.* San Francisco: Jossey-Bass, 1986.

Newman, Peter C. "The beaching of a great whale." *Maclean's*, 16 September 1991, p. 38.

Northrup, Terrell A. "The dynamic of identity in personal and social conflict." In Louis Kriesbergy, Terrell A. Northrup, and Stuart J. Thornson, Eds., *Intractable Conflicts and their Transformations.* Syracuse, NY: Syracuse University Press, 1989.

Oberschall, Anthony. *Social Movements: Ideologies, Interests, and Identities.* New Brunswick, NJ: Transaction Publishers, 1993.

Oliver, Daniel T. "Our needs outweigh animal rights . . ." Scripps-Howard News Service, November 1993.

Paris, Susan E. Letter to the Editor: "A rat is not a pig is not a boy." *Wall Street Journal,* 7 October 1992, p. 17.

Perrone, Janice. "Scientists tell of harassment by activists." *American Medical News* 23–30 March 1992, p. 3.

Picard, Andre. "James Bay II." *Amicus Journal,* Fall 1990: 13–16.

Reed, Susan, and Janice Carswell. "Animal passion." *People,* 18 January 1993, pp. 35–39.

Ritvo, Harriet. "Toward a more peaceable kingdom." *Technology Review,* February/March 1992: 55–61.

Rowan, Andrew N. Letter to the Editor: "Is justification of animal research necessary?" *Journal of the American Medical Association* 269/9 (1993): 1114.

Roy, G. L. Letter to the Editor: "More to a river than hydro development." *Montreal Gazette,* 17 September 1991, sec. B, p. 2.

Sanders, Scott, and James M. Jasper. "Civil politics in the animal rights conflict: God terms versus casuistry in Cambridge, Massachusetts." *Science, Technology, and Human Values* 19/2 (1994): 167–186.

Scott, Sarah. "Hydro will have to make a deal." *Montreal Gazette,* 1 October 1991, sec. A, p. 1.

Tribe, Laurence H. *Abortion: The Clash of Absolutes.* New York: W. W. Norton and Company, 1992.

Tu Thanh Ha. "Liberal, PQ stung by ad 'insulting to Quebecers.'" *Montreal Gazette,* 23 October 1991, sec. A, p. 1.

United Nations. Commission on Human Rights, Sub-Commission on Prevention and Discrimination and Protection of Minorities. *Transnational Investments and Operations on the Lands of Indigenous Peoples.* Report of the United Nations Transnational Corporations and Management Division pursuant to Sub-Commission Resolution 1990/26. 44th sess., 1992.

"U.S. defends use of animals by medical researchers." *Boston Globe,* 24 April 1990, p. 6.

Ury, William L., Jeanne M. Brett, and Stephan B. Goldberg. *Getting Disputes Resolved.* Cambridge, MA: Project on Negotiation Books, 1993.

Vance, Richard P. "An introduction to the philosophical presuppositions of the animal liberation/rights movement." *Journal of the American Medical Association* 268/13 (7 October 1992): 1715–1719.

Verhovek, Sam Howe. "Power struggle." *New York Times Magazine,* 12 January 1992, p. 26.

Volkan, Vamik D. *The Need to Have Enemies and Allies: From Clinical Practice to International Relationships.* Northvale, NJ: Jason Aronson, Inc., 1988.

Warren, Brad. "Heading off the by-catch boulder." *National Fisherman,* February 1995: 20.

Zitzkat, W. David. Letter to the Editor: "Use of animals in medical education." *Journal of the American Medical Association* 266/24 (1991): 3432.

Chapter VII. The Media

Abarbanel, Stephanie. "Toxic nightmare on Main Street." *Family Circle.* 14 August 1990, pp. 77–123.

Austin, Lisa. "'Public journalism' redefines the media's role." *Consensus* 24 (October 1994): 2.

Byrd, Joann. "The wonderful/horrible world of Disney." *Washington Post,* 22 May 1994, sec. C, p. 6.

Center, Allen H., and Patrick Jackson. *Public Relations Practices: Managerial Case Studies and Problems,* 4th ed. Englewood Cliffs, NJ: Prentice-Hall, Inc., 1990.

"Crisis management plan: Wash, rinse, spin." 1991. *Harper's Magazine* 284/1695 (August 1991): 21–27.

Cutlip, Scott M., Allen H. Center, and Glen M. Broom. *Effective Public Relations,* 6th ed. Englewood Cliffs, NJ: Prentice-Hall, Inc., 1985.

Finn, David. "Public invisibility of corporate leaders." *Harvard Business Review,* November–December 1980, pp. 102–110.

Gannon, James P. "Business and the media." *Vital Speeches of the Day* 46/5 (15 December 1979): 133–136.

Gilson, Gary. Face-to-face interview with the authors, 26 July 1995.

Greider, William. *Who Will Tell the People? The Betrayal of American Democracy.* New York: Touchstone Books, 1992.

Gruning, James E. "Image and substance: From symbolic to behavioral relationships." *Public Relations Review* 19/2 (1993): 121–139.

Hall, Jane. "Hazards of the trade." *Media Studies Journal* (Spring 1995): 35–41.

Hilts, Philip J. "Top manufacturer of breast implants replaces its chief." *New York Times,* 11 February 1992, sec. A, p. 1.

Jurkowitz, Mark. "A kinder gentler press?" *Boston Globe,* 1 May 1995, p. 15.

Keefer, Joseph D. "The news media's failure to facilitate citizen participation in the Congressional policymaking process." *Journalism Quarterly* 70/2 (Summer 1993): 412–422.

Khor, Karen L. "The media: Friend or foe?" *Consensus* 24 (October 1994): 4–5.

Lasch, Christopher. "Journalism, publicity and the lost art of argument." *Media Studies Journal* (Spring 1995): 81–91.

Lukaszewski, James E. "Managing bad news in America: It's getting tougher and it's getting worse." *Vital Speeches of the Day* 56/18 (1990): 568–573.

"News Council workshop will help media handle complaints effectively." *Newsworthy* [Minnesota News Council newsletter], Fall 1994, pp. 7–9.

Pacala, Mark. "In defense of Disney's America." *Washington Post,* 28 January 1994, sec. A, p. 23.

Powers, William F. "Eisner says Disney won't back down." *Washington Post,* 14 June 1994, sec. A, p. 1.

"The raspberry prescription." *Newsworthy* [Minnesota News Council newsletter], Fall 1994, p. 5.

Smith, Conrad. "News sources and power elites in news coverage of the *Exxon Valdez* oil spill." *Journalism Quarterly*, 70/2 (Summer 1993): 393–403.

Sonnenfeld, Sandi. "Media policy—What media policy?" *Harvard Business Review*, July–August 1994, pp. 18–30.

Squires, Richard. "Disney's Trojan mouse." *Washington Post*, 23 January 1994, sec. C, p. 1.

Wald, Matthew. "An ex-chemist's formula for Dow Corning. *New York Times*, 17 February 1992, sec. D, p.1.

Chapter VIII. Principled Leadership

Axelrod, Robert. *The Evolution of Cooperation.* New York: Basic Books, 1984.

Barzelay, Michael. *Breaking Through Bureaucracy.* Berkeley: University of California Press, 1992.

Bennis, Warren. *On Becoming a Leader.* Reading, MA: Addison-Wesley Publishing Co., 1989.

Field, Patrick, and Michael Wheeler. 1995. "Negotiating the right to know [draft]." Harvard Business School Case Study, N9-895-062, 1995.

Johnson, Peter T. "How I turned a critical public into useful consultants." *Harvard Business Review*, January–February 1993: 56–66.

Kouzes, James M., and Jarry A. Posner. *The Leadership Challenge.* San Francisco: Jossey-Bass, 1987.

Lyons, Richard D. "Atomic plant is still emitting radioactivity." *New York Times*, 30 March 1979, sec. A, p. 20.

Morgenstern, Joe. "The fifty-nine-story crisis." *The New Yorker*, 29 May 1995, pp. 45–53.

Powers, William F. "Eisner says Disney won't back down." *Washington Post*, 14 June, sec. A, p. 1.

Schwarz, Roger M. *The Skilled Facilitator: Practical Wisdom for Developing Effective Groups.* San Francisco: Jossey-Bass, 1994.

Susskind, Lawrence, and Jeffrey Cruikshank. *Breaking the Impasse: Consensual Approaches to Resolving Public Disputes.* New York: Basic Books, 1987.

Index